The Nisibis War
337–363

To the men and women of the California Army National Guard and the 40th Infantry Division, who, in the twenty-first century, have marched, fought, and died in the footsteps of the legions II Parthia, Joviani, and Herculiani.

The Nisibis War
337–363

The Defence of the Roman East
AD 337–363

John S. Harrel

Pen & Sword
MILITARY

First published in Great Britain in 2016
and reprinted in this format in 2020 by
Pen & Sword Military
an imprint of
Pen & Sword Books Ltd
Yorkshire – Philadelphia

ISBN 978 1 52678 206 9

A CIP catalogue record for this book is available from the British Library

Typeset in Ehrhardt by Mac Style Ltd
Printed in the UK by CPI Group (UK) Ltd, Croydon, CR0 4YY

Pen & Sword Books Limited incorporates the imprints of Atlas,
Archaeology, Aviation, Discovery, Family History, Fiction, History,
Maritime, Military, Military Classics, Politics, Select, Transport, True
Crime, Air World, Frontline Publishing, Leo Cooper, Remember When,
Seaforth Publishing, The Praetorian Press, Wharncliffe Local History,
Wharncliffe Transport, Wharncliffe True Crime and White Owl.

For a complete list of Pen & Sword titles please contact

PEN & SWORD BOOKS LIMITED
47 Church Street, Barnsley, South Yorkshire, S70 2AS, England
E-mail: enquiries@pen-and-sword.co.uk
Website: www.pen-and-sword.co.uk

Or
PEN AND SWORD BOOKS
1950 Lawrence Rd, Havertown, PA 19083, USA
E-mail: Uspen-and-sword@casematepublishers.com
Website: www.penandswordbooks.com

Contents

List of Maps

List of Diagrams and Illustrations

List of Photographs

Acknowledgements

Publishing a book is not a one-person endeavour; it takes a small army to finish such a project. The godfather of this project is Dr Frank L. Vatai, a professor at California State University, Northridge. Dr Vatai reawakened my interest in late antiquity and guided my journey through the world of Ammianus Marcellinus from Master's thesis to published book.

Compiling the plates and illustrations truly took an army. I would like to thank historian and actor Ardeshir Radpour and his photographer, Holly Martin, for her excellent photos of a Persian knight. The living history historians and re-enactors from the Britannia and Comitatus Societies provided photos of the arms and equipment of Late Roman soldiers to illustrate key points in the book. Thanks to graphic artist Ashley Harrel for designing the rough cover initially submitted to Pen & Sword. I would like to thank Lisa and Bill Storage for permission to use their photos of the Arch of Constantine; Dr J.C.N. Coulston, from the University of St Andrews, Scotland, for permission to use his photo of the Arch of Galerius; and Yale University, Connecticut, for permission to use photos from their Dura-Euopos Collection. Many thanks to LMarie Photo (aka Lisa Marie Harrel) and Cyrus Raymond Harrel for arranging the dioramas and photographing part of my miniature collection to illustrate military formations described in the book.

Once a manuscript is written, editing makes it come alive. I would like to thank William Creitz for editing the proceeding thesis and draft manuscript.

I owe a particular thanks to Philip Sidnell for accepting a project from a new unknown author; Dominic Allen, who did the final jacket design; Mat Blurton and his assistant, Katie Noble, who designed the book and plate section; and Matthew Jones, production manager and 'ramrod' for Pen & Sword who kept the project on track. I owe you all a 'pint.'

Finally, I would like to thank my wife, Linda, who hiked the mountains of Anatolia with me with her camera and who was the first and last editor of this book.

Key To Maps

Tactical Symbols
Imperial   Persians/Rebels/Barbarians

Strategic Symbols

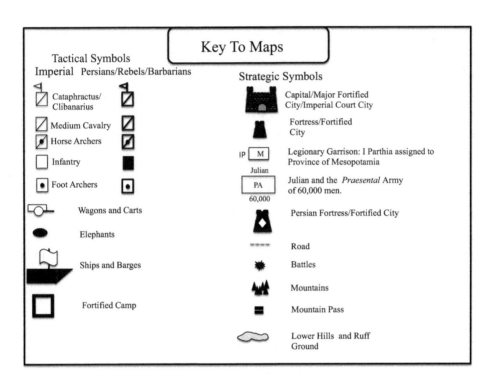

Cataphractus/
Clibanarius

Medium Cavalry

Horse Archers

Infantry

Foot Archers

Wagons and Carts

Elephants

Ships and Barges

Fortified Camp

Capital/Major Fortified
City/Imperial Court City

Fortress/Fortified
City

IP M Legionary Garrison: I Parthia assigned to
Province of Mesopotamia
Julian

PA Julian and the *Praesental* Army
of 60,000 men.
60,000

Persian Fortress/Fortified City

Road

Battles

Mountains

Mountain Pass

Lower Hills and Ruff
Ground

Introduction

It was only morning twilight and it was already hot. Count Victor, standing on a pile of rubble behind the first battle line, could see the Persians reforming 200 paces away in front of Ctesiphon's massive walls and towers. The previous night's battle to establish the Roman toehold had been utter confusion and terror as a rain of invisible arrows and fire fell on the disembarking legionaries. Despite their confusion and fear, Victor's legionaries stormed up the steep eastern bank of the Tigris to come to grips with the Persian antagonists. After an eternity of hand-to-hand fighting, the legionaries secured a small foothold as the Persians pulled back 200 paces to reform. During the lull in the combat, the centurions and tribunes shoved, pushed, and beat the legionaries into the traditional three battle lines. With only 12,000 men the battle lines of 4,000 were less than half a mile long. Victor could see the Persian cataphract formation extended beyond both flanks of his line. As the twilight continued to lighten he could make out masses of infantry behind the Persian cavalry and towering over them the massive bulk of elephants. He had to hold the beachhead until the midday heat would force the Persians to break off combat. But, prior to that, the Persian massed arrow storm would devastate his men, the elephants would break his formations, and the cataphracts would push the disordered remains into the river. As the sun crested the horizon, a blinding light reflected off the Persian armour. With the sun, the Persian host started singing praises to their King of Kings, Shapur II. As the Persians began their first chords of praise, Victor gave a signal. Roman horns blared, the 4,000 legionaries of the first line stepped forward as one, beating their spears on their shields, and started singing the first terrifying notes of the *Barritus*, the Germanic Roman war song.

The Battle of Ctesiphon, in late May 363 CE, was a tactical victory for Rome, yet it was the prelude to Rome's strategic defeat in June 363 and culminated in the fortress city of Nisibis reverting to Persian control. The Nisibis War (CE 337 to 363) was the first serious test of the strategic defence of the Roman East as formulated by Emperor Diocletian and finalized by Emperor Constantine I. Historians have studied and analysed the failed offensive led by Emperor Julian the Apostate in 363, but have generally neglected the overall conflict.

The Nisibis War provides the first campaign analysis of this important conflict between the Roman Empire and the Sassanid Kingdom. The Treaty of 298, which transferred Nisibis to Rome, and the Treaty of 363, which returned the fortress to Persia, were the only significant long-term adjustments of the Roman Eastern *Limes* during three centuries of incessant warfare. Thanks to the availability of primary sources, the Nisibis War lends itself to a detailed analysis – from the strategic conferences of emperors, the field tactics of generals, and the heroics of tribunes, to the unscrupulous activities of spies, scoundrels, villains, and usurpers. *The Nisibis War* examines the historical setting of the overall conflict, analyses the theatre of operations, and reviews the organization of the opposing armies. It evaluates the defensive strategy developed by Emperors Diocletian and Constantine I, with an assessment of the implementation of the strategy by Emperor Constantius II on the field of battle. While development of the strategy was simple, its implementation was (1) plagued by a lack of resources (due to Imperial politics and sibling rivalry), (2) undermined by the actions of traitors and usurpers and (3) ultimately derailed by King Shapur II and the Royal Persian Army.

The war can be divided into four phases. During the first phase (337 to 350) Emperor Constantius II faced the onslaught of King Shapur's Royal Persian Army with only a third of the Roman Empire's resources because his brother emperors were consumed with internal politics and sibling rivalry. Over the thirteen years of phase one, Nisibis was besieged three times and was the objective of several bloody, indecisive field battles. This phase culminated, in 350, with the third bloody siege of Nisibis.

The war entered a lengthy stalemate after the siege (the second phase). King Shapur II was distracted by nomadic incursions on Persia's eastern border, while Emperor Constantius II had to focus on defeating the Gallic usurper, Magnentius, and re-establishing Imperial authority in the Western Empire. *The Nisibis War* focuses on the period's military and political crisis and Constantius' often flawed solutions. The Battle of Murse (where Rome is reputed to have lost 50,000 legionaries in one day) and the civil war against three usurpers are analysed in detail, including their ultimate impact on the survival of the Western Empire. The rise, failure, and execution of Caesar Gallus are reviewed along with the rise and success of Caesar Julian the Apostate. Julian's development into a competent administrator and military commander is examined along with a battle analysis of his military operations in Gaul, placing the Battle of Strasbourg in its strategic context.

The return of King Shapur II and his offensive on the Rome's Eastern Empire heralds the beginning of phase three of the war (359 to 361). Emperor Constantius II, still distracted by events in the west, relied upon a passive defence to protect the Roman East. Unsupported by the field army, the *limitanei* legionaries were undermined by spies and traitors. King Shapur successfully planned and executed an indirect military campaign that unhinged the Roman defence. Extensive employment of espionage and diplomacy in support of military operations helped King Shapur neutralize Roman allies and undermine Roman civilian morale in besieged cities. The crumbling Roman defence and heavy casualties forced Constantius to return to the East before the West was stabilized. Julian's revolt in the west can be directly linked to Constantius' edict requiring forty per cent of the Gallic Army to reinforce the Roman East. Constantius' timely death prevented the empire from being plunged into another civil war and left Julian the Apostate in sole control of the Roman Empire.

The fourth and final phase of the war began with a new emperor at the helm of Rome and a return from Constantius' unpopular defensive strategy to the more traditional Roman strategic offence. For the last time in history, Julian massed the resources of the entire Roman Empire and attempted a knockout blow to the Persian Kingdom. Based on eyewitness accounts of Ammianus Marcellinus, campaign logistics are examined identifying operational flaws. Despite a sound operational plan and adequate logistical support, within less than six months of the massive Roman Army marching into Persia, Julian was killed in battle and the invading Romans were strategically defeated. The new Emperor Jovian was forced to cede Nisibis and its surrounding regions in exchange for Shapur allowing the trapped Roman expedition to return home. *The Nisibis War* will be of particular interest to historians of the Later Roman Empire and those interested in the military goals of Sassanian Persia. Military historians will also find it of interest as a thorough account and staff study of the Late Roman Army on campaign.

Chapter 1

The Nisibis War (337–363): Thesis, Sources, and Methodology

'Look With What Spirit the Cities Are Defended'

The study of military history has a wider scope than acknowledged by contemporary scholars. It is more than the story of campaigns and battles. It is a story of how societies form institutions to provide for their collective security and how those institutions operate during peace and war. It is a story of individual soldiers and their subcultures. It includes the entire range of economic, social, legal, political, technological, and cultural issues that arise from a state's need to use all means, including violence, to preserve its existence and achieve its collective goals.[1]

The Roman Empire historically attained success on the battlefield through its strategic offence ending with a decisive field battle or siege where the sword was the final arbiter. The first instance of Rome maintaining a war strategy of strategic defence was against Persia during the Nisibis War (337 to 363). After a twenty-four year defensive war, a change in emperors resulted in transition back to the strategic offence. However, instead of expected success based on historic experience, Rome was decisively defeated within six months. Historians have studied and analysed the failed offensive led by the Emperor Julian (the Apostate), but have generally neglected the overall conflict and its impact on Rome's survival. Eastern Rome's strategic defence, until the eighth century, was to defend against invading barbarians, Persians, and Muslims with small *limitanei* (border) armies based in fortified cities with limited operational offences by the regional *Comitatenses* (field) armies.[2] This book will focus on the importance of the Nisibis War and its resulting impact upon the defence of Rome's eastern provinces. Examination of Rome's eastern wars has become a current subject of interest as the United States and her allies are embroiled in a prolonged conflict in the Middle East, the same battlefield where Crassus' legions were destroyed, where Julian the Apostate was killed, and where Roman emperors and generals fought numerous fruitless wars against Parthian and Persian kings for almost six centuries.[3]

There are important issues addressed by this study: How did the Nisibis War differ from other wars between Rome and Parthia/Persia? Why was King Shapur II of Persia (hereafter, Shapur) obsessed with recovering the lands lost to Rome by the treaty of 298 and, specifically, with the recovery of the city of Nisibis after almost four decades of peace? Was the decision of Emperor Constantius to take the strategic defence a deliberate decision or was it forced upon him by circumstances? Did the strategic defence have any influence on the development of the Eastern Roman Army in relation to the development of the Western Roman Army? How did logistical support impact military operations during the Nisibis War? Why did Emperor Julian's transition to traditional Roman offensive strategy fail? Were Julian's objectives attainable with the resources at his disposal? What was the long-term impact of Julian's defeat on the subsequent defence of the Eastern Roman provinces?

Other than the Late Roman Republic, more contemporary accounts, routine records, and correspondence survive from the fourth-century Late Roman Empire than any other period of antiquity. In examining the Nisibis War, the most important primary sources are the fourth-century soldier historian, Ammianus Marcellinus, the fourth century Greek sophist, Libanius, and the fifth-century historians, Zosimus and Sozomen.

Ammianus Marcellinus was a staff officer who served with Julian's army during the Persian Campaign of 363. He was a pagan but his religious beliefs did not cloud his objective account of history. He was familiar with the Mesopotamian theatre of war. Born in Antioch around 330, he became a member of the *Protectores Domestici* staff/guard regiment when he was in his twenties and joined the staff of the *Magister Equitum per Orient*, Ursicinus in 354. By the time of the Persian Campaign, Ammianus was an experienced staff officer and would have attended staff meetings with Julian and his generals.[4] Historian Frank Trombley concluded that Ammianus 'demonstrates an organic understanding of "operations" in the modern sense of the term, with attention to personnel, intelligence, and timely movement of supplies and troops'.[5] Ammianus admired Julian (perhaps due to shared pagan beliefs).

Ammianus viewed Romans with a barbarian heritage negatively. He mentions Count (later *Magister Equitum per Orient*) Victor guardedly. Victor was repeatedly referenced, but without title, and Ammianus completely ignored the revolt of Queen Mavia from 375 to 378, which was a major event. Her defeat of a Roman army allowed her to dictate the peace terms, including a political marriage between Victor and her daughter.[6] Victor was a successful Romanized and Christianized barbarian (Sarmatian) Imperial general, and Queen Mavia was a Christianized Saracen (Arab).[7] Victor and Mavia personified two elements that Ammianus viewed with disfavour: they were both barbarians and both Christians.[8]

Ammianus was biased against Constantius because he suppressed the 'admirable' Julian, sacked Ursicinus (Ammianus' patron), and deployed a non-traditional defensive strategy. His analysis of events appears factually correct, but his analysis seems intentionally distorted to shift the blame for Julian's failures during the Persian offensive to Jovian and, to a lesser extent, to Procopius.[9]

Frank Trombley described Ammianus as demonstrating 'an organic understanding of operations', yet, of the hundreds of legions and regiments in the war, he mentions barely a dozen by name. Ammianus mixes unit descriptions between archaic and contemporary terms, and his writing is sloppy, especially when compared to Julius Caesar's *War Commentaries*.[10] Caesar was reporting contemporary war news to the citizens of Rome. Even though Ammianus had personal knowledge, he wrote years after the events to provide entertainment for Rome's elite and accuracy was less important than metre and timing.

Zosimus was a fifth-century Greek pagan historian and bureaucrat. His only surviving work, the *Historia Nova*, covers Roman history from 180 to 410. He was not a contemporary of the events. Much of his material is based upon the lost work of Eunapius. Eunapius, a pagan, was born around 345 and provided a pagan's view of events from 270 to 404. The two historians complement each other with Zosimus providing details not found in Ammianus' history.[11]

Sozomen (Salminius Hermias Sozomenus, c. 400 to c. 450) was a Christian church historian. His works cover the period 323–425 and are heavily dependent upon earlier historians. He preserved valuable information on the history of Christianity in Armenia and on the Sassanian Persians. Sozomen's second work, *Historia Ecclesiastica*, Book V, covers church history as influenced by the contemporary events from the death of Constantius I to Julian but is biased against Julian.[12]

Libanius (314 to 393), a Greek sophist and resident of Antioch, was one of the most influential pagans of his time. His speeches and letters provide a wealth of information on the Roman East. He corresponded with participants in the various campaigns of Constantius and Julian.[13] His most relevant work was his *Funeral Oration* to Julian that attacked the policies of Constantius and Jovian's treaty. In this oration, intended to praise Julian's accomplishments, Libanius suggests that Julian was assassinated. Despite his pro-Julian bias, he provides valuable insight into the decision not to besiege Ctesiphon and the subsequent march up the River Tigris.

Ioannes Mahala, a sixth-century historian, produced a minor work based on a lost history written by Magnus of Carrhae. Magnus was a soldier who participated in the Persian Expedition. His name is similar to that of a tribune noted by Ammianus for bravery.[14] Magnus disagreed with some facts recorded by Ammianus and Zosimus and is the only historian who attempted to record the reaction of King Shapur to Julian's campaign plan.[15]

Many of the lesser known ancient sources were not available in English until the twenty-first century. The study of Rome's Persian wars has long been 'bedevilled by' the diverse languages of the ancient sources (Latin, Greek, Arabic, Syriac, Hebrew, Palmyrene, Persian, and Armenian). Historians Geoffrey Greatrex, Samuel C Lieu, and Michael H Dodgeon performed a great service by publishing the source books *The Roman Eastern Frontier and the Persian Wars Part I AD 226–363 and Part II 363–630* translating many of these minor works into English.[16] Another source book by Beate Dignas and Engelbert Winter, *Rome and Persia in Late Antiquity*, focuses on political goals and military confrontations, and analyses diplomatic solutions.[17]

The *Notitia Dignitatum* is one of the most important documents to have survived from late antiquity. It is generally believed to be an official document recording the defence establishment of the Late Roman Empire from c. 395

to 420. The Eastern Empire section probably dates from c. 395 while the Western Empire materials were compiled in c. 420 to 430. The document is a directory of civil and military office holders and provides location and composition of frontier commands and the various field armies. Care must be used when relying on this document because mistakes and omissions are abundant.[18] Generally the section on the Eastern Empire appears to be more complete, perhaps due to its earlier date.[19]

Several ancient military treatises provide standards by which to judge Constantius, Julian, and Shapur as military leaders; the first is Sun Tzu's *The Art of War*.[20] Sun Tzu's work is a military classic, still guiding twenty-first century military leaders. Sun Tzu was a successful Chinese general for the State of Wu in the sixth century BCE. The military principles articulated by Sun Tzu are surprisingly similar to those found in the Late Roman Army military treatise *Strategikon*, written in the late sixth century. The *Strategikon* is a cavalry manual that provides general information about infantry tactics tacked onto a detailed work on cavalry training and tactics.[21] When the infantry section is compared to Aelianus Tacticus' second-century study of Macedonia military operations, the *Strategikon* is overly simplistic in dealing with the drill and internal tactics of the infantry battle line, and its recommendations sometimes violate basic norms of Roman infantry fighting.[22] The fourth work, Vegetius Renatus' *Epitoma Rei Militaris*, believed to have been written during the reign of Roman Emperor Flavius Theodosius (Theodosius I, 347–395), also provides applicable military leadership standards.[23] Vegetius was not a soldier, but his work on military theory contains basically the same principles found in *The Art of War* and the *Strategikon*. The three works entitled *Three Byzantine Military Treatises*, translated by George T Dennis, demonstrate that the Roman art of war survived to the tenth century. The first text, *The Anonymous Treatise on Strategy*, appears to have been written by a combat veteran and engineer during the sixth century. The remaining two, *Skirmishing* and *Campaign Organization and Tactics*, were written during the tenth century.[24] In all of the surviving Roman-Byzantine treatises, the keys to success were training, drill, discipline, the establishment of a fortified camp, and reconnaissance.

Reviews of Late Roman Empire military operations have been popular from the eighteenth through to the twenty-first centuries. George

Rawlinson's seven-volume history *The Seven Great Monarchies of the Ancient Eastern World*, and Edward Gibbon's six-volume *History of the Decline and Fall of the Roman Empire* are still relevant today.[25] While some discoveries in the twentieth and twenty-first centuries made some portions of these works dated, these great historians were not working under the handicap of modern technology. These and other seventeenth through nineteenth century authors retained a historic appreciation of time and distance and would have used similar travel methods as their Late Roman counterparts. Hardy explorers produced maps and travel logs published in nineteenth and early twentieth-century scientific journals. They would have walked or ridden a horse over the same terrain that Shapur's cavalry or Julian's legions marched.[26]

Any modern study of the Late Roman Empire should begin with A H M Jones' scholarly work *The Late Roman Empire 284–602.*[27] Jones' work is a social, economic, and administrative survey of the Empire. The information gleaned from Jones is a prerequisite for *The Limits of Empire: the Roman Army in the East* by Benjamin Isaac, *The Roman Near East, 31 BC–AD 337* by Fergus Millar; and *The Roman Empire of Ammianus* by John Matthews.[28] Isaac's work traces Rome's goals and objectives in the eastern provinces, whether they achieved their results and what impact Rome's activity had on its eastern subjects. Millar's work complements Isaac's as a social history tracing the development of the East by the Roman Army in relation to geography and changes in society imposed by the development of the new Imperial system in the early fourth-century. Matthew's analysis of Ammianus traces the transformation of the Roman world through the quill and experiences of the last great historian of the classical Latin tradition.

Study of the Late Roman Army is very popular with contemporary scholars. Authorities relevant to this book are: *The Late Roman Army* and *Roman Cavalry*, by Pat Southern and Karen R Dixon; *Byzantium and Its Army 281–1081*, by Warren Treadgold; *Twilight of Empire: the Roman Army from Diocletian Until the Battle of Adrianople*, by J Nicasie; *The Rise and Decline of the Late Roman Field Army*, by Richard Cromwell, and *Frontiers of the Empire* and *Warfare in Roman Europe AD 350–425*, by Hugh Elton. While these historians may disagree on the details of the transition of the Roman Army to the army that would be known as the Late Roman Army, and whether the Late Roman Empire had a grand strategy, they generally agree on the process of transformation and the beginning and end states.[29]

Unlike the first-century BCE, campaign analysis of the Late Roman military operations are rare. Those that have been published deal primarily with the sixth through tenth centuries.[30] No historian has published a work on the entire Nisibis War or attempted to reconstruct the defence of the East during the mid-fourth century. In 1982 Lightfoot explored the fourth century defence of the East in a dissertation but never published his work.[31] Those who have published articles have focused on specific sieges or Julian's campaign in 363.[32] Historian W E Kaegi has published a short article on 'Constantine's and Julian's Strategies of Strategic Surprise', and B H Warmington has published a short article on the 'Objectives and Strategy of Constantius II'. Both articles are excellent but of limited focus; they address strategy without a detailed analysis of the terrain, weather, or the opposing commander, Shapur.[33]

No detailed study of the Late Roman logistical system has been undertaken. The classic study of ancient army logistics is Donald W Engels' *Alexander the Great and the Logistics of the Macedonian Army*.[34] Published in 1980, this study has been the primary foundation for the analysis of Roman military campaigns until Jonathan P Roth published *The Roman Army at War (264 BC–AD 235)* in limited edition in 1999).[35] Both studies are relied upon herein since the technology of logistics did not change from the fourth century BCE to the mid-fourth century, and the daily food and fodder requirements did not change for man or beast until modern processed foods of the twentieth century replaced unprocessed rations in the military diet.

Archaeological evidence supports and elaborates upon the ancient sources. The Roman fortress city of Dura-Europus, on the Middle Euphrates, was stormed, sacked, and abandoned by the Persians in the mid-third century. It has become a time capsule for the study of Persian siege techniques, Roman defensive tactics, and social interaction between the civilian population and the Roman Army.[36] Most of the key fortress cities in the Roman East have remained inhabited down to the twenty-first century and, as a result, have been extensively studied.[37]

What is known of third and fourth century Sassanian* dynastic history has been derived from distorted versions of an early tenth century historical

---

* Alternate spelling is 'Sassnian.'

compendium presented by al-Tabari (839–923) and a massive epic completed by Firdawsi in the early ninth century.[38] Historian James Howard-Johnson concludes that both of these sources have pockets of authentic information augmented by anecdotes, romantic and heroic stories, and 'triggers for fanciful elaborations'.[39]

The secondary sources on Sassanian Persia are many and varied and cover all aspects of Sassanian society.[40] The main sources used in this study are Touraj Daryee's *Sassanian Iran (224–651 CE)*, Ahmad Tafazzoli's *Sassanian Society*, Kaveh Farrokh's *Shadows in the Desert: Ancient Persia at War* and James Howard-Johnson's *East Rome, Sassanian Persia and the End of Antiquity*.[41] As the Sassanian Army matured over the centuries, from a feudal host to a semi-professional army, it developed a series of military texts similar to the *Strategikon* and *Epitoma Rei Militaris*. Unfortunately, these texts did not survive other than as cited sources in early Islamic military texts.[42] As a result analysis of King Shapur's war plans must be deduced from terrain analysis and data derived from Roman and Armenian sources.

This thesis is a military history and, as a result, will follow a methodology similar to a modified campaign analysis. Military history cannot be viewed as a separate 'quaint' subset of history. It is a reflection of society and all of its complexities.[43]

As historian Stephen Morillo observed '[M]ilitary history is not the most respected branch of historical inquiry in academic circles.'[44] There is an opinion among academics that to write about war is to approve of it and to glorify it. As Herodotus so aptly stated, 'No one is so foolish as to prefer war to peace: in peace children bury their fathers, while in war fathers bury their children.' This is not only the opinion of the first ancient historian. Modern generals are more pacifists than their civilian leadership, liberal or conservative. War is not glory, as General Robert E. Lee observed: 'It is well that war is so terrible lest we grow too fond of it.'[45] Arthur Wellesley, Duke of Wellington, stated: 'Nothing except a battle lost can be half as melancholy as a battle won.'[46] As we enter the second decade of the twenty-first century despite our alleged advancements, war remains an aspect of mankind's existence and to remain ignorant to its causes and impact on society is folly.

Despite the objections of some of their colleagues, military historians today have published as broad a range of material based upon their political, ideological, and methodological interests as any other branch of history.[47] On fourth century Rome, there are more books and articles on the social and political aspects of the Roman military than there are on wars, campaigns, and battles. This study helps bridge that gap.

Knowledge of military terminology is critical to understanding how the Nisibis War changed Roman military methodology. 'Strategy' deals with the preparation for and the waging of war at the national level by kings and emperors. Historically, it has often been linked with the art of planning and directing campaigns. Today the 'art of campaigning' is known as operations. 'Tactics', strategy's partner, is the art of executing plans and handling troops in battle. Strategy is used herein with its modern connotation as the art of employing all the resources of an empire or kingdom to achieve objectives in war or peace.[48] An empire may conduct offensive operations with its armies (attacking enemy cities, raiding into enemy territory, etc.), but if its strategic objective is to maintain the status quo it is considered here to be on the strategic defensive. If a kingdom conducts a defensive campaign against an empire's offensive operations but has the objective of recovering territory lost in previous wars or causing a regime change in an opponent's government, it is considered in this work to be on the strategic offence. As Shapur and the various Roman emperors fenced for control of Mesopotamia, tactical success did not necessarily develop into strategic success, and tactical failure did not necessarily lead to strategic defeat.[49]

In the fourth century, educated Romans spoke Greek and Latin, but employing both transliterated terms in this work would be confusing. Technical terms and names, where possible, are in their Latin form or an English version: 'Constantine' rather than '*Konstantinos*' and 'legion V Parthia' instead of '*legio V Parthica*'. In Persian and Greek names macrons on long vowels are not used in this work.[50]

To reconstruct the defensive system of Diocletian that Constantius inherited when his father Constantine I assigned him to the East, circa 335, a detailed analysis of relevant sections of the *Notitia Dignitatum* is provided and two situational templates for 337 have been created. Templating is a modern military intelligence technique used to determine an enemy army's positions by studying its doctrine and historical methods of operations.[51] Once created, the template is adjusted for terrain and other factors into a situational template. Theorized enemy positions are plotted on a map and then confirmed or denied with reconnaissance. In this case, the recorded Roman deployment pattern circa 395 is applied to the portion of Mesopotamia lost in the treaty of 363. Reconnaissance is provided by Ammianus, the *Notitia Dignitatum,* as well as nineteenth, twentieth, and twenty-first century archaeological and historical field surveys.[52]

This study starts with the peace of Nisibis, forced upon the Persians by Diocletian in the Treaty of 298. Like many wars, the Nisibis War (337 to 363), had its beginning in the forced peace of the previous war. A detailed understanding of the terrain, weather, and economic factors of the Roman East and its interaction with Persia and Parthia is essential. After reviewing the Roman Eastern Theatre of Operation, a summary of the perpetual conflict between Rome and Parthia/Persia ending in a treaty of peace in 298 will set the stage for this study. Identification of the Roman leaders, their military structure, and the factors that influenced Constantius' decision to adopt an apparently non-Roman defensive strategy against the Persians, follows the terrain analysis. Next is the examination of King Shapur and his Persian army. As with other wars, the Nisibis War had its beginning in the forced peace of the previous war, and the next section examines the secular, religious, and military events that made the war inevitable.

The four phases of the war are then examined and analysed in detail. The first phase considered is the period 337 to 350 where the Romans successfully executed an active defence, wearing down the Persians in a war of attrition. Phase two, 351 to 358, became a stalemate as Shapur was forced to defend his eastern border against Hunnic tribes and Constantius marched west to defeat a usurper. Phase three examines why the Romans were forced by circumstances to adopt a passive defence strategy relying exclusively on their eastern *limitanei* armies between 358 and 360 and how Shapur's maturity as a general unhinged the Roman Mesopotamian defensive zone. The war's final phase, 362 to 363, concludes with Julian's return to the traditional offensive strategy that led to his decisive defeat. The conclusion summarizes the overall events that led to the Roman defeat and the establishment of a new defensive strategy that protected the Empire's eastern provinces for the next 300 years.

Chapter 2

Background of the Nisibis War

Rome and Parthia, and then Persia, had been at war off and on for five centuries prior to the outbreak of the Nisibis War in 337. During the Parthian period, with the exception of some spectacular Roman defeats, Rome dominated the wars but could not turn victory in war into permanent territorial gain. The Parthian ineptness at siege warfare combined with incompetent logistics and internal dissention made long-term occupation of raided Roman provinces unsuccessful.[1] This changed with the rise of the first Persian king, Ardashirs I, who defeated his Parthian overlords and established the Sassanian Dynasty in 224.

Upon establishing dominance over other Parthian clans, Sassanian and Roman ambitions clashed. During the third century, Rome, beset with internal civil wars and barbarian invasions, lost a series of wars with Persia. During these wars, Roman Syria and Mesopotamia were overrun, several large armies were lost, and an emperor was captured.[2] Despite improved Persian military capability in siege warfare, logistics, and internal organization, no significant territorial gains by either side were realized until 296. In that year, Caesar Galerius surprised King Narses' Persian army during a night attack near Satala, Armenia and destroyed it.[3] During the plundering of the Persian camp, King Narses' family was captured. Narses, wounded, barely escaped with his life. With the Persian army destroyed, Narses was unable to prevent Galerius from marching into the Persian homeland. Emperor (Augustus) Diocletian's war aims did not include the conquest of Persia and, therefore, Galerius was restrained from penetrating the Iranian Plateau. Diocletian viewed the victory at Satala as the termination of the conflict and did not advance further due to severely limited resources damaged by almost a century of conflict and civil wars.

The root cause of the Nisibis War was the humiliating terms of the treaty imposed upon the Persians by the Romans in 298. The treaty no longer exists but is described in a commentary by Peter the Patrician (circa 500–564). The treaty established the Tigris River as Rome's new eastern boundary with the eastern Trans-Tigris regions of *Intilene* (aka *Ingilene*), *Sophene*, *Arzanene*, *Corduene* (aka *Cordyene*), and *Zabdicene* ceded to Roman control. The Tigris became the new border. The fort of Zintha, on the border of Media, became the boundary of Armenia. Iberian and Albanian kings received their authority from Rome. The city of Nisibis, ceded to Rome, became the main centre for the silk and spice trade and Rome's administrative centre for the region.[4] Bezabde was established as a fortified town to safeguard the newly acquired Trans-Tigris region.[5] It is possible that at least one *limitaneus* legion, with supporting units, was established to occupy and patrol the Trans-Tigris region.

Historian R C Blockley puts the treaty in perspective. It placed the former Persian-occupied Armenian satrapies under Rome extending the Roman sphere of influence to Lake Van positioned to threaten Persian-controlled Adiabene. It provided for Roman possession of northern Mesopotamia and extended Armenia into Persian-held Adiabene, thus confirming Roman suzerainty over Armenia. Additionally, it recognized Roman suzerainty over Iberia and the strategically important east-west corridor between the Caspian and Black Seas south of the Caucasus Mountains. Finally, it designated Nisibis as the sole location for trade between Persia and Rome and granted Rome the ability to monitor the movement of merchants.[6]

The terms of the treaty imposed redress for Roman humiliation and losses endured at the hands of the Persians during the third century. However, they humiliated King Narses in the eyes of his nobility, threatened his western territories, and barred the Persians from Armenia and Iberia. In the intervening years between the signing of the treaty and Shapur II's majority (325), there was some unrest and raiding along the Roman-Persian frontier, but no outright breach of the treaty.[7]

In 325, Shapur turned sixteen and assumed the responsibilities of the King of Kings. He was obsessed with recovering the lost provinces, but he was not reckless. Prior to Shapur's majority, advisors and senior nobles guided the kingdom. While the humiliating treaty of 298 burned in his mind, Shapur faced more pressing problems from Saracen inroads into Persian Mesopotamia. According to Arab historian al-Tabri (circa 839–923), Shapur attacked with 1,000 warriors and seized the coast of the Persian Gulf and Arabian Peninsula driving the Saracens back into the desert.[8]

Shapur's Arab Wars were more complicated than a young warrior king leading 1,000 Savaran (knights) into battle. While the details are elusive, al-Tabri's account describes not only land campaigns but amphibious operations. The Persian military forces subdued not only the desert Saracens but also the city-states and small Arab kingdoms on the Arabian Peninsula granting Persia control of the trading ports along the India Ocean except for Roman Africa and Palestine. The evidence suggests that Shapur's 'Arab Solution' was part of an overall strategy to control the trade between India and Rome. Shapur's engineers built the 'Wall of Arabs' to keep the Saracens confined to the desert and to protect the settled Persian-Arab villages. This field fortification was a moat and wall that protected loyal Arab settlements from Hira to Bosera.[9] It is unclear whether this wall was a continuous barrier manned by Persian-Arab militias or a series of smaller walls and moats around individual villages. What is clear is that Shapur was interested in hydraulic, civil and military engineering from an early age and, as a young king, he gathered around him advisors with diverse military skills.[10]

Shapur's Arab Wars were not unnoticed by Constantine. Despite limited documentation of this period, historian Irfan Shahid concludes that Shapur's wars altered the balance of power in Arab lands causing pressure along the Arabian *Limes* and the *Strata Diocletiana* as the Saracen Lakhmid and Tanukhid Tribal Confederations rebounded from the Persian offensives.[11] This upheaval disrupted trade as evidenced by the alleged Persian pilferage of a gift from an Indian king sent to Constantine and carried by the philosopher Metrodorus. This event is estimated to have occurred in 326 or 327, but was not, as Ammianus argues, a *casus belli* for Constantine to go to war against Persia ten years later. Instead of being goaded into war, Constantine focused upon the establishment of his new capital at Constantinople and pacifying the Danube *Limes* from the Goths and Sarmatians, a task he completed in 334.[12]

The incident demonstrates that Rome had economic and diplomatic interests in India during the fourth century. Shahid argues that Constantine pursued a vigorous trade policy in the 330s as he prepared for war against Persia.[13] This was the period when the Roman Red Sea ports of Berenike

Map 1. King Shapur's Saracen Wars 324–335.[14] Shapur II's Arab Wars disrupted Rome's trade for incense with the kingdoms on the Arabian Peninsula and cause increased pressure from displaced Saracen tribes along Rome's desert *limes*. Despite this fact, Constantine I chose not to address the Persian problem until he settled the conflict with the Goths along the Danube.

and Myos Hormos were expanding.[15] While the fourth century trade may not have been at the same volume as the first and second centuries, it was overcoming the slump of the third century. Based upon records of port activities, many skilled captains sailed between Roman Africa and India, propelled by monsoon winds and bypassing Persian controlled ports.

Rome's adoption of Christianity created a religious aspect to the friction between the empires. Once Constantine defeated his last competitor, Licinius, in 324 he established Christianity as the de facto religion of the Roman Empire. Constantine mandated Christianity as part of his foreign policy. In concluding treaties with the Goths in 332 and the Sarmatians in 334, he insisted on religious stipulations. Constantine assumed the role of protector of Christians and the responsibility for converting pagans. These personal attitudes shaped his policy toward Persia and the Christians living under the domination of the Zoroastrian King Shapur.[16]

Constantine wrote a personal letter, recorded by Eusebus, to Shapur during routine political discourse in 324. The letter was polite but proselytized Christianity. Shapur's response is unknown. The conversion of the Kingdom of Iberia to Christianity around 330 and Constantine's foreign policy along the Danube would have troubled the Persians with their large Christian minority. Shapur would have been aware that, as a young officer, Constantine had marched with Galerius to Ctesiphon in 298. Shapur likely concluded that Constantine intended war on Persia once his other borders were pacified.[17] Before 337, with the exception of a brief period at the end of the third century, Christians had been tolerated in Persia. The result of Constantine's proselytizing was the creation of a perceived internal threat to the Persian monarchy that resulted in renewed persecution.[18]

The traditional Roman Imperial military strategy could be defined in modern terms as political high-intensity warfare. As historian Matyszak explains, Rome was not interested in seizing strategic areas of real estate or disrupting lines of communication. Roman generals headed directly toward the enemy's governmental centre intending to destroy the enemy's will to resist by capturing the capital and destroying, en route, the enemy army. The defeated nation or tribe would negotiate terms and a Roman civilian administrator or collaborator would be placed in charge.[19]

This strategy, as applied in the fourth century, required a large, readily available army deployable at the emperor's personal command and explains the creation of the *comitatus* or elite central field army despite criticism that it weakened the empire's defence. Blockley asserts that Constantine's *comitatus* was an '…instrument of a policy that was militarily and politically aggressive, even expansionist'.[20] Yet, Constantine only created a single field army and could not attack the Persians until the Danube region was pacified.[21] It was not until around 335 that he could turn his attention toward Persia. Believing an attack was imminent, Shapur struck while Constantine was engaged along the Danube. Constantine sent his son, Constantius, as caesar to Antioch to guard the eastern frontier. In 336, a Persian army marched into Armenia and installed a Persian nominee to the throne. Constantine responded by fielding an expedition with religious overtones of a crusade that included, for the first time in Roman history, a contingent of Christian bishops.

From the limited evidence available, Shahid theorizes that Constantine's campaign envisioned two armies striking into Persia. His plan entrusted Constantius to command the army at Antioch and his nephew Hannibalianus to command the second army in Cappadocia. Constantine would take the field in person as commander-in-chief to direct operations. It appears his ultimate goal upon defeating Persia was to replace Shapur on the Persian throne with Hannibalianus.[22] Hannibalianus was the son of Constantine's half-brother Flavius Damatius. Constantine elevated Hannibalianus to the thrones of Pontus and Armenia with the eventual intent of replacing Shapur. As Potter points out, this arrangement was unique. 'No other previous emperor had made plans for succession that depended upon the occupation of new territory or installation of a relative upon a foreign throne.'[23]

In Walter E Kaegi's essay, based upon John Lydus' sixth century summary of Constantine's and Cornelius' fourth century records, the Romans were planning a surprise attack on Persia in 337. Constantine's plan involved a two-prong attack with one army attacking through Armenia and a second army attacking through Mesopotamia.[24] As historian A D Lee notes, advance warning of pending invasions always reached the enemy. In this case, a Persian embassy arrived in Constantinople with the aim of dissuading Constantine from his plan.[25]

Julian explains in his oration 'In Honour of the Emperor Constantius', written circa 355, that when Constantius assumed command of the regional ad hoc Army of the East circa 335, it was unprepared for war.[26] Training had been relaxed and recruitment had declined. Units were not fully manned and military supplies had not been stockpiled. Constantius recruited or drafted veterans' sons of military age and implemented training and drill for the infantry. The cavalry was expanded with new *cataphractarii* regiments. Supplies were stockpiled.[27]

These preparations did not go unnoticed by the Persians. In 336, the Persian general Narses, possibly a brother of Shapur, stormed Amida and marched into Roman Mesopotamia. Constantius marched out with his regional army and defeated and killed Narses at the Battle of Narasara.[28] He then marched on Amida and reoccupied and rebuilt it. The new fortifications included high walls and stout towers armed with artillery.[29]

Rome's war plans failed when Constantine fell ill in April 337 and died on 22 May near Nicomedia.[30] According to historian Benjamin Isaac: 'the mechanism of [Roman] decision-making was influenced primarily by the interests of the emperor in safeguarding his position and enhancing his glory....'[31]

Constantine had shared his Imperial power with five relatives raised to the rank of Caesar. Three were sons by his second wife Fausta (Constantine II, Constantius II and Constans) and two were sons of his half-brother Flavius Dalmatius (Dalmatius and Hannibalianus). He also awarded the title of Augusta to his daughter Constantia (born after 306 and before 317, she died in 354) While most historians view this as merely an honorary title, Constantia grew to become a political force in her own right.

After winning a number of civil wars in the wake of the failure of Diocletian's succession scheme, Constantine became the sole ruler of the Roman Empire; it is difficult to take Eusebius' assertion at face value that he intended his three sons to rein as co-heirs. It is difficult to imagine that after establishing a system of one augustus assisted by five caesars that Constantine did not plan to have Constantine II, his eldest son, reign as sole augustus. The regions assigned to Constantine II, Spain, Gaul and Britain, were where Constantine I's father had established his power base in 306. The caesars in question were all young men in their late teens or early

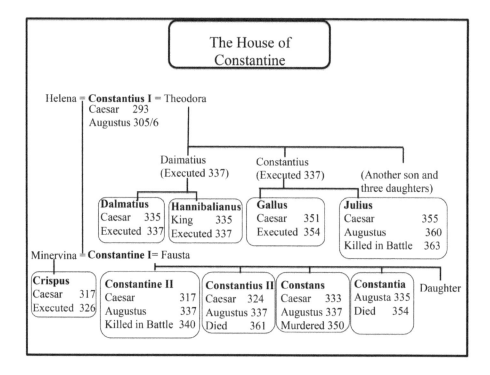

The House of Constantine

Helena = **Constantius I** = Theodora
Caesar   293
Augustus 305/6

Daimatius
(Executed 337)

Constantius
(Executed 337)

(Another son and three daughters)

Dalmatius
Caesar   335
Executed 337

Hannibalianus
King   335
Executed 337

Gallus
Caesar   351
Executed 354

Julius
Caesar   355
Augustus   360
Killed in Battle   363

Minervina = **Constantine I** = Fausta

Crispus
Caesar   317
Executed 326

Constantine II
Caesar   317
Augustus   337
Killed in Battle 340

Constantius II
Caesar   324
Augustus 337
Died   361

Constans
Caesar   333
Augustus 337
Murdered 350

Constantia
Augusta 335
Died   354

Daughter

twenties and had all been assigned competent senior advisors to assist them in ruling.[32] The fact that Constantine II attempted to assert himself over Constans, which led to his death in 340, indicates that at least in Constantine II's mind he should have been senior augustus.

While many historians blame 'the Army' for a vicious coup and blood bath that left Constantine's three sons in power, this assertion is unrealistic. The contemporary and near contemporary historians of Late Antiquity were reluctant to blame high or mid-level civilian officials or army officers for these executions. Tribunes, counts, dukes, civil servants and generals controlled Roman armies, not the rank and file. A *pedes* did not decide with his tent mates in a tavern to murder a caesar or declare their general or count an emperor. It is more likely that some agent of the ruling class stirred up dissent and or distributed gold to turn grumbling soldiers into rebellion in support of a political agenda.

The first of the five caesars to arrive in Constantinople after Constantine I's death was 19-year-old Constantius. Being the centre of Constantine I's power, Constantinople was the hub of the Imperial administration and communication network. The key functionaries of the Roman civil service and army administration were also located in the capital city. It would not have been in the interest of the Roman government for the five caesars to start fighting for control of the empire. It would therefore not be surprising that the 19-year-old Caesar Constantius would have been easily persuaded by his advisors to take steps to prevent the empire descending back into civil war. The fact that the army declared they would serve only the sons of Constantine I and murdered Dalmatius in the Balkans and Hannibalianus in Anatolia was not a spontaneous revolt of the rank and file of those armies. The caesars were not the only male relatives of the Imperial family that were purged. While there is no direct evidence that Constantius gave the order, the fact that he was in the Imperial capital at the time surrounded by the senior civil and military officials of the empire, makes him the prime suspect for issuing the order of execution.[33]

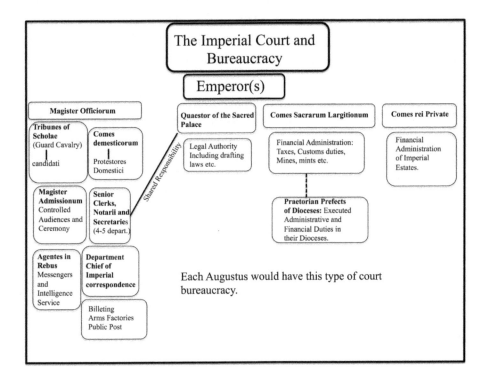

With three court bureaucracies to fill ambitious court officials saw opportunities.

Additional murders carried out on the orders of ambitious clergy, civil administrators and military officers were not likely usurpation attempts but designed to secure the independence of the new augusti from the advisors appointed by their father and to secure positions for themselves as new advisors.[34] Flavius Ababius, Prefect of the East heads the list of the prominent non-family government officials that were purged. Following the purge of the caesars, princes and high ranking officials the three co-augusti met, in Sirmium, in September 337 to determine the division of the empire.[35] Sirmium was the capital of Constans' prefecture, the place of Constantius' birth and a major logistics centre for the Danube campaigns that Constantine II participated in with his father in 323.[36]

Besides addressing the major issue of their areas of responsibilities the brothers issued coins and strengthened the fortifications along the Danubian *Limes*. Commemorating these joint activities Constantius' Duke Sappo (prefect of the *Limes* of Scythia) erected a monument giving credit for the repairs of the fortress of *Troesmis* (Turcoaia) listing the brothers augusti in order of age: Constantine, Constantius and Constans.[37] The seniority of the three augusti would disrupt the harmony of the triumvirate within three years.

During Constantius' absence, the Armenians revolted.[38] Shapur took advantage of the situation and, with his army, massed earlier to oppose the Roman invasion, marched on Nisibis and besieged it, possibly as early as May 337 but at least by mid-summer 337.[39] A twenty-five-year war followed.

Chapter 3

The Military Aspects of the Geography

Climate, and Weather of the Roman East

'The nature of the ground is often of more consequence than courage.'[1]

The Treaty of 298 forced a geopolitical disaster upon the Persians. Most historians fail to recognize that the terms of the treaty handed the Romans two daggers pointed at the heart Persia.[2] A portion of Media was attached to Armenia, five regions were torn from Persia, the Kingdoms of Iberia and Albania were added to the Roman sphere of influence, and the Tigris was established as the new boundary between Rome and Persia. Persia's northern and western frontiers were vulnerable to Roman assault. Roman armies were stationed at the very edge of the Iranian plateau within 'a fortnight's march' of the Persian heartland.[3] The theatre of operations of the Nisibis War stretched from the Caucasus Mountains and the Caspian Sea in the north to the Indian Ocean in the south and from Antioch on the Mediterranean Sea east to the fortified oasis city of Merv. This theatre encompassed scorching deserts, fertile steppes, river valleys, and desolate alpine passes.[4] An examination of the geopolitical factors within the Tigris–Euphrates Valley is critical since the majority of military operations occurred there. The terrain and weather in the Tigris–Euphrates Valley, or Mesopotamia, was far different than the Mediterranean climate prevalent in the province of Syria and the major centres of Greco-Roman civilization. The climate of the Tigris–Euphrates Valley, as described by primary sources in the fourth century, was similar to its current climate. The climate within the valley itself differed significantly from that in the city of Nisibis in the north to the city of Ctesiphon in the south.

In the northern end of the valley lies the Mesopotamian Plain, bounded on the north by the Tarsus Mountains, on the south by the Sanjara Ridge, on the east by the Tigris River, and on the west by the Euphrates River. This region, basically the Roman provinces of Mesopotamia and Osrhoene,

Map 2. Nisibis War Theatre of Operations 337–363.[5] In the fourth century the Oxus River flowed into the Caspian and Aral Seas, supporting trade routes and nomad pasture land outside Persian controlled territory. Because of this trade route the semi-independent kingdom of Iberia between the Black and Caspian Seas was of strategic importance to both Rome and Persia.

received sufficient rainfall for dry farming and wild grass that survived the summer dry season. The central and southern portions of the valley required irrigation, and those areas that were not irrigated remained desert. The daily high temperature in the middle and southern parts of the valley reached 120 degrees Fahrenheit in June 2010 and, based upon Ammianus' account, the temperature in 363 was equally debilitating. The harvest in the upper, middle, and lower valley – then and now – takes place in June.[6] The harvest in the eastern Mediterranean region was earlier than in the Tigris-Euphrates Valley. Legumes, such as lentils, are harvested in April and May, barley in April, wheat in May, and chickpeas as late as June. The campaign season for northern Mesopotamia was from March to October. The winter season, November to March, subjects the region to heavy rains and freezing temperatures that are also common as far south as the modern city of Mosul. Olives ripen in the fall and do well after a cold winter. Campaigns normally started in the spring and ended with the onset of winter, normally in November.[7]

Supplementing food supplies into Roman Syria and Mesopotamia for military stockpiling or overcoming effects of famine required detailed Imperial planning. The Eastern Mediterranean was dangerous between 22 September and 27 May and closed to shipping between 11 November and 10 March. Individual shipper's grain fleets were often tied up for up to twenty-four months on a single run from Alexandria to Constantinople. It took months for the Imperial government to shift the flow of grain from its routine sea lanes to build up supplies for a military expedition or alleviate the effects of famine. Only the Imperial government could afford to move grain long distances over roads. As a result grain was more expensive in cities than in villages due to the distance it had to travel. In 362, the Emperor Julian prided himself on bringing to Antioch the help needed to overcome the effects of the famine. He moved the grain using the Imperial wagons of the *cursus publicus* from the City of Hierapolis, a mere 100 miles inland from Antioch.[8]

The Sassanian Empire was a highland empire with the Iranian Plateau as its centre of gravity. These mountainous regions, particularly the mountain spine of the Zagros, provided Shapur with manpower, horses, and other vital resources.[9] The key to decisively defeating Persia was penetrating the Iranian plateau. The same passes used by the merchants of the Silk Road during the summer became impassable during the winter months increasing the effectiveness of the Zagros Mountains as a natural fortification. The map of Persia is deceptive. A large part of the centre of the kingdom was desert. The Persian heartland followed the Zagros Mountains northwest to the vicinity of the City of Hamadan, turning east along the forested shores of the Caspian Sea and the Elburz Mountains. The central part of the empire was arid desert with pockets of habitation where water was available. The eastern border stretched from the grasslands of Gurgaon abutting the mountains of Khurasan to the deserts to the southeast.[10]

One of the four Great Fire Temples of Zoroastrianism was located at Takht-I Sulsimun in Atroatene (aka Media and modern Iranian Azerbaijan) where the Persian heartland turned east. This was an important religious location with a fire temple built at the site in Achaemenian times. It remained an important religious site throughout the Parthian and Sassanian periods. The crusading Roman Army of Emperor Heraclius destroyed it in 624.[11]

Three main trade routes from the Roman Empire lay open to the Far East. The most dangerous northern route started at the Black Sea, headed east through the river valleys of the Caucasian country, across the Caspian Sea, and up the Oxus River into China or India. This route avoided Parthian and Persian-controlled territory. The second route started at Roman-controlled Nisibis and followed the Tigris River down to Ctesiphon crossing Persia toward China or India. The southern route was by sea, beginning at the Romans' Egyptian Red Sea ports following the monsoon wind pattern to India and back.[12]

Historian M P Charlesworth argues that during the Parthian period, Roman operations in Iberia, Albania, and eastern Armenia were not aimed at defending against Parthian raids, but rather to secure the northern trade route. This northern trade route circumvented Parthian-controlled territory. Trade along this route followed the Oxus River west, crossed the Caspian Sea, and then continued west up the Araxes River. Charlesworth argues, based upon Tacitus, that the Roman General Corbulo utilized the Araxes River, Caspian Sea, and Cyrus River as supply lines during his first century campaign. While the Araxes Valley suffered some Parthian raids, the Cyrus River and Oxus River route to Samarkand were never threatened by Parthian or Persian domination. During antiquity, the Oxus River (modern Amur River) emptied into the Caspian and the Aral Sea.[13] Charlesworth argues that first and second century Romans secured this region west of the Caspian Sea due to its value as a trade route.[14]

The central route was the Silk Road passing through the Persian heartland. From Ctesiphon, the route climbed the Zagros Mountains via the Diyala River to the Iranian Plateau and continued past the great rock at Behistun to Ecbatana. The route continued though the cities of Hamadan and Damghan east to Merv. At this point, the route split into a southern route leading to Alexandropolis (modern Kandahar) and a northern alternative through Bactra that eventually arrived at the 'stone tower' where the Chinese merchants were met.[15]

The Indian Ocean was the third route and it bypassed Parthia/Persia. Despite Shapur's control of Arabian Peninsula ports, Roman-Indian trade flourished during the fourth century thanks to monsoons that enabled shipping to bypass the Persian ports. The Greek sea captain Hippalus rediscovered the monsoon wind pattern during the first century. Ships departing Egypt in July reached India in September by sailing directly across the Indian Ocean without entering a Parthian or Persian Port. They returned by sailing west in November landing at a Roman Red Sea port and arriving in Egypt in February.[16] The deep sea monsoon route to India did not preclude local coastal trade routes. Silks and other products from China and Southeast Asia continued to arrive at Roman provinces via these routes as well.[17] The routes that utilized Persian ports or crossed Persia converged at Ctesiphon and then flowed up the Tigris to Nisibis were subject to a hefty Persian tariff and could be easily interdicted during wartime.[18]

While little is known about the northern route it was important to Rome because it bypassed Parthia and Persia. During the first and second centuries, Roman emperors campaigned to gain control of Iberia and Albania through which the northern route traversed.[19] During the late third century, Persia campaigned in the region and brought the Kingdoms of Iberia and Albania within its sphere of influence, thereby cutting off Roman trade along this northern route. The Treaty of 298 returned Iberia and Albania to the Roman sphere of influence supporting a hypothesis that Diocletian, or someone at his court, wanted to re-establish Roman dominance of this route. The eastern part of this route skirted Persian territory following the Oxus River possibly through the territory of King Grumbates of the *Chionite* (a tribe of Huns).[20]

Michael Loewe contends that Roman merchants used this route to avoid the consequences of travelling through Persia.[21] During the early empire a large part of the state's income came from taxing international commerce.[22] It is reasonable that these trade considerations would have influenced foreign policy in the fourth century and explains why the Indian Ocean once again became a Roman interest.

Since the discovery of the monsoon wind pattern during the first century, Roman trade with India was brisk. Rome had extensive economic ties with the kingdoms along the Indus River and west coast of India.[23] Trade flourished during the second century but suffered during the mid-third century crisis but rebounded toward the end. A Roman soldier, *Optio* Aurelius Gaius, claims to have served in India on a grave marker he erected for his wife at the close of the third century.[24] The India reference is listed as the fourteenth location Aurelius served, and the voyage may have been in the 290s. The Indian posting follows *Optio* Aurelius Gaius' service at Alexandria and in Egypt. It is possible that his century was sent with merchant ships to protect them from pirates on the sea and brigands at Roman trading ports in India.

Stability during the early and mid-fourth century resulted in the resurgence of Indian Ocean maritime trade. In the middle of the fourth century, the Roman Red Sea port of Berenike expanded operations linking Indian Ocean trade with Egyptian markets via caravan routes.[25] Roman and Indian ships bypassed Persian ports thereby excluding the Persian middlemen and evading revenue collection. The Nisibis War interfered with merchant traffic along the Silk Road, and Persian merchants took to the Indian Ocean to compete with Romans in the Indian markets.[26]

Prior to the Treaty of 298 Rome benefited from merchants using these three trade routes. Two of these routes provided access to and overlapped potential invasion routes: the northern and the central Silk Road; however, Rome did not control these trade routes. After the Treaty of 298, the border and the parties' spheres of influence shifted and Rome acquired military access to two of these trade routes: the northern route and the central Silk Road route. Rome also acquired access to a third route that had not been used for trade but was suitable for an invasion route.

The Treaty of 298 provided Rome access to three invasion routes into Persia, Armenia, and Media on the Iranian Plateau. The first and northernmost invasion route was from the Araxes River and the Kingdoms of Iberia and Albania (modern day Georgia) into the Persian heartland. The Roman General Corbulo campaigned in this region during his first century campaign. The second central route was a fourteen-day march from Bezabde across the Tigris River, across the Greater Zab and through the Zagros Mountains via the Rawanduz Pass into the vicinity of the Fire Temple at Takht-I Sulsimun in Atroatene.[27] Another fortnight's march would have brought a Roman army to Hamadan, the hub of the Silk Road. This route, in reverse, was used by Heraclius to invade Persian Mesopotamia from the Persian heartland.[28]

The third southernmost route required the Roman army to take Ctesiphon before marching up the Diyala River through the Zagros passes in order to attack Hamadan. This route was weather dependent since the passes were blocked by snow until as late as June.[29] This invasion route had two branches into Persian Mesopotamia that followed the Tigris and Euphrates Rivers. In 363, the Euphrates avenue of approach was defended by a series of island city fortresses, supported by the heavily fortified city of Peroz-Shapur, downstream from the major canal intake that linked both rivers.[30] The second invasion route followed the Tigris. Little is known about fortifications along this route. On the eastern bank of the Tigris, the intersecting rivers of the Great Zab, Lesser Zab, Adheim, and Diyala formed natural defensive barriers. The west bank was primarily desert. During the Roman Emperor Heraclius' 627 Campaign, the Lesser Zab had fortifications defending its four bridges and was probably defended in the fourth century as well.[31] The Euphrates River was fed by the melting snow packs on the Anatolian plateau. The melting snow on the Anatolian plateau and Zargos Mountains fed the Tigris making the crossing of four major rivers difficult.[32] Until the passes melted in June, an invading army attacking from Ctesiphon could not march into the heart of Persia.

Both avenues of approach led to the key city of Ctesiphon. Ctesiphon was the Persian Imperial capital and was one of the great cities of Late Antiquity. Ctesiphon's importance was due to its being the main distribution centre for the overland spice and silk route and sea trade with China and India.[33] Today, the ruins of this great metropolis lie 20 miles southeast of modern Baghdad and comprise 18.7 square miles. In comparison fourth century

Map 3.[34]

Rome was only 8.5 square miles.[35] Ctesiphon was originally one huge city. It is unclear when, but sometime prior to the fourth century, the Tigris jumped its banks, shifted east, and divided the city. In 337 Ctesiphon was actually two fortified cities at the time of the Nisibis War: Ctesiphon on the east bank and Coche on the west bank.[36] The configuration of the Tigris combined with challenging regional conditions such as canals, flooding, swamps, insects, extreme humidity, and scorching heat, made capturing Ctesiphon a complicated military problem in the fourth century.[37] Despite these obstacles, the city was captured four times in the second and third centuries and was last threatened by the Romans when the crusading army of Emperor Heraclius marched on it in 627.[38]

Chapter 4

The Mid-Fourth Century Roman Army and the Strategic Defence of the East

rom the third century on, the Roman Army faced a variety of threats and was constantly at war along its long frontier or within its borders. In the east, Rome faced the large conventional army of Sassanian Persia capable of raiding, launching full-scale invasions of conquest, and siege warfare. Along the Rhine-Danube *Limes*, barbarians of various origins, ranging from small war bands to large tribal confederations, threatened penetration of Roman defences and engaged in hit-and-run raids. Saracen (nomadic Arab) tribes harassed the trade routes of the East, and North African tribes harried Egypt and Rome's other African provinces. The Roman Army itself posed a threat as it sporadically supported usurpers and contenders for the throne. Finally, the *Bagundae*, small bands of insurgents or bandits, terrorized civilian populations and occasionally grew strong enough to form a sizable force to offer open battle with the Roman Army.[1]

The defensive system that Diocletian implemented, which was finalized by Constantine, differed from the Servian system by the creation of a two-tiered military force: the *Comitatenses* and the lower and less prestigious tier *Limitanei*. 'Limitanei' was the general term for all units along the *limes*.[2] All *limitanei* regiments that formed the frontier armies were descendants of the Roman Army of Principate, were tasked with the mission of defending the *limites* and were based in fortified cities, fortresses, and forts.[3] The *comitatenses* units were originally created from detachments of the old Roman Army. These regiments and legions were stationed in the provincial interiors with the strategic mission to intercept border incursions or invasions that the *limitanei* could not defeat or control.[4] Two other types of units are referenced in historical sources. The *Scholae* regiments were guard units created by Constantine after the Praetorian Guard was disbanded. They were the personal guards of the emperor. Finally, there was the *Protectors Domestici.*

This special regiment was partly guard regiment, officer candidate school, and Staff College, and it provided staff officers for the various army generals.

A *Praesental* (in the presence of the emperor) Army of *scholae* and *comitatenses* legions and regiments was attached to the court.[5] In 364, the empire's massed *Praesental* Army for the Persian war was estimated by Cromwell to contain 137 regiments and legions with theoretical strength of between 90,000 and 100,000 men, but may have been reduced by losses in the Nisibis War to 30,000.[6] In March 363, sources arguably indicate Julian's *Praesental* Army mustered 85,000 to 95,000 men. Constantine's massed *Praesental* Army in 337 could have matched Julian's army and may have been larger.[7]

Under Constantine, the command and control of the *Praesental* Army was simple. He commanded the army and was assisted by a *magister per peditum* (master or field marshal of infantry) and a *magister per equitum* (master or field marshal of cavalry) with dukes (*duces*) commanding the *limitanei* units in their provinces. After Constantine's death, the empire and *Praesental* Army was divided among his three sons. While there are no sources detailing the split of the army, an even split would have provided the three co-emperors with approximately 30,000 to 40,000 men each.[8] The three brothers appointed their own *magister per peditum* and *magister per equitum* to assist them in the command and control of their regions.

Constantius' share of the empire included not only the East but the region of Thrace, as well. Because both fronts were at war, and Constantius could not be in both places at once, he initially did not want to detach his *magister peditum* or *equitum* from his *Praesental* Army.[9] His solution was to create the position of *comites rei militaris* (military count) who commanded small regional *comitatus* field armies detached from the *Praesental* Army. The military counts were generals in their own right and were normally given commands of limited duration. Count Lucillianus commanded Nisibis during the 350 siege, while Count Aelianus commanded a small army to reinforce Amida and took command of its defence upon his arrival in 359.[10] There were exceptions to limited-term commands of the military counts such as the count Constantius placed in command of Thrace and the count commanding the *limitis Aegypt* (Egypt).[11]

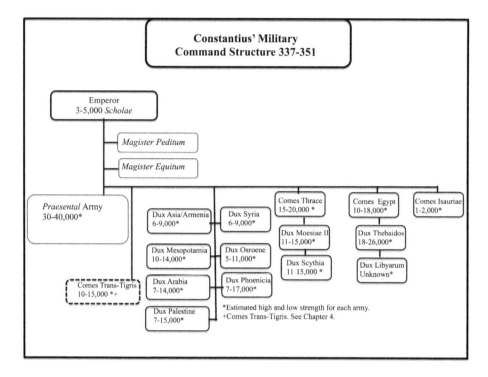

Eventually, Constantius detached his *magister peditum* to command in Thrace, and he was assisted in the East only by his *magister equitum*. After 353, when Constantius ruled the empire alone, he commanded his *Praesental* Army assisted by a *magister peditum* and *equitum*. Each of the three regional field armies (Gaul, Illyrucum, and the East) were commanded by their own *magister militum*.[12]

Two generals (*comes* or *magisters*) were normally placed in command of large operations. While in theory the lines of seniority and command responsibility appear clear, in execution they were modified by the character and temperament of the individuals involved. In 357, Barbatio, the *magister peditum*, commanding an army of 25,000 men, and Caesar Julian, commanding 13,000 men, failed to cooperate in a joint operation against the Alamanni.[13] Sabinianus' failure to cooperate with Ursicinus was one of the primary causes of the Roman defeat in 359.[14] Despite these notable failures due to the violation of the principle of 'unity of command', the Roman system of appointing two commanders for large armies when the emperor was not present did not normally distract from military operations.

The Roman field armies evolved from the third century and early fourth century chaos of Persian and Germanic invasions and civil war. Full ten cohort legions (hereafter, antique legions) could not be withdrawn from the *limites,* so detachments known as *vexillationes* were sent to reinforce the threatened region.[15] Historian H M D Parker theorizes that, in the army of Constantine and his successors, a legion *comitatensis* numbered about 1,000 men and was commanded by a tribune. Such legions began as *vexillationes* from antique legions.[16]

The creation of some *comitatenses* legions can be traced, if not accurately dated. A case in point was the legion III (tertia) *Diocletiana* (Diocletian). Starting life as an antique legion during Diocletian's reign and stationed in Egypt, the *Notitia* lists III Diocletian under the command of the Count of the Egyptian Border, a legion III Diocletian under the command of the Duke of Thebes, and a legion III Diocletian *Thaeorum* under the command of the *Magister Militum* in Thrace.[17] It appears that these units were created as detachments from the antique legion III *Diocletiana* and never returned to their parent organization.[18]

In tracing the organization of fourth century Roman Army units this study addresses the problem from traditional Roman organizations as modified by the original sources. The Roman logistics system was based upon the *contubernium* (tent group) of eight, the infantry century of eighty, and the cavalry *turma* of thirty-two with a *modii* of grain feeding eight men for one day. Divining a military organization from reported troop strength is futile. No professional military unit has ever been at its recorded strength. Real units are over or under strength. Units are normally under strength until the beginning of a campaign when they are built up to strength or over-strength. Once the campaign starts, attrition immediately starts to reduce the formation. Disease and injury in pre-twentieth century armies killed or maimed more friendly soldiers than enemy action. For example, the two legions (*Lanciarii* and *Mattiarii*) providing the security screen for Julian's advance in March 363 averaged 750 men each while two cavalry regiments providing security in 359 for Amida are reported totalling 700 men or an average of 350 men each.[19] Determining the authorized strength for these four units is futile without some knowledge of their internal structure.

The smaller fourth century *comitatensis* legion organization reflected a modified version of their parent organization. The structure was based upon two antique cohorts: six centuries of eighty men, each century commanded by a centurion who was assisted by an *optio*.[20] The antique cohort did not need a command structure, but the sources indicate that a tribune commanded the new cohort. The *vicarious* was second in command; *primicerius*, chief of staff; *adjutor*, cohort clerk; *campidoctor*, drill instructor; *actuarii and optiones*, quartermasters; plus heralds, standard-bearers, and musicians; in total, 501 men with the fighting strength of 480 men and a command and staff headquarters of twenty-one. Treadgold's research concludes that two cohorts, plus a command and staff headquarters, put the theoretical strength of the fourth century *Comitatensis* legion at approximately 1,023. Unlike Jones, Treadgold concludes that a prefect commanded the *comitatensis* legion. Jones has prefects commanding legions and tribunes commanding cohorts only in *limitanei* legions.[21] Ammianus refers to *comitatensis* legionary, *auxilia*, and cavalry commanders as tribunes, and Jones considers the term 'tribune' as a general term for regimental commander.[22] Both scholars could be correct with 'prefect' being the fourth century title of a legion commander and tribune being the rank or pay grade of the officer. A similar situation occurs in modern navies where a lieutenant commander may command a ship but he is also 'the captain' of the ship with all of the titles, operational and legal responsibilities.

The *limitanei* legions varied in size depending on the number of *comitatenses* legions created from their original organization and the number of major fortresses and cities they garrisoned. The basic organization referred to above applied to the *limitanei* legions, but the number of cohorts varied. Most historians, when computing the size of the *limitanei* legions of this period, depending upon their responsibilities, put them at between 2,000 and 4,000 men or three to five cohorts.[23] The *limitanei* rank structure would have been based upon the traditional rank structure with a prefect commanding the legion. Some legions, like the IV Parthia, held key fortresses such as Circesium on the Euphrates River, and may have maintained the strength of an antique legion well into the late fourth century.[24]

Auxilia regiments, not to be confused with the older auxiliary cohorts, formed an elite corps within the fourth century Roman Army. The first regiment was raised in 306 from a Germanic war band.[25] They were instrumental in declaring Constantine I Augustus, and their valour in battle was instrumental in his victories in the following civil wars. Unlike the earlier auxiliaries, the new *Auxilia* Corps was not a supporting organization for the legions. They fought alongside the legions in the main battle line and may have been similarly equipped.[26] Since the third century, the arms and equipment of the legionaries and auxiliary became standardized with both corps equipped and trained to fight in open and close order.[27] Equipped similarly to the legionaries, the new *auxilia* were versatile but often ill-disciplined warriors from the Rhineland. These new Roman soldiers were capable of skilfully swimming major rivers using their shields as paddle boards, surprising Persian soldiers or Germanic warriors alike, and standing within the shield wall with their legionary counterparts.[28] Once enrolled in the armies of Rome, they had no qualms about fighting their kinsmen and plundering and burning their villages. It is not clear whether they only accepted recruits from the tribes that originally made up the newly formed regiment.

As newly formed units, without a legacy from the antique legions, they may have followed the alternative organization with *auxilia* junior officers bearing the titles *circitor, biarchus, centenaries*, and *ducenarius* instead of the traditional *optio* and centurion.[29] This also suggests that the maniple of two or three centuries was important as the title *ducenarius* means commander of 'two hundred'. Logistically, they would have been divided into *contubernum* 'tent-groups' of eight and centuries of eighty. With the rank of *circitor* or *biarchus* replacing the traditional *Decurion* (commander of eight), the full regiment would have mirrored the *comitatensis* legion. Based upon the *Notitia Dignitatum*, by the 390s, the *auxilia* corps provided a large part of the main infantry fighting force of the Eastern and Western *Praesentalis* armies and Western regional field armies. They were the primary force that declared Julian Augustus.

Despite their versatility, the *auxilia* corps did not provide all the capabilities of the legions. Being initially recruited from upper class Germanic warriors, they thought the normal fatigue work of the legionaries beneath them. According to Vegetius in the later fourth century, the weight of arms and armour of the *auxilia* corps may have been lighter than the legions. As a result, new western recruits flocked to the *auxilia* regiments in preference to joining the legions.[30]

Experts agree that the cavalry regiments of the fourth century had an official strength of between 500 and 600 men.[31] Cavalry before the reforms of the later third century were generally organized into four basic organizations. The majority of the cavalry were organized into auxiliary regiments (*alae* or wings) of approximately 500 to 1,000 men and a mixed formation of infantry and cavalry. The antique legions organized 726 *equites legionis* (legionary cavalry) into *turmae* and attached two of them to the ten cohorts. The basic tactical organization of all third century cavalry was the thirty-two-man *turma* (troop) commanded by a *decurio* (decurion). Sixteen *turmae* formed an *ala quintgenaria* of 512 men and twenty-four *turmae* formed an *ala milliaria* of 768 men. The adjective '*milliaria*' suggests that the unit's strength was 1,000 men, but like the term 'century', Roman traditional unit naming practices did not equate to unit strengths.

In the legionary cavalry, a centurion may have commanded two *turmae*. Thus the antique legions contained twenty-two *turmae* for a total of 704 men instead of 1,000.[32] In reviewing these organizations logistically, they are divisible by eight making logistical requirements such as rations, tents, and barrack rooms simpler and uniform throughout the empire.[33]

The reforms of Gallienus, Diocletian, and Constantine left fourth century emperors with cavalry regiments of approximately 500 men. The regiments bore titles of *cunei, equitum, equites, alae,* and *vexillationes.* The *alae*, descendants of the old auxiliary cavalry, were found only in *limitanei* armies and *vexillationes* were found only in *comitatenses* armies.[34]

The Roman Army of the fourth century required between 15,000 and 30,000 new recruits yearly, depending on whether its total strength was 300,000 or 600,000.[35] The two main sources of recruits from inside the empire came from volunteers and conscripts.[36] The typical Roman soldier was conscripted in his late teens or early twenties, was by law 5′10″, usually from a rural area, and was often the son of a veteran.[37] Vegetius reported that, traditionally, peasants made better recruits than city dwellers because they were accustomed to hard labour.[38] Despite the fact that Christianity was the dominant religion of the Roman government during the first half of the fourth century, the majority of Roman soldiers were not Christian.[39]

Recruits were to be in good health and not fully enrolled (branded) in the army until they were found fit for military service.[40] Veterans' sons were required to serve but not necessarily in the same unit as their father.[41] The Abinnaeus Archive indicates that the civilian populations were aware that men conscripted into *limitanei* units might remain in their home province.[42] Sons of veterans, if they enlisted with a horse, were allowed to join the cavalry.[43]

Men from outside the empire could join the army as individual volunteers, be conscripted as part of a treaty, or recruited from prisoners of war. While the majority of barbarians serving in the Roman Army were Germanic, all barbarian groups provided recruits. The majority of barbarian volunteers were attracted to the lifestyle of a Roman soldier, which would have been luxurious compared to their tribal home. These individual volunteers would have been absorbed into the society of their regiment learning Latin and becoming completely assimilated, often forgetting their native tongue.[44] Laws against military service evasion and prohibitions against pacifist churchmen opposing conscription should not be used to support the conclusion that most of the population were against military service in the east.[45] A large number of the eastern units on the *Notitia* are listed as indigenous (*indigenae*) or raised and recruited from the local population.

To face a herd of charging armoured elephants with only an eight-foot spear, a three-foot sword, shield, and a handful of darts required a brave man. The Romans recognized that:

'Scientific knowledge of warfare nurtures courage in battle. No one is afraid to do what he is confident of having learned well. A small force which is highly trained in the conflicts of war is more apt to victory; a raw and untrained horde is always exposed to slaughter.'[46]

The Roman method of war recognized that only training, discipline, and teamwork would ensure victory.[47] Roman training methods developed recruits into soldiers with endurance and expertise in the use of their weapons. Before being enrolled, the conscript or volunteer was tested to ensure that they could sustain the rigors of military training. The *campidoctor* and his junior drill instructors were responsible for training the recruits.

Recruits were trained to swim and to march twenty Roman miles a day carrying weapons, equipment, and rations weighing sixty Roman pounds in five hours.[48] Vaulting and jumping obstacles was part of the training regime. Twice daily, recruits performed sword and shield drills with heavy practice weapons against wooden posts. They were trained in the use of javelins, bows and arrows, slings and lead-weighted darts (*mattiobarbuli*). They were taught the basics of horsemanship. As their individual skills improved, they graduated to century, maniple and cohort manoeuvres. At least until the reign of Gratian (circa 375 to 383), all infantry were equipped with helmets, mail, or scale body armour no matter what their combat specialty was within the legion.[49] When the recruit (*tiro*) completed his training, he was promoted to *pedes* (infantry) or *eques* (cavalry trooper). If a perspective recruit enlisted with a horse, he was enrolled as an *eques*.[50] It is unlikely that enlisting with a horse allowed a recruit to skip the recruit training, but it guaranteed him a billet in the cavalry and higher pay.

It took time to turn a recruit into a soldier, and sending untrained troops into battle was to waste their lives.[51] The 'Achilles' heel' of the Roman Army was the time it took to train recruits to replace battle casualties. Vegetius states that recruit training took approximately four months and, at the end of that period, the recruits took the oath and were tattooed or branded.[52] The new *pedes* then joined a veteran *contubernium* of eight to ten men. These veterans incorporated the new *pedes* or *eques* into their mess and ensured that they continued to develop as members of their file within the century or *turmae* battle formation. While it is not clear from the sources, the *contubernium* probably formed a file in its century's battle formation with the *caput-contubernii* or or *decani* (squad leader) being the file leader and a veteran being the file closer.[53] Training continued within the legion under the watchful eye of the *campidoctor*. Heavy casualties normally equated to a proportionally high loss of veteran leadership from *decani* to tribunes. Contemporary historians ignore the loss of veteran junior leaders and record heavy losses as the number of tribunes (regimental commanders) lost in combat.[54] It required two years to train a newly formed unit for battle.[55] It took twenty years to train the average centurion or regimental command tribune. A shortage of veteran leaders equated to lower training standards and lack of discipline. As will be seen, Roman indiscipline during the pursuit of defeated Persian forces on two occasions turned a Roman tactical victory into a bloody operational draw or strategic defeat.

The training process for non-legionary fourth century units has not survived the ravages of time. Newly recruited *auxilia* regiments were formed from Germanic war bands and led by tribal chiefs. When enrolled into Roman service, they were given Roman ranks and pay. Eventually, as they became institutionalized, they would have had to establish a Roman training system to replace losses from war, service, and retirements. Vegetius and Ammianus state that *auxilia* units thought the fatigue duty of the legions was beneath their dignity as warriors.[56]

In the Late Roman Army, only men in the staff corps, regimental commanders, and higher would be commissioned on the emperor's authority. Today, this rank is referred to as 'field grade': officers in the rank of major, lieutenant colonel, colonel, and general. Roman non-commissioned officers performed the function of modern junior officers. *Ducenarius* and centurions were the equivalent of modern company commanders. They were given small independent commands, such as escorting foreign dignitaries to the court of the emperor. In the fourth century, officers could be appointed from the ranks, or through patronage, into the *Protectores Domesticus* in service to the emperor.[57] In this corps, the potential regimental commanders were trained and tested to determine whether they were fit to command. Regimental commanders were called *tribuni* (tribunes), *prefects*, or *praetositi*. The title 'tribune' was also used for army staff officers (*tribuni vacates* or protector*)*. Many *tribuni vacates* or protectors like Ammianus, were attached to generals like Ursicinus to serve in the field. In 357, the Emperor Valentinianus I (321 to 375) was promoted from the staff regiment to command a *Comitatensis* cavalry regiment at age thirty-six. Flavius Abinnaeus, spent thirty-three years in *limitanei* cavalry regiments rising to the rank of *ducenarius* when posted to the staff corps at fifty-one.[58] After serving twenty-eight years in the *Palatinai* Legion *Joviani,* Flavius Memorius was elevated to *Protector Domesticus,* where he served for six years before being appointed prefect of the *Comitatensis Legion Lanciarii Seniores.* He must have been fifty-five when appointed prefect. After three years as prefect, he served five years as a count, first as *comes ripae* and then *comes Mauretania*.[59] The evidence indicates that successful, experienced soldiers could achieve appointment to regimental command, regardless of the status of their regiment. Also, heavy casualties could reduce the available experienced manpower pool required to provide competent legion and regimental commanders and reduce the training and discipline level of newly formed and rebuilt units.

This system of training future military tribunes, dukes, and counts by apprenticing them as junior officers of the *Protectores Domesticus* to senior military leaders had advantages not readily apparent. The realities of protecting the empire from invaders and usurpers still required independent combat formations the size of the antique legions. These forces, between 2,000 and 5,000 men, were detached from the main armies for specific missions. Prior to the late third and fourth centuries, one senatorial legate would command a force of this size. In the fourth century, with a portion of legionary and regimental commanders promoted to their commands from the *Protectores Domesticus,* there were five to ten senior officers who owed their career to the current emperor(s) and whose presence served to rein in the ambitions of any count with an eye on the purple robes of emperor. In 351, despite Magnentius' usurpation in Gaul, part of his army (led by Silvanus) deserted back to the sole remaining legitimate emperor at the first opportunity. Based upon the length of Constantius' and Constans' reign, the majority of these legionary and regiment commanders would have owed their position to the legitimate ruling emperors, not to the usurper. It is therefore not surprising that Magnentius executed those commanders he suspected of remaining loyal to the House of Constantine.

The Roman Army pay in the first half of the fourth century was primarily 'in-kind,' but still received some coin. Coin was paid as donatives given on special occasions such as the emperor's birth and accession days. These sums could be quite large as on Julian's accession to augustus he paid the sum of five *solidi* (gold coins) and 1lb of silver (valued at four *solidi*) to each soldier. However, the primary income of a soldier was his rations (*annona*) and fodder (*capitus*) for his horse. Veteran soldiers and non-commissioned officers received multiple *annonea* and in cavalry units *capitus*. As an example, centurions received two-and-a-half *annonea* while *ducenarius* (commanders of 200) received three-and-a-half *annonea*, and a *primicer* received five *annonea*.[60]

The rations issued normally consisted of bread, meat (veal, pork, or salt pork), wine or sour wine, and oil. Loaves of bread or biscuits were often baked for the army by local bakers and transported to the campaigning army. The only ration scales come from sixth century Egypt and indicate that each man received 3lbs of bread, 2lbs of meat, two pints of wine, and one eighth of a pint of oil. Jones considers this ration a little extravagant and theorizes that the unit did some financial juggling to eat this well and may have short-changed its horses. The horses' rations consisted mainly of barley supplemented by hay and chaff. In spring and summer, soldiers or their slaves were expected to cut grass for fodder or turn their horses out to graze in public or military pastures.[61]

The standard of living for the Roman soldier of this period was substantially higher than for that of the peasantry. They received ample clothing and rations and, at intervals, cash donatives. They were allowed to maintain wives and children on their extra rations. Often, deductions were made from their rations for the benefit of their officers and, in some cases, their officers cheated them out of rations, clothing, and money. But these abuses were balanced by their ability to extort extras from their civilian hosts who often were forced to billet the soldier and his family without compensation. Slaves were owned by members of the rank-and-file and officers alike to serve as batmen. While more elite regiments enjoyed higher compensation, all soldiers enjoyed a higher standard of living than the civilian population. After twenty to twenty-four years of service, they could retire and were either provided a sum of money to establish a business or a plot of land with two oxen, cash, and 100 *modii* of grain to establish a farm. The discharged veteran was exempt from the poll tax and, depending upon which corps he served in and the length of service, he could receive up to four additional tax exemptions.[62]

Tactical Organization

Legions were the primary eastern infantry force until after 363, while *auxilia* regiments were an important element of western armies. Both eastern *comitatenses* and *limitanei* legions and their third century ancestors included archers and skirmishers along with their traditional infantry armed with body armour, large shield, sword, and various types of spears, javelins, and darts. The early third century funeral monuments of II Parthia depict a skirmisher (*lanchiarii*) with bundles of javelins, an archer (*sagittarius legionis*), an artilleryman (*scorpio*), and a close-formation trainee (*discens phalangarius*).[63] Based upon the career of Aurelius Gaius, *vexillations* during the late third century contained legionary cavalry, close order infantry, and *lanchiarii*.[64] In a papyrus pay record from circa 300, a full twenty per cent, or the equivalent ten centuries (878 to 899 out of 5,000) of legion III Trajan stationed in Egypt was composed of *lanchiarii*.[65] Vegetius' recommendation that recruits be trained in archery may have compensated for the lack of archer (*Sagittarius*) regiments in the eastern order of battle as illustrated by the *Notitia*. *Lanchiarii* legions are listed on the *Notitia*, and most of the unit names were derived from names of border provinces. Historian Nicasie theorizes that they were originally formed by withdrawing *lanciarii* from border legions.[66] This conclusion does not mean the *limitanei* legions lost *lanciarii* capabilities. These *lanciarii* centuries could have been reformed after the reorganization over time. There is no evidence that *comitatenses* legions would not have been affected by this reorganization.

In place of *auxilia* units, the eastern army contained legions trained primarily for skirmishing and scouting. At the siege of Amida in 359, the Count Aelianus commanded a small army of six legions, including the light legions *Superventores* (catchers) and *Praeventores* (interceptors).[67] Fifteen hundred skirmishers from the legions *Lanciarii* (spearmen or spear throwers) and *Mattiarii* (club wielders) are mentioned as the forward security screen of Julian's army.[68]

Despite the increased number of cavalry units, the Roman legionary and *auxilia* remained swordsmen.[69] The spear, whether *pilum* or *lanceara*, was only a primary weapon when fighting cavalry or elephants, otherwise it was thrown – with darts and javelins – before entering into hand-to-hand combat. Both the *Epitoma Rei Militaris* and the *Strategikon* agree that training with sword and shield was critical for the infantry.[70] Until the end of the fourth century, infantry was the 'queen of battle' for the Roman Army and it dominated the battlefield due to its discipline and training.

The expanded fourth century Roman cavalry retained the four basic types of cavalry from its third century predecessor: horse archers and javelin-armed light cavalry, various types of general-purpose medium cavalry, and heavily armoured *cataphracti/clibanarii* heavy cavalry. Up to the fourth century the various types of cavalry – whether armed with bow, shields, spears, javelins, or two-handed pikes (*kontus*) – wore some form of body armour.[71] There was a significant difference between the versatility of the Roman medium cavalry and the heavily armoured *cataphracti/clibanarii*. Constantius improved the Roman cavalry by expanding the *cataphracti/ clibanarii* arm as noted by Julian in his *Oration I* as a response to the superiority of Persian and Gothic cavalry.[72] These heavily armoured men on armoured horses, supported by horse archers, were crucial to Constantius' victory against the usurper Magnentius at the Battle of Mursa in 351. The exact number of these regiments in the early fourth century is unknown. The *Notitia* lists sixteen *cataphracti* and *clibanarii* regiments, of which seven were stationed in the east.

During the fourth century, Roman light and medium cavalry provided key support functions to the infantry. Due to its relative speed and manoeuvrability over marching infantry columns, cavalry provided reconnaissance during the advance, screened the army from enemy reconnaissance and ambushes, covered foraging parties, and provided dispatch riders.[73] Roman light and medium cavalry's primary task in battle was to protect the infantry's flanks, support attacks of the *cataphracti/clibanarii*, and if possible, drive off the opposing cavalry. If successful in defeating enemy cavalry, Roman cavalry attacked the flanks and rear of the enemy infantry. A potential problem for all types of cavalry was loss of cohesion, resulting in uncontrolled charges or disorderly withdrawals. In the fourth century, Roman cavalry played a secondary role in battle, but were soldiers of choice in their constabulary roles within the Roman east.

Roman Battle Tactics 337 to 363

The tactics employed by the Roman Army of the fourth century had adapted to changing conditions but were firmly grounded in Roman military traditions. The demise of the antique legions complicated command and control on the battlefield. As described by Vegetius and Julius Caesar, antique legions formed one to three battle lines of cohorts (battalions) depending on the tactical situation.[74] The *Strategikon* recommends that the lines of a cavalry army be deployed a bowshot apart (100m to 300m).[75] This would be the maximum distance between infantry lines. Running 300m in full armour to conduct a passage of lines on foot would reduce the effectiveness of the fresh infantry formations. In large battles during the first to early third centuries, a legate, assisted by six tribunes, commanded a legion (up to ten cohorts and support troops) and supervised the battle, feeding fresh cohorts into combat as required. During the fourth century this mid-level command staff of the antique legions disappeared with the creation of and reliance on regimental-size legions. At first glance, there appears to be no replacement mid-level command structure during the fourth century.

In battle, Roman armies of all periods divided battle lines into right, left, and centre with a general in charge of each sector. In the case of a large army like Julian's Persian invasion force, each of these generals had thirty small legions or regiments within their sector of responsibility. In the heat, dust, limited visibility, and friction of battle, command and control of more than ten units would have been impossible. The antique legion's battle formation, as described by Vegetius, had four cohorts in the first line and three cohorts in the second and third lines. The antique legionary legate controlled a 400m frontage occupied by ten cohorts in three battle lines. There are passages in Ammianus that indicate a mid-level command structure did exist: unit pairs. There are seven unit pairs listed by Ammianus, and they include paired legions and *auxilia*.[76] When these units are listed in the narrative, they are always listed as fighting together as if they were organic to a brigade structure.

Command and control of battle in the fourth century was a continuation of traditional Roman methods. Roman success on the battlefield depended upon discipline and drill, not Homeric heroics. The fifth, sixth, and seventh centuries would see Roman command and control drift away from the rule of discipline and drill, and Roman commanders and senior officers would begin to fight duels with opponents before the beginning of formal battle.[77] But in the fourth century, Roman generals stayed near the fighting but only joined it in emergencies – with the exception being Julian.

In field battle, the Romans initially only committed thirty to forty per cent of their forces to combat. Commitment of the second and third battle lines was the responsibility of the commanding general or his immediate subordinates who commanded the left, right, or centre of the army formation. The emperor or senior general present surveyed the battle mounted while being protected by a mounted bodyguard. By judging the ebb and flow of battle, the commander could encourage his men, commit reserves, or ride to a point of crisis to prevent disaster.

Levy is the only ancient historian who describes in detail the method the Roman second and third battle lines used to relieve a line in combat. In a description of a drill field manoeuvre, Levy states that the engaged line falls back through the gaps of the supporting line, which takes over the battle.[78] In many battle descriptions the support line charges in to combat to reinforce the combat and the engaged lines do not withdraw from combat. It is clear that Roman historians assumed their audiences knew how the tactics worked off the parade field and felt no need to state the details of the drills used in legionary tactics.

The Eastern Roman Army, according to the *Notitia Dignitatum,* contained few archer or light infantry legions. In a theatre where Rome's primary enemy's decisive arm was heavily armoured horse archer-lancers, this omission seems unusual. Based upon Ammianus' and other eyewitness battle descriptions, the Eastern Roman Army's decisive arm in the fourth century was its legions rather than its *cataphract* cavalry. The evidence indicates that, since the third century, the legions serving in the Persian and Parthian theatre were combined arms and, when the new smaller legions were formed, they kept this combined arms organization.

An infantry army fighting a cavalry army faces a number of challenges. Formal field battles with the Persian Royal Army tended to last six to twelve hours in extreme heat. Horses are not very intelligent, but they are not stupid. They will not charge into a wall of spears or a wall of compact men. As a result, a cavalry force fighting well-trained and disciplined legions resembles the ebb and flow of waves upon a beach. If the legions stand like a large rock on the beach, the cavalry flows around the rock to its limit and then withdraws. If the legions stand as a rock barrier, the water smashes into the rock halting its momentum and then the water recedes and the process is repeated. If the legions are untrained, they stand like a sand castle and each wave of cavalry will erode the legionaries' cohesion until, like a sand castle, the legion formation crumbles and the fleeing infantry is washed away like individual grains of sand. Initially, to face the ebb and flow of the Persian cavalry tactics, the basic tactical formation of the Eastern Roman Army was a combined arms cohort of six centuries which, by the middle of the third century, was evolving into a large combined arms maniple, cohort or *numero* of 300 to 400 men. Vegetius informs us that, within a Roman six-rank battle line, the first two ranks consisted of seasoned veteran soldiers whose job was to hold the line. The third rank consisted of young and fast armoured archers and soldiers armed with heavy javelins, light spears (*lanceae*), and possibly lighter shields. The fourth rank consisted of young archers and javelin throwers that used lighter javelins and darts (*plumbatae*) and carried lighter shields. The fifth rank consisted of staff slingers, slingers, and crossbowmen (*manuballistarii*). The sixth rank consisted of experienced veteran soldiers like the first two ranks and most likely served as a file closer to prevent the faint of heart from leaving the formation upon seeing a charging war elephant. Carriage-mounted *ballistas* fired in support over the heads of the battle line. Each file occupied three feet and each rank was six feet deep. This space was needed for the javelin and dart throwers to take a short hop to launch their missiles. One thousand six hundred and sixty-six files occupied a Roman mile of frontage and a six-rank line equalled 9, 995 soldiers or ten full-strength legions.[78]

In battle, the first and second ranks stood their ground while the third and fourth ranks would rush out as skirmishers and challenge the enemy with arrows, darts, and javelins. When pressed, these skirmishers would fall back into the formation and resume their positions in their ranks while the first and second ranks would fight off the enemy.[79] While not mentioned by Vegetius, the heavier missile weapons (staff slings, *manuballistarii*, and carriage-mounted *ballistas*) were intended for the Persians' heavily armoured *savarin* cavalry. These armour piecing weapons with slow reload times would launch their missiles over the heads of their comrades into the confused ranks of the Persians after the forward momentum of their charge was halted. As the Persian cavalry started to turn and withdraw, the third and fourth ranks would sally forth, hamstring the Persian warhorses, and attack the Persian knights with swords, javelins, and clubs. The increase of missile capacity of the legionary formations could explain the alleged decrease in the penetrating capacity of Persian arrows. The greater missile capacity of Roman infantry formations would have forced Persian horse archers to loose their arrows from a longer range.

Legionary formations with mixed weaponry were not an invention of the fourth century Eastern Roman Army. During the second and third centuries BCE, Republican Roman legions were comprised of 3,000 close order infantry and 1,200 *velites* (young skirmishers). Arrian, writing in the second century, describes his preparations to fight the Alans. In his essay, he describes legionary formations with mixed weaponry and combining close order and skirmishers in the same formation. Adapting to changed battlefield conditions within existing traditional force structure was nothing new for the Romans.[80] It is significant that the *Strategikon* supports Vegetius and recommends the ratio of close order infantry to skirmishing infantry as 2:1 and that the skirmishers should be young and nimble and, based upon the tactical situation, able to operate within and without the close order infantry formation.[81] Whether the differently armed and armoured soldiers were found within the same century or whether they formed specialized centuries is still an open question. The career of Aurelius Gaius suggests that moving from legionary cavalry to skirmisher (*lanciarius*) to close order infantry (*optio* of *triarius*, *ordinatus* and *priceps*) could be a normal career progression.[82] Light infantry and skirmisher drill is a young man's game.[83] As soldiers were wounded, injured, or simply became less nimble over their twenty to twenty-five year career, shifting from skirmisher to close order duty may have been simply a normal career progression.

As mentioned, there are indications that the basic tactical formation in battle was a maniple size unit and each cohort contained two. Ammianus records Roman Army units organized into centuries, maniples, and cohorts. Detachments are recorded as maniple size. In 360, Constantius ordered Julian to provide him with massive reinforcements to replace his losses from the Persian campaign. The reinforcements ordered equated to over thirty per cent of the Army of Gaul. With the exception of three named units ordered to be transferred, the reinforcements were to be provided as 300-man detachments from each unit in the Army of Gaul.[84] When Count Sebastianus formed a special command to fight the Goths, he was assigned 300-man detachments from units in the local army.[85] Three hundred men equals four centuries (320 men) or three over-strength centuries (300 men). If the legions were of a combined arms nature and the ratio of heavy infantry to light infantry was 2:1, then detachments consisting of two heavy infantry centuries and one *lanciarius* century seem probable. Sending three over-strength centuries ensures that, despite the attrition of moving long distances in winter, the detachment will arrive in fighting strength. Written 200 years later, the *Strategikon* describes the basic heavy infantry formation of the past as 256 men.[86] Three normal strength centuries equals 240 men and equates to the formation the *Strategikon* refers to. The type and size of reinforcements to the Eastern Theatre becomes important when determining the size of the Roman forces opposing Shapur's 360 Campaign. A cohesive organic maniple, cohort or *numero / numerous* of 300 men is more tactically useful than a 'marching unit' of 300 soldiers thrown together for administrative purposes.

The 'marching camp' continued to constitute a critical aspect of Roman tactics into the fourth century but sources hint at significant changes in the establishment of such a camp from the first, second, and third century model. The marching camp provided the Roman soldier a safe haven in hostile territory. Its uniform layout provided the psychological security for the Roman soldier where he could relax in relative safety. Tactically it was so important to the Roman method of warfare that it remained a main stay of successful Roman military operations from the republic to late antiquity. The *Strategikon* recommends a safety ditch, caltrops, defensive ditch, and wall made from the army's supply wagons instead of the former traditional ditch, turf wall, and wooden palisade.[87] This different configuration would prevent a surprise cavalry and elephant attack into a Roman camp and compensate for the lack of wood in the Tigris and Euphrates Valley. As early as Julian's expedition (363), the Roman Army was adapting its marching camp to the conditions of Mesopotamia by using shields and wagons instead of a wooden palisade.[88] Even as late as the tenth century, Byzantine military theory still considered the march camp extremely important. Its basic organization was still based on its Imperial Roman predecessor.[89]

Logistics: The Key to Military Victory

Vegetius observed that time and opportunity may help reverse misfortune, but 'where forage and provisions have not been carefully provided, the evil is without remedy. An exact calculation must, therefore, be made before the commencement of war of the number of troops and the provisions needed to support all aspects of the operations.'[90] Food, wood, fodder, and water were the four key requirements of an ancient campaign. Availability of these commodities dictated the time of year campaigns commenced and concluded, as well as the routes. The basic requirements for man and beast would have been similar for both the Roman and Persian armies.

Donald W Engels' study of the logistics of the Macedonian Army provides a baseline of an ancient army's support requirements. A soldier required a minimum of 3lbs of grain and two quarts of water per day. Based upon weather and activity, the water requirement could increase to two or more gallons per day. Horses and mules needed 10lbs of fodder and 10lbs of grain per day, plus eight gallons of water. Along with the combatants and their warhorses, non-combatants and supply animals needed the same rations. Pack and draught animals were required to carry an army's non-consumable supplies (tents, siege machinery, cooking equipment, extra weapons, etc.). A force of 5,000 infantry required 1,200 pack animals (mules can carry 200lbs and camels 300lbs for extended periods).[91] It was theoretically possible for an army to carry grain for about twenty days' supply for the men on the soldiers' backs. When the 60lbs of food (twenty days' rations) was added to the weight of a soldier's weapons and equipment, the load could exceed 100lbs. Without water transportation, the army's supply train could only carry about ten days' supply of grain for man and beast.[92] Alexander's Macedonians did not use wagons because they reduced an army's march rate and manoeuvrability. Romans used wagons drawn by oxen, which increased their carrying capacity but reduced the army's rate of march.

Rome relied heavily on wagons. In the Roman period wagons are depicted as two and four wheel vehicles pulled by a team of two oxen or mules. The carrying capacity is difficult to determine, but the Theodosian Code sets the limit at 1,075 Roman pounds (775lbs or 352kg) while Diocletian's Price Edict attests to a wagon load as 1,200 Roman pounds (865lbs or 393kgs). A tariff from Palmyra, dated during the second century, equates a wagon load with four camel loads or approximately 1,540lbs or 700kgs.[93] Fourteen hundred mules carried 140tons (280,000lbs) of supplies and equipment while 350 ox wagons (700 draught animals) carried the same load (800lbs per wagon). Oxen can only maintain a rate of march of fifteen miles per day at a speed between 2½ to 3mph over an extended period of time. Horse and mule teams could maintain over fifteen miles per day at a faster rate of march.[94]

To move large armies like Julian's *Praesental* Army of 65,000 with a minimum daily consumption of 251 tons of grain and sixty-five tons of fodder for the soldiers and cavalry horses alone, all manner of draught animals were required, plus 1,100 boats and barges. These figures do not take into account the grain to feed the thousands of pack and draught animals and their handlers.[95] The forage requirement for the thousands of pack animals and cavalry mounts for preindustrial armies was difficult to procure, which was why they normally waited until late spring or early summer to begin a campaign when foraging parties could gather the fodder from the seasonal grass.

In 507, chronicler Joshua the Stylite recorded the events of the Roman-Persian War of 502 to 507. During the 501 to 502 Campaign, two Roman armies, totalling 52,000 men, were operating in the vicinity of Edessa. The army bakers were unable to make sufficient biscuits for the combined force so the Commissary-General, Appion, ordered the people of Edessa to make the biscuits (*bucellatum)* for the army at their own cost with 630,000 *modii* of grain.[96] One *modii*, approximately eight dry quarts, weighs about 20lbs and fed a *contubernium* (tent group or squad) of eight soldiers for one day.[97] The grain recorded could feed 52,000 men for approximately ninety days and weighed nearly eleven million pounds or 5,040 tons. Joshua only takes note of the grain made into biscuits and lists the event as a first baking. A document from 360 lists individual daily rations in a garrison at the equivalent of three pounds of bread, two pounds of meat, two pints of wine, and one-eighth of a pint of oil.[98]

If one adds the grain and fodder for the cavalry horses and fodder for the draught animals to the tonnage required to feed the army for ninety days, totals are doubled to a minimum of 10,080 tons. When these logistical planning factors are applied it becomes apparent that a besieging army of 50,000 men must either capture a fortified city within ninety days or pack up and march home. If the army's operation exceeded the ninety day limit, it starved or needed to import supplies from another region. During the 359 Campaign, Ammianus claims the Persians left 30,000 dead in the Roman province.[99] The siege lasted seventy-three days, and the manoeuvres before the siege were between fifteen and thirty days. Shapur's total operation lasted between ninety and hundred days. Most of the 30,000 deaths would have been caused by starvation and related diseases, not Roman weapons.

Expendable weapons required for a campaign, such as javelins and arrows, were included in an army baggage train. In the tenth century, a Byzantine army of 34,000 requisitioned 800,000 arrows and 10,000 javelins. A Byzantine or Late Roman archer carried thirty to forty arrows. If this army only contained 9,000 archers the requisition would have provided eighty-eight arrows per man.[100] The weight of the expendable weapons in the baggage train would have been insignificant compared to the weight of the food and fodder required for the campaign.

The Roman government established arsenals (*fabricate*) for the manufacture of weapons and armour. According to the *Notitia,* there were arsenals for weapons, armour, and shields at Damascus, Antioch, Nicomedia, Sardis, Adrianople, Marcianopolis, Horreum Margi, Ratiaria, Thessalonica, and Naissus. Cavalry armour was produced at Antioch, Caesarea in Cappadocia, and Nicomedia.[101] A D Lee points out that the arsenals in the east were located a significant distance behind the *limites* to guard against capture, but they were also located in the vicinity of the greatest threat to the security of the empire.[102]

The difficulty of supplying an army limited its size. Despite the Roman Army's size during the fourth century (varying between 345,000 and 600,000 depending on the historian), armies in the field rarely exceeded 40,000 men, and the majority of armies in the Late Roman period never exceeded 25,000.[103] Vegetius recommends the optimal size of an army at 20,000 infantry and 4,000 cavalry for a *magister militum* – a ratio of four infantry to one cavalryman.[104] Based upon this ratio, Julian's *Praesental* Army of 65,000 would have contained 52,000 infantry and 13,000 cavalry. Larger armies, like Julian's 95,000 man invasion force in 363, were divided into two or more operating armies that coordinated manoeuvres but operated in different regions.[105] Any other approach would have over-taxed the land and the army would starve.

Ammianus and other historians, including Julius Caesar, fail to record time-distance factors of marching armies, which have a bearing on their narratives. Understanding these factors often clarifies passages made cloudy over time. Marching in a close column (six soldiers wide) of 5,000 men occupied 1,334 yards of road space. Fifty-two thousand infantry in close march column occupied at least 13,340 yards of road space or between six and seven miles. Adding the baggage train extended the column to over twelve miles.[106] When the advance guard reached the site of a new camp, at 3mph, it would have taken over four hours for the rear guard to reach the camp.[107] Julian solved this problem by marching his army in parallel columns, but wanting to appear stronger than he was, he had the column extended to ten miles by having greater intervals between units.[108] Recruits during training were expected to conduct route marches at 4mph carrying a 60lbs load.[109] During campaigns this rate of advance would have been reduced considerably by the soldiers' load increased with twenty days rations and the maximum speed of the siege and supply trains.[110]

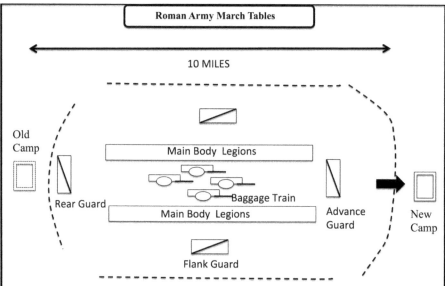

A Roman Army marching at 3.5 MPH, and taking up 10 miles of road space, would take six hours to cover the distance from its old camp to its new camp. The advance guard would reach the new camp in three hours as the rear guard marched out of the old camp. It would take an additional three hours for the rear guard to close on the new camp.

Defence of the Roman East

Scholars debate whether the Late Roman emperors, and specially Emperors Diocletian and Constantine, had a grand strategy for the defence of the Roman Empire.[112] The Roman *limes* stretched over 3,738 miles/6,000kms from the North Sea along the Rhine and Danube Rivers to the Black Sea, along the Tigris River, along the edge of the Arabian Desert to the Red Sea and then along the edge of the Sahara Desert to the Atlantic Ocean. The historian Whittaker is of the opinion that there could not have been a grand strategy due to the length of the *limes* and the diverse threats along its length.[113] Isaac bases his opposition to the probable existence of a grand strategy on his conviction that Roman emperors' policy considerations were primarily focused on maintaining political power rather than establishing a systematic defence of the empire.[114]

There are no documents proving Diocletian and Constantine formulated a grand strategy. Only criticism of their strategy by near contemporary historians like Zosimus provides testimony that it existed.[115] There is circumstantial archaeological evidence, however, that indicates not only was there a grand defensive strategy but that it was successful. Massive public and private resources were expended to develop fortified zones along the Eastern *limes* and the army was reorganized and expanded in order to defend the empire. This proves the Emperors' obvious defensive intent.[116] The Treaty of 298 illustrated Diocletian's intent not to expand the empire into Persia proper. The fact that emperors, counts, and dukes attacked across the *limes,* winning battles and burning barbarian villages or sacking Persian cities does not negate the fact that the empire was on the strategic defence and was not attempting to add new provinces.[117]

Diocletian's organization of the security of the East put Rome on the strategic defence against the Persians. No emperor who followed Diocletian, with the notable exception of Julian, made any serious attempt to expand the empire into Persia. Based on the *Notitia*, completed circa 395, Jones argues that the defensive system established by Diocletian survived almost intact in the eastern portion of the empire, having been relocated only due to the Roman defeat and the resulting Treaty of 363.[118]

Historian Hugh Elton asserts that the *limitanei* provided three functions on the border: policing, intelligence gathering, and deterring raids.[119] Due to the open terrain in the east, the policing function fell to the *limitanei* cavalry. Surviving military records indicate the *limitanei* were also assigned responsibilities for recruitment, tax collection, and administration of justice in the communities around the forts.[120] The police function included preventing deserters from leaving and spies from entering the empire. *Limitanei* interaction with the tribes along the border provided intelligence on Persian military matters.[121]

Roman literary sources of the time did not record minor events.[122] Ammianus admits that he failed to record battles that were indecisive or insignificant.[123] In the east, Saracen raids targeted isolated travellers and small groups but left cities unmolested. The main roads and pilgrimage routes in Palestine were patrolled and protected by small forts. Important pilgrims were provided military escorts.[124] Bloody skirmishes were never recorded since they were unimportant by the standards of contemporary historians. Church historians had different criterion and, as an example, they recorded an event in 276 where a large Roman combat patrol returning from Persian territory mistook a local regional agricultural ceremony as a Persian encampment.[125] This patrol was recorded due to its tragic results: 1,800 civilian casualties and attempted cover up of the incident.

The impetus for the improvement of fortifications during the fourth century was their failure to prevent Persian incursions into Roman Syria during the third century.[126] Emperors Diocletian and Constantine turned the province of Mesopotamia into a defensive zone of fortified cities to protect the rich province of Syria and city of Antioch.[127] During the first through third centuries, the Roman military constructed towers flush with their fort's wall. Fighting was expected to take place outside the walls, not upon them. In the middle of the third century, forts were built with towers projecting out from the fort wall. This change in military construction signified a change in tactics and forts were now intended as fighting platforms.[128] These towers allowed defenders to protect vulnerable walls and gates from assaulting troops with enfilading fire from mural artillery, archers, and slingers.[129] When not stationed in cities, *limitanei* units were stationed in forts ranging in size from garrison forts (accommodating a legion of 2,000 to 3,000 men) to small watchtowers and blockhouses occupied by a rotating eight-man garrison.[130]

Roman armies of the East, fighting mostly from fortified positions, relied upon torsion artillery: *ballistae* and scorpions, also known as the *onagri* (onager).[131] The ballista functioned like a huge crossbow firing a bolt or stone and were produced in various sizes, some small enough to be transported on a small cart or hand carried by its crew while others were so large they had to be disassembled to be transported. The onager ('wild ass') was just beginning to be deployed in the fourth century. It was simpler in design but 'kicked like a wild ass'. The larger versions were mounted on fortresses and required reinforced walls and towers due to the stresses produced by their operation. Regardless of the size of the weapon, both types were primarily anti-personnel weapons.[132] These machines were very dangerous for the crews to operate. Ammianus delights in describing the gruesome death of a crewman of an onager when the weapon malfunctioned, tearing itself and the soldier to pieces.[133] With that appalling picture in mind, it is understandable why the Gallic legionaries at Amida were not helpful in defending the walls of the city and preferred sallies outside the walls to engage the Persians with swords.[134]

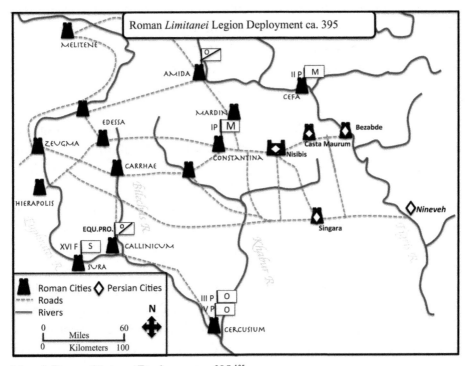

Map 4. Roman *Limitanei* Deployment c. 395.[135]

By studying the deployment of the *limitanei* armies of the provinces of Phoenicia, Syria, Euphratensis, Osrhoene, and Mesopotamia in 395, the Roman defensive strategy for 337 to 363 can be templated. The provinces of Phoenicia, Mesopotamia, Syria, and Osrhoene contained a higher proportion of cavalry regiments than did other regions.[136] The legions were stationed in fortress cities on possible Persian avenues of approach and guarded the main caravan routes and major road junctions. With the exception of Phoenicia, the cavalry was stationed along river lines forming a defensive screen connecting the legionary fortress cities.[137] In close support of each legion (either stationed with the legion or in a nearby fortified town) was an *equites promote* cavalry regiment. Former antique legion cavalry contingents, these regiments were promoted into independent cavalry units prior to the commencement of the Nisibis War.[138] The legions and *equites promote* were deployed in such a way as to give each duke a provincial rapid reaction force or strike force.[139]

The cavalry was also stationed in depth along the Belikh River and the crossing point at Zeugma on the Euphrates River. Most of the cavalry was stationed in the Mesopotamian steppes or Tigris-Euphrates River valleys. The limited old auxiliary infantry cohorts were stationed to patrol rough ground and mountainous passes. This deployment allowed these armies to scout the *limes* for raiders, protect caravans, enforce trade regulations, and provide early warning of a Persian invasion. The Romans could have dispatched legionary detachments, supported by *equites promote*, in response to intermediate threats and, in the case of serious assault, they could have defended their fortresses until the Eastern Field Army from Antioch deployed. In 395, the Eastern Field Army contained nineteen legions, two *auxilia* regiments, and eleven cavalry regiments.[140] Assuming Jones' regimental totals are correct and that the regiments were at full strength, the Eastern Field Army was comprised of approximately 21,000 infantry and 5,500 cavalry.[141]

Phoenicia had no river line for its *limes*. The *Strata* Diocletian, which connected Damascus to the legionary fortress of Palmyra and the legionary fortress at Oresa and Sura, became the border. Phoenicia's problem, not being on the Euphrates' avenues of approach, was Saracen raiders rather than Persian invaders. Its *limitanei* army was deployed in two echelons. The first echelon of tightly grouped regiments stretched along the *Strata* Diocletian from Damascus to Palmyra along the edge of the desert. The second echelon was deployed on the hilly terrain along the road network north of the *Strata* Diocletian centred on Danaba, headquarters of the legion III *Gallica*.[142] A few cavalry regiments were deployed in the Syrian Desert southeast of the *Strata* Diocletian at oases to deny Saracen raiders key watering points. This deployment was not surprising considering the Saracen warrior Queen Mavia's revolt in the 370s over a Christian theological issue.[143]

As a final note on the circa 395 deployment, Dodgeon and Lieu argue that the cavalry regiment *Ala quintadecima Flavia Carduenorum* (Corduene) and the infantry regiment *Cohors quartodecima Valeria Zabenorum* (Zabdicene) were raised in the five Trans-Tigris regions. If they are correct, there would have been at least three other Trans-Tigris regiments that did not survive the Nisibis War. Based upon its title the *pseudocomitatenses* legion *Transtigritani* from the Eastern Field Army may have been one of the missing Trans-Tigris units. The Trans-Tigris regiments would have been raised to police and patrol their home regions operating from forts east of the Tigris and turned over to the Persian's by the Treaty of 363. Empires often recruit local soldiers from tribal regions to help police tribal lands. The British Khyber Rifles and the American Apache and Navaho Scouts are nineteenth century examples of this technique. The Persians treated such soldiers as traitors and, after the fall of Amida in 359, captured survivors were executed.[144] Finally, Dodgeon and Lieu argue that legion I Parthia *Nisibena*, stationed at Constantina in 395, had been stationed at Nisibis during the Nisibis War. Established by Septimius Serverus, I Parthia was originally stationed at Singara. Shapur's three attacks on Nisibis and the legion's honorific '*Nisibena*' support the proposition that sometime before the war commenced the legion's headquarters was shifted and only a detachment deployed forward as part of the garrison at Singara.[145]

In determining the Roman defensive strategy in the 330s, primary sources provide a partial picture and archaeology fills in the blanks. The only province that was greatly impacted by the peace treaty of 363 was Mesopotamia. During the period 298 to 363, the defensive foundation for the Province of Mesopotamia was the fortress cities of Amida in the north on the Tigris, Bezabde in the west on the Tigris, Singara on the southern

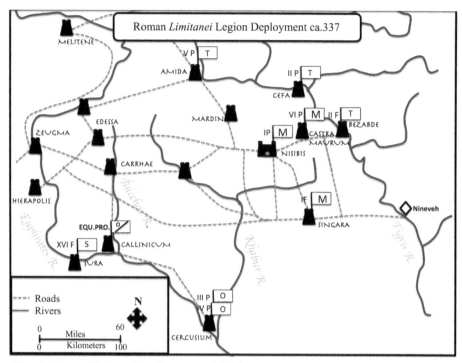

Map 5. Roman *Limitanei* Deployment c. 337.[146]

slope of Mount Jebei Sinjar, and Nisibis in the centre of the Mesopotamian steppes.

Castra Maurorum in the Tur Abin Mountains reinforced Bezabde. Taking the example of the defensive pattern in the *Notitia*, each city would have been supported by cavalry forts in open terrain and infantry forts in rough terrain. The Singara *Limes* surveys completed in the nineteenth and twentieth centuries supported their fieldwork with the *Peutinger Itinerary.* Their finding located structures that may have been forts controlling routes from the desert into the Singara *Limes*, as well as possible crossing points of the Tigris River near Nimrud and Nineveh.[147] The Amida *Limes* were supported by forts along the Tigris River as depicted in the *Notitia* and described by Ammianus in 359.[148] The Bezabde *Limes* were supported by Castra Maurorum just west of Bezabde on the road to Nisibis and other forts such as Seh Gubba along the Tigris River.[149] In addition, the Bezabde

Limes projected a forward presence as forts and routine patrols in the Trans-Tigris region of the Roman sphere of influence east of the Tigris.

Based upon the information available and following Diocletian's and Constantine's formula of two legions per province, the situational template in 337 for the *Limitanei* Army of Mesopotamia has I Parthia *Nisbena* headquartered at Nisibis with a legionary detachment in Singara. II Parthia occupied Cefa, Bezabde, and Castra Maurorum. In 395, Amida did not rate a legionary garrison. This may have been the case at the beginning of the war in 337. The legion V Parthia was Amida's primary garrison in 359 and was probably created and/or deployed there after Amida was sacked in 337 when the city was rebuilt and heavily fortified.

Hierapolis, just south of the bridges at Zeugma, was the yearly mustering point and training ground for the field army. Constantius, Gallus, and Julian all mustered their armies at this city before starting campaigns.[150] In 354 Flavius Abinnaeus escorted Egyptian recruits to Hierapolis.[151] The city was located in a central position blocking the three Persian avenues of approach toward Antioch (Mesopotamian plain, Singara *Limes*, and Euphrates) while acting as a staging and training area for the field army so that it could use the same avenues as invasion routes into Persia. Edessa, with its weapons factories and storehouses, acted as a forward assembly area for the field army. While walled, Edessa was not considered part of the fortified zone. It was the field army when located at Edessa that made the city a significant military threat to the Persian Royal Army operating in the region.

The actual manpower required to man the defence along the *limes* is still an open issue. The Arabian *Limes* provide a baseline for the study of the practical rather than the theoretical manpower required for Eastern frontier defence. Unlike the Rhine-Danube *Limes*, the Arabian *Limes* never collapsed during the fourth and fifth centuries, neither were they adjusted due to a defeat as were the Mesopotamian *Limes*. Unlike the old re-built forts along the Rhine-Danube *Limes*, Diocletian and Constantine established new forts east of the Jordan River and Dead Sea along the military road, *via Nova Traiana*. The *limitanei* armies of Arabia and Palestine were organized much like the other ducates (*ducatus*) of the East.[152] The official strength of the armies varied depending upon which theory of Late Roman regiments strength is accepted. Using the *Notitia*, Jones (writing in 1964) estimated that the Ducate of Arabia was garrisoned by a *limitanei* army of between 13,500 and 19,500 (consisting of two legions, twelve cavalry *equites* and *alae* regiments, and five infantry cohorts).[153] Parker (writing in 2006), and his team that excavated the Arabic *Limes,* place the effective strength of the Arabian *Limitanei* Army at between 6,050 and 8,050.[154] While Jones and Parker agree on the number and type of units, Parker bases his reduced regiment size upon the small size of the fortresses and Roman military records found in Egypt. These records and excavated barracks suggest that *limitanei* cavalry regiments were comprised of 120 horsemen and 160 footmen in the cohorts rather than Jones' theorized strength of 500.[155] After the war started in 338, it would be surprising if Contantius maintained the two legion per province deployment. By 359 five additional legions are found garrisoning key fortresses within Mesopotamia.

The two-legion provincial defence formula is not realistic for the decades-long Nisibis War. It is more suited to the relatively peaceful period circa 395 when the *Notitia* was compiled. A dissertation by Lightfoot, ignored primarily because it was never published, he points out that scholars disregard the policing of the Trans-Tigris Region when trying to unravel the deployment of legions after the Treaty of 298. Lightfoot provides a defensive deployment for the Roman East by templating *pseudocomitatenses* legions found on the *Notitia* and mentioned by the sources operating in the region during the Nisibis War. Lightfoot concludes that the legions I and II Armenia, I and II Flavia, and VI Parthia were deployed along the Tigris River prior to the beginning of the Nisibis War.

The key fortress cities of Amida, Cefa, Bezabde, and Casta Maurorum not only guarded the approaches to Nisibis but also provided administrative, law enforcement, and military control of the Trans-Tigris Regions. Amida was responsible for Greater Sophene, Cefa for Arzanene, and Bezabde for Zabdicene. It is proposed here that there were elements of additional legions assigned to Mesopotamia prior to or after 337. Adjusting the template for the additional legions, the deployment would be as follows: IV Parthia at Circesium, III Parthia at Apatna, I Parthia at Nisibis, I Flavia at Singara, VI Parthia at Castra Maurorum, II Flavia at Bezabde, II Parthia at Cefa, V Parthia at Amida (assigned after the city was sacked in 337), I Armenia in the Anzitene Region, and II Armenia in the Lessor Sophene Region.[156]

Speculative Legion Deployment 337-363			
Province/Fortress	Legion	358-361	Location/Status 395
Osrhoene:			
Circesium	IV Parthica	Ciresium	Ciresium/ *Limitanei*
Apatna	III Parthica	Apatna	Apathna/ *Limitanei*
Mesopotamia:			
Nisibis	I Pathica	Nisibis	Constanina/ *Limitanei*
Singara	I Flavia	Defeated/Singara	FLD Army Thrace/*Comit.*
C. Mauroum	VI Parthica	C. Mauroum	FLD Army East/ *Pseudo-Comit.*
Trans-Tigress:			
Bezabde	II Flavia	Defeated/Bezabde	FLD Army Thrace/ *Comit.*
Cefa	II Parthica	Cefa	Cefa/ *Limitanei*
Amida	V Parthica	Destroyed/Amida	------
Anzitene?	I Armeniaca	Defeated/Bezabde	FLD Army East/*Pseudo-Comit.*
L. Sophene?	II Armenia	Julian's P/ Army	FLD Army East/*Pseudo-Comit.*

Lightfoot discounts the value of Bezabde as an obstacle to a Persian attack south of the fortress. But a concentration of two or three legions and their supporting cavalry would be a threat to the Persian lines of communication that could not be ignored. A significant blocking force would have had to be detached from the Royal Army to prevent VI Parthia, II Flavia, and II Parthia, and their supporting units, from interdicting the Persian lines of communications. It is, therefore, not surprising that the Persian attacks took place along the Singara axis of advance, which was defended by only one legion: I Flavia. This wartime deployment placed five legions and elements of a sixth in the province, instead of the normal two, but the command responsibility may have been divided between the duke of Mesopotamia and a military count. Giving a military count command of a troublesome region was not unusual. Isaurian, Egypt, and, originally, Thrace were commanded by military counts. The responsibility for the garrisons at Amida and Cefa may have belonged to such an official. That official could have been Count Aelianus, reported by Ammianus as general of the unusual brigade of the light legions *Superventores* (catchers) and *Praeventires* (interceptors) who mysteriously appears to take command of the defence of Amida in 359.[157] Roman units with unusual functional titles normally were associated with intelligence and reconnaissance functions.[158] These types of activities would be needed to police and administer the Trans-Tigris Regions.

It is proposed here that after 337 there were five *limitanei* legions with elements of a sixth within Mesopotamia with a combined legionary strength of between 10,000 and 20,000 men. In the *Notitia*, the Province of Mesopotamia contained 13 cavalry regiments and two infantry auxiliary cohorts. In 337, at least an additional three auxiliary cavalry regiments should have been added for the three Trans-Tigris regions not represented in the *Notitia*, in addition at least one additional *equites promoti* regiment. Assuming Jones' figures of 500 per regiment, the cavalry and auxiliary strength in the whole region would have been 10,500 men (9,500 cavalry and 1,000 infantry). Applying Parker's figures of approximately 200 men per regiment and cohort, the total would be 4,200 (3,800 cavalry and 400 infantry). Pre-twentieth century armies commonly allowed regimental strength to drop below fifty per cent when engaged in constabulary operations, which could explain the discrepancy between the two figures.[159]

In addition at least three additional legions would have been responsible for the east side of the Tigris River and a military count appointed to have supervised those activities. The legion Trans-Tigris probably occupied an unidentified fortress on the east side of the Tigris supported by the normal auxiliary cavalry and infantry units. Count Aelianus commanded a brigade, consisting of the legions *Superventores* (catchers) and *Praeventires* (interceptors), to provide a reaction force to counter stronger Persian incursions. Their skirmishes would have been too small for Ammianus to take notice.

This defensive strategy employed between 10,000 and 20,000 men in fortified positions across the Province of Mesopotamia with at least 3,800 cavalry patrolling the *limites*. For the defence strategy to work properly, the field army had to advance into the defensive zone and counter any large Persian invasion. Added to these numbers would be the small Trans-Tigris garrison and constabulary brigade. As the Nisibis War unfolded, considerations in other regions of the empire dictated where the Eastern Field

Army was committed. As a result, the five legions assigned to Mesopotamia successfully defeated Persian invasions, often alone, unsupported by the emperor for most of the twenty-five-year war.

This historical data supports the conclusion that the emperors of the fourth century expended the empire's wealth by creating an eastern defensive system of improved border forts and city fortifications. They pinched pennies by subdividing the army and creating a border army, the *limitanei,* which had lower status, lower pay, and fewer benefits than the more prestigious *comitatenses* regiments. All legions, regiments, and cohorts were provided cheaper equipment than in previous centuries. The emperors compensated for their tight-fistedness by providing regiments with experienced commanders, many being long-service professionals, instead of court-appointed favourites. Battlefield performance often had more to do with training and leadership than regimental status. The new defence system was tested in 337, while the emperor Constantine lay dying on his deathbed.

Chapter 5

The Persian Army and the Strategic Offence

T he most striking difference between the Parthian and Sassanian Empires was the latter's emphasis on charismatic leadership by the king, a centralized government, and a link between the king and Zoroastrianism, which became the state religion in the third century. During the rise of Persia in the third century under Ardashir I and Shapur I, Persia was a warrior-kingdom built on the desire for glory, booty, and expansion. The Sassanian Empire was based upon the union of the seven great Parthian families, led by the Sasan family, which held the kingship. Unlike the Parthians, the Sassanians created a centralized feudal state, which eventually developed a central administration that, to an extent, eliminated the independence of the hereditary kingdoms.[1]

Persian society was divided into four classes: clergy, warriors, bureaucrats, and commoners. The three upper classes overlapped and were often drawn from the same families. These classes formed the Persian nobility. Within the nobility there were four grades. The highest class was the *Shahrdars* comprised of the provincial governors belonging to the Sassanid family. Six principal families dating back to the Parthian period led the nobility. The most important were the Surens and Karans who owned vast estates throughout the empire and occupied hereditary posts in the government. Heads of families were the *Vaspuhr*. The principal ministers formed the third grade as *Vuzurgan* or Great Ones. The fourth grade consisted of a great number of lesser nobility, the *Azadha*, 'Free Men or Barons'. Below them were the *Dehqans*, 'village squires', who ruled their village and functioned as the local tax collectors. It was from the nobility that the *Savaran* (knightly cavalry) were drawn.[2] The commoners consisted of the farmers, town artisans, and country peasantry. The peasantry was tied to the land similar to serfs and performed statutory labour for the kingdom and their landlords.

They paid land and personal capitalization taxes to the Royal Treasury. In time of war they were drafted as an infantry levy.[3]

It has been commonly assumed that the Persian Army mustered by Shapur was a feudal host consisting of landed elites and their retainers supported by a simple logistics system limited to good roads, supply dumps, and defended forward positions. Howard-Johnson argues that by the mid-fourth century the Persian Army was a sophisticated semi-professional army, and the defence of Persian Mesopotamia resembled the fortified zone of Roman Mesopotamia.[4] The evidence indicates the kingdom had regional armies guarding its borders, garrisons in its cities, and a royal field army led by the king.

The kings of Persia faced a strategic dilemma similar to that of the Romans.[5] They faced the Romans and Saracens on their western border, and they had to contend with nomadic tribal confederations on their northern border. After Rome became Christian in 325, they had an additional, perceived internal threat from their Christian population. Like Rome, Persia had developed Mesopotamia into a fortified zone. Persian Mesopotamia had developed fortified cites along the Euphrates similar to the Romans. The cities of Anatha, Thilutha, Achaiachaia, Baraxmialcha, and Pirisabora on the Euphrates River and Maozamalcha on the canal between the Tigris and Euphrates Rivers were significant fortifications.[6] In addition to the fortified Euphrates cities, there was a system of moats and earth walls west of the Euphrates to hinder raiding Saracens and defend Shapur's loyal Arab settlements. A moat and fortification system was constructed from Hat to Basra and settled Arab militia garrisoned the villages. It is reported to have been a continuous fortification.[7] Ammianus verified the existence of this defensive system but described it 'as mounds along the banks [of the river] to prevent Saracens from raiding Assyria'.[8]

The Tigris River lacked the same level of man-made fortifications as the Euphrates. However, four large rivers (Great Zab, Lesser Zab, Adheim, and Diyala) intersected the Tigris from the Zagros Mountains and formed natural defensive barriers. The west bank was primarily desert. During the Roman Emperor Heraclius' 627 Campaign, the Lesser Zab had some fortifications defending its four bridges, and these minor fortifications probably existed in the fourth century.[9]

The region east of the Caspian Sea and north of the main Persian lines of communication and trade between Damaghan and Merv (aka Marv and Mulu) was where the Eurasian steppes met the Iranian plateau. After 350, this section of the Persian *Limes* would be under constant pressure from tribal confederations. The situation became so troublesome that, in the late fifth or early sixth century (scholars disagree as to the date), the Persians built a 120 mile wall between the Caspian Sea and the Elburz Mountains just north of and parallel to the Gorgan River. The wall had fortresses along its length with a barracks capacity of up to 30,000 men.[10] The fortified oasis city of Merv anchored the Persian *Limes* in the east. In addition to the city walls, there was a wall around the oasis that was almost 150 miles long. It is unknown whether these outer walls were operational during the fourth century.

While the details of the Persian command structure are limited, Roman accounts indicate that they had a regional command structure in the mid-fourth century and that it was more sophisticated than a simple feudal host. The ultimate commander-in-chief was King of Kings Shapur. Shapur was a storybook king. Brave in battle, chivalrous to the weak and, at the beginning of his reign, wise beyond his years. In 325, at 16 and without military experience, he allegedly masterminded a long complicated land and sea campaign to subdue the Arabian coast and pacify the Arab tribes along Persia's western border. Such exploits made good poetry for the bard; however, it is known that he had capable advisors and generals from the beginning.[11] It is clear that the Persians developed a sophisticated command structure based on both feudal and centralized elements.[12] Shapur's command system produced competent field commanders who successfully operated independently of the king's Royal Army.[13]

The Persian army that followed Shapur was significantly different from the Roman Army of the fourth century. Ammianus described the Persian army in battle array outside of Ctesiphon:

…with squadrons of [*cataphractarii/clibonarii*] drawn up in serried ranks that their movements in close-fitting coats of flexible mail dazzled our eyes, while all their horses were protected by housings of leather. They were supported by detachments of infantry…in compact formation…. Behind them came elephants looking like moving hills.[14]

The Persian cavalry was the decisive arm of the Persian army from its foundation in the third century to its destruction in the seventh century. The army's dominant arm was the noble armoured knights known as *Savaran* but referred to by the Romans as *cataphractarii* or *clibanarii*.[15] The *Savaran* were divided between armoured lancers and armoured horse archers. Artefacts and rock reliefs of Persian kings, observations of Ammianus, and later Persian records provide a detailed description of *Savaran* arms, equipment, and tactics.[16] In open battle the *Savaran* were heavily armoured on armoured horses armed with kontos (cavalry pikes, not lances), swords, shields, and bows.[17] In skirmishes, they most likely wore less armour. Fully armoured in formal battle, they were formidable opponents even for Roman infantry.

In skirmishes with Roman cavalry, they were a terror. Prior to the battle outside Ctesiphon, Julian was plagued by the operations of the Surena's Persian cavalry in league with Emir Podosaces' Assenite Saracens (Arabs). These nimble horsemen ambushed Julian's cavalry security screen, raided the Roman supply trains, disgraced four Roman cavalry regiments in combat, and shadowed the Roman advance.[18] They became such a nuisance that when the Romans pitched camp to besiege Maozamalcha they had to take 'precautions against any sudden attack by the Persian horse, whose daring in open country inspires unspeakable dread in all peoples'.[19]

The Persian infantry, which could comprise two-thirds of a Sassanian army in the field, supported the cavalry.[20] Ammianus described Sassanian infantry as armed with shields, spears, and bows. A large percentage of the infantry was levies who lacked the training and discipline of their Roman counterparts. There appears to have been regular, or at least professional, infantry within the Persian military structure. The garrisons of the Persian cities provided reliable infantry, which at the Battle of Ctesiphon (363) fought for over six hours before withdrawing back into the city. While these troops may not have been as well trained or armed as their Roman counterparts, no Roman historian of the fourth century reports Persian infantry being routed in terror by a Roman legionary charge. During sieges, they assaulted breaches in Roman fortress walls, a bloody and gruesome task. Persian foot archers were highly regarded by the Romans. Their mission in open battle was to shower arrows down upon the Romans in order to weaken their defence against the charge of the Savaran. The mass archery was only effective at a maximum of 200m. At this extreme range it forced the Romans into various close order formations but caused few casualties. To penetrate shields and armour the engagement range would have to be less than 100m and to be very effective the range would have to be less than 50m. Within 50m the archers would have been susceptible to Roman hand thrown weapons and a quick charge. In theory, spearmen with large shields protected the archers from Roman infantry. Ammianus mentions Persian armoured infantry capable of resisting Roman attacks. Farrokh theorizes that the Persians were developing a core of professional infantry from the early days of the kingdom.[21] The centralization of the kingdom and the requirements of garrisoning the cities and fortified walls would lead to the development of professional infantry. While archery was extremely important in Persian warfare it was only decisive in the Battle of Singara, after the Roman Army broke formation to plunder the Persian camp.

Finally, the Persians deployed elephants in support of the *Savaran*. Elephants were important to the Persian method of warfare until the destruction of the Persian Empire by the Arab conquest.[22] While striking terror into Roman soldiers and horses, elephants were used to ambush and assault marching Roman columns and to provide high platforms for accurate archery.[23] Shapur used trained war elephants in all of his major battles and sieges and would have required access to a steady supply of these beasts from India. In the pre-Mughal India, elephants were often used in place of close order infantry. Their massive bulk and thick hides, often reinforced with armour, made them very difficult to injure let alone kill. A charge of a mass of trained war elephants was extremely difficult to stop. Their impact on cavalry horses required cavalry to retreat and only the most disciplined and trained infantry could stand and receive an elephant charge. Eventually, during the Early Modern Age, improvements in firearms forced the elephant into a solely logistics role.[24] Modern classical scholars ignore the dominant role of the elephant on the Indian subcontinent in pre-gunpowder warfare when dealing with warfare in the Roman sphere of influence. Persian kings, with one boot in the Tigris Euphrates Valley and the other boot in the Indus Valley, needed elephants to successfully engage and defeat Indian armies. In addition, they were very effective in 363 in almost destroying the Roman invasion force. Modern scholars and Ammianus try to downplay the elephants' effectiveness due to their reputation for panicking as exhibited by the untrained elephants during the battle of Zama where they were routed through their own support troops. Based upon Ammianus, accounts of the battles of 363, Persian war elephants were extremely effective in frontline combat.

Female Persian soldiers were reported by Roman sources. Zonaras notes that, after a battle in 260, women dressed and armed like men were found among the Persian dead of Shapur I's army.[25] Libanius notes that, at the battle for Singara in 343, women had been conscripted as sutlers into the Persian army.[26] These Roman observations are reinforced by Persian epic poetry that mentions women fighting as Savaran knights. Gurdafarid, daughter of Gazhdaham, was one of the heroines of the *Shahnameh* (The Book of Kings) written in the tenth century but referring to pre-Islamic events. Gurdafarid fights a duel in defence of the fortress of *Sepid* against warlord Sohrab who was leading an invading army. She fights mounted in full *cataphract* armour with bow, *kontos*, sword, and Roman helmet. Gosasb Banu, daughter of the Persian hero Rostam, was another Persian heroine who fought as a *Savaran*. She is the heroine of an epic poem entitled *Banu Gošasb-nama*, written by an unknown poet between the fifth and sixth century (or eleventh and twelfth century). Sir Richard F Burton's translation of *The Book of the Thousand Nights and a Night* tells the story of Princess Al-Datma who was 'accomplished…in horsemanship and martial exercises and all that behoveth a cavalier'.[27] Epic poems are difficult to pin down to a specific period. Persian female Savaran disappear from western sources after the fourth century but remain in Persian tradition.

The known historical Persian and Parthian women *Savaran* include Sura (circa 213), daughter of Ardavan V, last king of Parthia; and Apranik (632), a Persian commander and daughter of Piran, and general of King Yazdgird III. Female guerrilla commanders against Islamic rule include Azad Deylami (circa 750); Negan (circa 639); and Banu, wife of Babak Khoramdin.[28] Historic and legendary female Savaran were all daughters of members of the noble class.

Fourth and fifth century sources do not address the size of Shapur's Royal Army. Later sources record Persian field armies ranging from 20,000 to 60,000 men. In 578, the Persians had 70,000 registered warriors.[29] Most likely, this number represents the total number of Savaran and not the lower class infantry. There was no known basic building block of the Persian army such as the Roman legion. Historian Farrokh speculates that the basic Persian formation followed its Parthian predecessors and that the 1,000-man regiment (*drasfsh*) was made up of companies or battalions (*vasht*) of undetermined size. Each *drasfsh* had its own standard and heraldry, and several of these regiments formed a corps or small army (*gund*) commanded by a general (*gund-salar*). The Immortal Guard Division (*Zhayedan*) numbered 10,000 Savaran, but may not have been formed in the mid-fourth century. The 1,000-strong Guard Regiment (*Pushtighban*) was stationed at Ctesiphon during peacetime.[30] The first references to the Immortal Cavalry Corps start appearing during the fifth century. Ammianus noted that Shapur added a contingent of the royal cavalry to a sunrise surprise elephant/cavalry attack on Jovian's camp, but the passage is unclear as to the size of this contingent or if it was a subdivision of the Immortals.[31]

It is theorized that the Persians used the decimal system of organization with companies of 100, regiments of 1,000, and divisions of 10,000. Farrokh theorizes that Shapur's Royal Army consisted of 12,000 cavalry and infantry and would have been reinforced with regional forces.[32] Ammianus informs us that in 359 the Royal Army was reinforced by the armies of the kings of Albani and the nomadic Chionitae along with contingents of Gelani and Segestani, but does not provide the estimated total strength of this invasion force.[33] In 530, Procopius recorded that the Persians invaded Roman Mesopotamia with 40,000 cavalry and infantry, reinforced with 10,000 men from the Persian Nisibis garrison. Based on fifth and sixth century precedents, it may be assumed that Shapur's Royal Army – with the addition of feudal, allied, and regional contingents – numbered between 40,000 and 50,000 men, excluding garrison and frontier regiments.[34] Like the Roman army, logistics would have limited the size of any Persian field army.

Persian Tactics

Persian tactical manuals have not survived. However, the *Strategikon* provides descriptions of Persian tactics and analysis from the Roman sixth century perspective and would have applied to the tactics utilized by Shapur. For the most part, Persians preferred planning and generalship to blind attacks.

They stressed an orderly approach rather than a brave and impulsive one. They easily endured heat, thirst, and lack of food. They were formidable when laying siege and being besieged. They coped bravely with adversity, often turning adverse circumstances to their advantage. When giving battle in the summer, they took advantage of the region's heat to dampen the morale of the Romans, often delaying battle for extended periods of time.[35] The Persians were skilled adversaries often underestimated by the Romans.

The decisive arm of the Persian army was its cavalry. The best description of an eastern cavalry army fighting the legions is the Battle of Nisibis in 217 pitting the Eastern Roman Army against the Parthian Army of King Artabanus. During this three-day battle, the ebb and flow of a cavalry battle becomes apparent. The legions on day one formed into multiple battle lines with light infantry stationed between the lines and gaps between cohorts. The Parthian's showered the Roman formations with arrows before rushing into close combat with armoured cavalry and mail-clad dromedary riders armed with kontos. During one of the ebbs of the Parthian tide, the Romans dropped caltrops and, after covering them with sand, fell back. When the Parthian mounted troops charged forward again, the points of these devices mauled their mounts' hooves and feet. As the cavalry attack dissolved into a disordered mass of bucking animals and thrown riders, the Roman troops, in open order, attacked killing and capturing a large number of Parthians after they were thrown from their mounts.[36]

On closer investigation, Sassanian tactics combined waves of armoured cavalry supported by massed arrow storms. The Persian cavalry would approach the Roman line in waves divided into columns of horse archers followed by a wave of Savaran armoured cavalry. The wave of horse archers would shower the Roman line with arrows, hoping to disrupt the formations, wheel, and then ride to the rear. The second wave of armoured cavalry would charge the Roman line with kontos. If the Roman cohorts and maniples did not break, like an ocean wave, the Savaran would wheel and withdraw to the rear as the horse archers rode forward to renew their missile assault.[37] Roman historians and writers of tactical manuals misinterpreted this ebb and flow of Sassanian cavalry tactics as disinclination for close combat.[38] But all cavalry tactics, including Roman, have the same 'ebb and flow' pattern.[39] These eastern open field battles were not short affairs. They tended to start in the early morning and last until the heat of the midday sun would force both sides to disengage.

During the retreat of Julian's army from Ctesiphon, the Persians employed cavalry and elephants. The Savaran cavalry and elephants worked effectively together and twice came near to destroying Julian's army. Ammianus' account makes clear these task forces were not last minute ad hoc groupings of combat units. Their successful performance against the Romans indicates that the Persians took the time to train their elite cavalry horses and elephants to fight together, since untrained horses were afraid of the 'frightful hideous' animals.[40]

All Persian armies of the fourth century described by Roman historians were combined arms formations. The Persian arm of decision was its cavalry, but Roman commanders took Persian infantry, and especially its infantry archers, seriously. The Roman victory at the Battle of Singara (see Chapter 6) was turned into a bloody draw by a Persian arrow storm. Learning from previous errors, in 363 Roman legionaries repeatedly charged Persian cavalry and infantry instead of exchanging missiles as they would have done with Germanic enemies.

Persian Strategy

Throughout the entire war, Shapur's policy was to use the strategic offensive to regain the cities and regions lost as a result of the Treaty of 298. During the period 337 to 350, the Persians engaged in at least five major offensives where they massed the full resources of the kingdom against Rome. In three of the offensives they were able to break through the ring of Roman fortresses and unsuccessfully besiege the fortress city of Nisibis. The terrain limited the Persians to three avenues of approach to attack Nisibis. The first route required the Persians to assemble at Ctesiphon and move west along the canals to the Euphrates. The army would then march north along the Euphrates bank to Syria. This route was supplied with well water and, during the campaign season, would provide adequate fodder for the Persian animals. Its main problem would have been supplying rations to the army, and a supply fleet would have had to be towed against the Euphrates' current. Ammianus informs us that 20,000 soldiers would have been required to pull Julian's 1,000 logistics boats and barges up the Tigris. It is likely that, if the

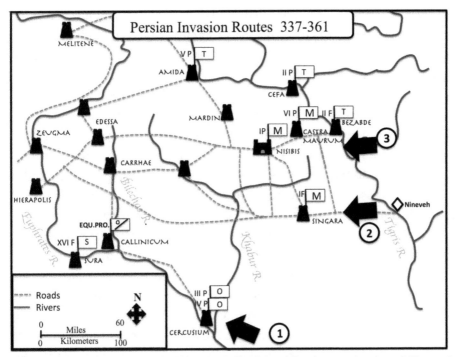

Map 6. Persian Invasion Routes 337–361. 1. Traditional Persian attack route of Shapur I during the third century. 2. Shapur II's primary fourth century attack route. 3. Alternate third century attack route blocked in the fourth century by two forts occupied by two legions and support regiments.

Persians used the Euphrates avenue of approach for a large army, they would have had to overcome an equally difficult supply problem. A fast moving cavalry force could use this route to appear suddenly in Roman Syria, but it would be impractical for a large moving infantry heavy army.

Despite its disadvantages during the 250s, at least one Persian expedition used the Euphrates avenue of approach. Due to the confusion of this period no official written records remain of this offensive. There is an extensive archaeological record of this attack in the ruins of the fortified City of Dura-Europos. Between the years 165 to 255–256, Dura-Europos guarded the middle Euphrates for the Romans. After a successful siege, the Persians apparently deported the population and the Romans never reoccupied the site. Ciresium, at the confluence of the Euphrates and Khabur Rivers, became the new Roman bastion on the Euphrates. Garrisoned by the legion

IV Parthia, and closely supported by III Parthia at Apathna, Ciresium blocked any Persian offensive up the Euphrates.[41] During the Nisibis War the records indicated that Shapur did not use the Euphrates avenue of approach for a major invasion.

During the third and fourth centuries, routes two and three seem to have been the traditional Persian invasion routes into Roman Syria. The Royal Persian Army would assemble at Ctesiphon. As it marched north, it would increase its strength with contingents and allies debouching from the Zagros passes. In the vicinity of Nineveh it would cross the Tigris behind a large reconnaissance and security screen of cavalry. Not burdened with slow marching infantry, elephants, and logistics trains, this cavalry advance guard would be raiding and scouting deep into Roman territory before the Persian main body crossed the Tigris. During the third century, Shapur I used this avenue of approach during all three of his successful campaigns into Roman Syria. In the third century, the legions, including II Flavia and VI Parthia, did not garrison Bezabde and Castra Maurum. As a result King Shapur I treated routes two and three as one avenue of approach. During the fourth century, the legionaries at Bezabde and Castra Maurum complicated the problem of using the route in the vicinity of these fortresses. During the third century, Roman soldiers and civilians in bypassed fortified cities and fortresses actively fought Persian outriders and raiding parties.[42] There is no reason to believe that their descendants were any less valorous. Because of these fortresses, Shapur II favoured route two through the Singar *Limes* for his invasions throughout the war.

Chapter 6

Roman Active Defence, 337–350

hapur's first major military operation of the Nisibis War was a direct attack on the centre of Roman Mesopotamia: Nisibis. If the attack took place in 337, as is argued here, the attack was a target of opportunity based upon the stalled Roman offensive and not pre-planned for a 337 campaign. The events of this siege are clouded by the sources, both religious and secular. There were three sieges of Nisibis – 337, 346 and 350 – of which the best documented were the sieges of 337 and 350. With the loss of Ammianus' account of the first phase of the war (337 to 350), it is difficult, but not impossible, to analyse the strategy employed by Shapur and Constantius during this period. As events unfolded during the first phase of the war, Constantius and Shapur were evenly matched tactically, with Constantius being superior operationally and strategically.

Constantius left the East in 337 to secure his throne, thus leaving the Roman offensive in shambles. He probably took a detachment of the army mustering at Antioch with him to support his claim to the throne. Shapur seized the opportunity to besiege the unsupported city of Nisibis. According to Theodoret's (circa 393 to 466) *Historia Religiosa*, and *Historia Ecclesiastica* (stripped of supernatural intervention) and the *Historica S. Ephraemi*, upon Constantine's death, Shapur marched against Nisibis with a vast army composed of cavalry, infantry, and elephants. His combat engineers raised siege works, including towers, so his archers could shower arrows down upon the Romans defending the walls. Persian engineers undermined the city's walls and dammed the Mygdonius River. Then they dug dikes to direct the river against the city's walls. On approximately the seventieth day of the siege, the water was released and the torrent struck the walls like a massive battering ram. Entire sections of the city wall collapsed into the river. The rampaging river passed through the city and knocked down the opposite wall as well. The Persian assault was postponed because the approaches to the breaches were impassable due to floodwater, mud, and debris. While the Persians paused, Bishop Jacob of Nisibis prayed for deliverance as soldiers and civilians worked all night to block the breaches and raised ballista positions to cover the approach to the damaged walls. By dawn, both breaches were closed with a barrier high enough to stop a cavalry charge and which required assault troops to use scaling-ladders. Shapur's army assaulted the breaches as Bishop Jacob and the 'blessed Ephrem' walked the walls praying and encouraging the defenders. The assault was repulsed and a few days later the Persians lifted the siege.[1] Significantly, this was the first siege where Christianity had a significant impact on maintaining the morale of Roman soldiers.

Some historians discount the narrations of the siege due to the nature of the Mygdonius River and the topography of the area in the vicinity of Nisibis.[2] But to do so disregards the sources as well as Persian capabilities. Such feats of military hydro-engineering were recorded as early as the fifth century BCE during the capture of Babylon by Cyrus the Great and by the Chinese in the third century BCE.[3] The control of lower Mesopotamia required an advanced understanding of hydro-engineering techniques to build and maintain the irrigation canals without modern pumps. The excavations at Dura-Europos attest to the skills the Persians possessed in siege warfare.[4] A Persian engineer and 20,000 peasant labourers could move a mountain in sixty days. The successful first defence of Nisibis does not validate Constantine I's defensive strategy. There was no field army marching to relive the beleaguered defenders or harassing Persian lines of communication. Constantine I's *Praesental* Army was busy elsewhere deciding the Imperial succession. Nisibis held solely based upon the bravery and tenacity of its garrison and population.

With the death of Constantine I, his *Praesental* Army was divided between his three sons. The friction between the brothers that quickly developed and military requirements of the unstable Rhine-Danube *Limes* resulted in Constantius' *Praesental* Army being unsupported by the rest of the empire during the first phase of the Nisibis War. Julian stressed that Constantius controlled only one-third of the empire's resources at the beginning of the war.[5]

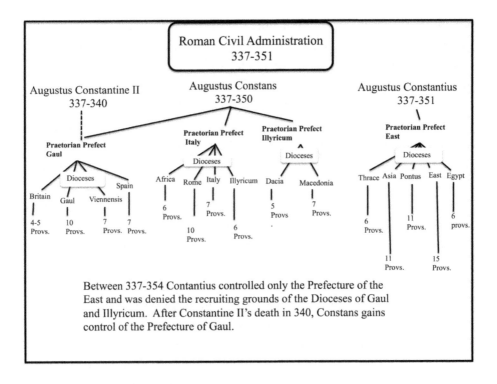

Roman Civil Administration
337-351

Augustus Constantine II
337-340

Augustus Constans
337-350

Augustus Constantius
337-351

Praetorian Prefect
Gaul

Praetorian Prefect
Italy

Praetorian Prefect
Illyricum

Praetorian Prefect
East

Dioceses

Dioceses

Dioceses

Dioceses

Britain   Gaul   Viennensis   Spain

Africa   Rome   Italy   Illyricum   Dacia   Macedonia

Thrace   Asia   Pontus   East   Egypt

4-5
Provs.

10
Provs.

7
Provs.

7
Provs.

6
Provs.

10
Provs.

7
Provs.

6
Provs.

5
Provs

7
Provs.

6
Provs.

11
Provs.

6
provs.

11
Provs.

15
Provs.

Between 337-354 Contantius controlled only the Prefecture of the
East and was denied the recruiting grounds of the Dioceses of Gaul
and Illyricum. After Constantine II's death in 340, Constans gains
control of the Prefecture of Gaul.

With only these limited resources, Blockley concludes that the object of
Constantius' foreign policy was to maintain the territorial integrity of the
Roman Empire as set forth in the Treaty of 298.[6] The means by which he
executed this policy varied based upon a realistic assessment of the available
resources.[7] Complete reliance upon the fortified zone would have handed the
Persians the initiative, something no Roman of the time with an undefeated
army would have willingly done. While a full-scale invasion of Persia was
not possible, Constantius' operational plan included military and political
offensive elements.[8]

Constantius' *Praesental* Army took to the field in 338 and reinstalled
a Roman nominee to the throne of Armenia.[9] Shapur's losses during the
siege of Nisibis must have been heavy since he did not take the field in 338
and declined a general engagement between 339 and 343. The alternative
possibility was that Shapur was having problems on his northeast border,
and he and the Royal Army were not in Mesopotamia, leaving the defence of
the region to his local generals. A war of attrition was conducted during this

period as skirmishes were fought mainly on Roman territory.[10] Finally, in 343, Constantius captured a small Persian city on the east bank of the Tigris and transported the population to Thrace while adding the title *Adiabenicus* to his official titles.[11]

The sacking of a Persian city and relocation of its population may have goaded Shapur into action. In 344, Shapur attacked Singara. Constantius marched his army to Singara to block the Persian advance. Shapur must have attacked in the spring or early summer because, according to Ammianus, during late summer or fall there was insufficient water along the western approaches to the city to support a relieving Roman army.[12] Libanius, Julian, and Festus provide details of the battle. With minor differences, Libanius and Julian, stripped of their artistic rhetoric and anti-Persian bias, provide similar accounts of the battle, while Festus provides a key element to the battle's climax.[13] The Persian army deployed by Shapur included Persian cavalry, horse archers, foot archers, heavy infantry, and allies from their borders, underage levies, and women conscripted as sutlers. Elephants are not mentioned as accompanying this army. The infantry levies were trained on the approach march.[14] With such a large number of levies to provide labour, it is evident that Shapur was planning to besiege Roman cities.

Upon receiving intelligence of the Persian army's approach, Constantius instructed the *limitanei* to retreat and not oppose the Persian crossing of the Tigris and not raid their camp once they crossed the river. Constantius wanted to bring the Persian army into a decisive field battle because he held a major geographical advantage. The Tigris would have blocked a Persian retreat in case of a Roman victory and turned defeat into a complete Persian disaster. The Persian army built a fortified camp on the road between the Tigris and Singara while Constantius built his camp sixteen miles from the Persian camp, most likely in the immediate vicinity of Singara.[15]

Shapur, aware of his army's strengths and limitations, devised a battle plan to capitalize on both. On the morning of the battle, he deployed foot archers upon the battlements and on the hills surrounding his camp. He then formed his heavy infantry and Savaran *cataphracts* in front of his battlements. The remainder of his Savaran (most likely without horse armour) and lighter cavalry, possibly under command of Shapur's son, rode the sixteen miles to the Roman camp.[16]

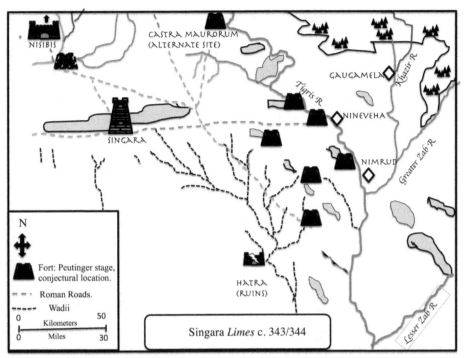

Map 7. Singara *Limes* c. 343/344.

On the morning of the battle, when the Romans observed the large body of the enemy approaching their camp, they marched out into battle formation. The engagement started mid-morning with the Persian and Roman cavalry and light infantry skirmishing using bows, javelins, and darts. As the Romans attempted to close to hand-to-hand combat, the Persians withdrew. As the skirmish continued, the Persians slowly withdrew toward their camp enticing the Romans to follow. While Julian and Libanius reported the Persians fled and the armoured Romans 'ran after them' such dramatic developments were improbable. The Roman infantry carried up to 40lbs of armour and weapons and running sixteen miles with this load is not realistic, even for our heroic ancestors. The Persians enticed the Romans to cover the sixteen miles from where their initial battle lines had been formed to the Persian camp. From the reports of his scouts, Constantius would have known the location of the Persian camp and that to attack it he would have had to conduct an approach march of sixteen miles. The fact that he followed the fighting withdrawal of the Persian screening cavalry indicates that he was confident of victory.

Yet, Shapur's battle plan was to entice the Romans to advance the sixteen miles away from the sheltering walls of Singara and the Roman camp. It would have taken the Roman infantry at least four hours to cover this distance during the heat of the day. It was a favourite Persian tactic to use the

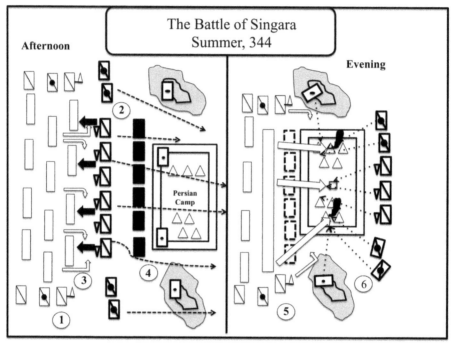

Map 8. The Battle of Singara, Summer 344. 1. Upon reaching the Persian camp the Roman army deploys for combat. 2. The Persian Savaran heavy cavalry and infantry deployed in front of their camp supported by archers on the camp walls and surrounding heights. The Persian heavy cavalry attack on the Roman front line fails and the Roman infantry break into the milling Persian cavalry formation. 4. After one or more cavalry attacks are unsuccessful, the Persian cavalry withdraw behind their infantry. In the confusion Shapur's son is captured and executed. 5. The Roman battle line immediately charges the Persian infantry defeating it and turning the Persian cavalry withdrawal into a route. At dusk the Romans break into the Persian camp desperate for water and eager for plunder. 6. As the Romans plunder fires break out illuminating the camp. Roman soldiers cluster round cisterns desperate for water. The Persian rear guard unleashes an arrow storm on the disordered Romans causing heavy casualties.

heat of the day to wear down the Romans before battle.[17] From the Persian perspective the Romans took the bait and would have arrived at their selected battlefield tired and parched by the scorching sun.

The Roman battle line arrived at the Persian Camp in the late afternoon. The fresh Savaran *cataphracts* now took up the battle. As their momentum was stopped by the Roman front line, *lanciarii* and other light Roman infantry charged out to meet the *cataphracts* from the intervals in the Roman line and engaged the Persians in hand-to-hand combat with clubs.[18] A *cataphract's* armour protected horse and rider from edged weapons and arrows, but provided no protection from the blunt force of clubs. In 272, Aurelian's Palestine auxiliaries were the first Romans recorded to have used clubs against Queen Zenobia's *cataphracts*.[19] In 312, Constantine's cavalry used clubs with metal heads to defeat Maxentius' *cataphracts*.[20] The clubs were effective at Singara as the skirmishing Roman infantry was able to dodge the *cataphracts' kontos* and swords and unhorse them with blows from their clubs. The use of skirmishing infantry to defeat a stalled cavalry charge was a Germanic tactic the Romans incorporated. With the unexpected defeat of their elite cavalry, the Persians broke and fled back to their camp before the main Roman battle line engaged them in combat. During the confused fighting that followed, Shapur's son was captured and executed. As night fell, the Roman legionaries stormed the camp cutting down all in their path.

The Roman army had been marching or fighting since morning in the heat of the sun. Constantius attempted to organize a pursuit of the Persians but failed to re-form his army due to their plundering the camp and search for water. During the confusion, the Persians rallied east of the camp in the dark and formed a rear guard. The Romans discovered cisterns in the Persian camp and soon clustered around them. Torches or the burning Persian camp itself illuminated the Romans around the water points. The Persian archers posted upon the hills around the camp and the Persian rear guard loosed an arrow storm at the illuminated cisterns causing heavy casualties on the disordered Romans. The Roman pursuit was abandoned and the Persians left the Romans in control of the field as they crossed back over the Tigris.[21]

The battle at Singara was technically a Roman victory because they held the field and prevented the Persians from successfully obtaining their objective. Roman casualties caused by dissolution of discipline made it a 'pyrrhic victory'. Operationally, Constantius demonstrated his superiority by enticing Shapur into a field battle with a river blocking a Persian retreat. The battle demonstrated that both Constantius and Shapur were skilled and resourceful adversaries. Both were evenly matched tacticians understanding the strength and weakness of the enemy and their own army.

The sources for the period 345 to 350 record very little activity on the part of Constantius and his *Praesental* Army. The battle at Singara did little to deter Shapur from his goal of recovering the territory lost in the Treaty of 298. Nisibis was besieged a second time in 346. In that year, it is recorded that Constantius was in or around Antioch but made no attempt to lift the siege.[22] The heavy Roman casualties at the battle of Singara could not have been severe enough to knock Constantius' *Praesental* Army out of contention. Ammianus hints at a defeat of Constantius when he fled with a body of companions to the unguarded frontier post of Hibiuta.[23] The date of this defeat is uncertain and, if it took place in this period, would explain the *Praesental* Army's failure to intervene in the second siege of Nisibis. The details of the second siege have not survived. Shapur besieged Nisibis for seventy-eight days and then lifted the siege.[24]

Based upon the details that have survived, the Persian army apparently utilized the avenue of approach through Singara to attack Nisibis throughout the 340s. The Persians blockaded Singara again in 348. Aelianus, a member of the *Protector Domesticus* and most likely a *tribunus vacans* (staff officer), on his own initiative led the two recently-recruited light infantry legions, the *Praeventores* and *Superventores*, on a night-time raid of the Persian camp, slaying a great number of them in their sleep.[25] There are hints from Ammianus that Singara fell to the Persians, but the fortress city was not occupied and the Romans reoccupied the site and repaired the fortifications.[26]

In mid-January 350, Magnentius, an army officer of German descent (*laeti*), overthrew and murdered Constantius' brother and co-ruler, Constans, in Gaul.[27] Shapur invaded mid-spring and besieged Nisibis for the third time. On the horns of a dilemma, Constantius left the defence of Mesopotamia and the city of Nisibis to Count Lucillianus, a competent and respected officer. The sources do not identify the garrison, but it most likely included the *limitanei* legion I Parthia *Nisibenae* and other *limitanei* units of the Ducate of Mesopotamia.[28] There is no indication that Constantius sent Lucillianus any reinforcements from the field army. It is assumed that Shapur, as was his custom in 359 and 360, upon his arrival before the walls of Nisibis, tried to persuade the garrison to capitulate. The details of the siege are preserved by Julian, Theophanes, Libanius, Zosimus, and a number of minor passages in other works.[29]

The Persians besieged the city for between 100 and 160 days. The Persian engineers used every siege tactic, which Count Lucillianus successfully defeated. Finally, the Persian engineers brought down a section of the wall by a novel, and unclear, use of the Mygdonius River. Unlike the first siege where the River Mygdonius was dammed and then unleashed against the walls, Julian records in his oration that the Persians created a lake around the city and used boats with siege engines to knock down the wall on one side. Unlike the first siege, as the walls fell, the Persian assault troops, supported by a mass of war elephants, immediately entered the breach and were met by the desperate garrison fighting to hold the breach.

The use of massed war elephants in an enclosed area at first may seem folly. Yet, in Indian warfare elephants were used effectively in assaulting fortifications. They were very effective at destroying gates and hasty fortifications, similar to those the Nisibis defenders would have thrown up to block the breach in their walls.[30] However the initial assault failed to break through the breach and the attack stalled. Hand-to-hand combat, supported by arrows and bolts from the walls and towers, checked the Persian assault and panicked the elephants, while a sortie from a gate forced the Persians to withdraw. Shortly after this failed assault, the Persian Army lifted the siege and retreated after suffering heavy casualties from combat and disease. The lifting of the siege represented another humiliating defeat for the Persians. They had taken advantage of a favourable opportunity when the *Limitanei* Army of Mesopotamia was unsupported to attack the fortress. The garrison showed a remarkable degree of resistance, both physical and psychological, to the Persian onslaught.[31] Constantius lingered in Antioch while the siege played out, and may have visited the city after the siege was lifted before marching west to confront Magnentius. The *Praesental* Army made no attempt to intervene at either the strategic or operational level. Constantius needed his *Praesental* Army, reinforced with Eastern units, to protect his throne. After the siege concluded, Constantius and advance elements of his army crossed over into Europe. After failing in his third attempt to capture Nisibis, Shapur appears to have abandoned all hope of capturing the city by direct assault.

It was difficult for Shapur to maintain the sieges for longer than 160 days as he was hampered by the need to provide food and fodder for his army. By expanding his army with large numbers of levies and conscripts to provide the labour for the sieges, he greatly expanded the supply requirements. The sources indicate that sieges lasted from 70 to 160 days. This appears to be the maximum time that the Persian army could remain stationary. At the end of this period, the Persians would have consumed all foodstuffs within a region and the besieging army would have starved.

During this phase of the war, Shapur employed the direct approach and fought in accordance with the Roman defensive plan. Even when Constantius' *Praesental* Army was defeated, the fortress cities disrupted communications and supply routes to the Persian army besieging Nisibis. Shapur failed to learn from his mistakes during this phase of the war and blindly continued 'banging his head' against the walls of Nisibis.

Chapter 7

Stalemate in Persia 350–358

As historian James Howard-Johnston observed, the Sassanians fought their way to power in the third century during benign geopolitical circumstances. The era of Kushan domination of the Eurasian steppes was ending. The rulers of the eastern approaches to Persia from the Oxus River to Bactria could not successfully contest its expansion. Persia had no rival in the east until the appearance of the Huns in the middle of the fourth century.[1]

A Han uprising in 349 led to genocidal slaughter of the Hunnic tribes (aka Xiongnu and known as the Chionitae by Ammianus) and pushed them west out of the Chinese sphere of influence onto the steppes northeast of Persia.[2] By 350, the leading edge of the Chionitae nomads were raiding into the Persian sphere of influence and were such a serious problem that Shapur was forced to suspend his operations against Rome without a negotiated truce and concentrate his empire's military power for the campaign years 351 to 358 against the Chionitae incursion. Persian military operations in the west were left to the initiative of local commanders.[3] During this period, Persian and allied Saracen raids continued to disrupt life in Roman Mesopotamia.[4] Other historians conclude that because Ammianus did not report raids into Mesopotamia by Persia there must have been a truce. However, Ammianus admits that he only recorded events of significance. He omitted details regarding small Germanic war bands that overran Gaul between 354 and 357 and completely ignored the Saracen Queen Mavi's revolt in 376. Based on his silence, it may not necessarily be concluded that an unofficial truce descended upon the Roman East between 350 and 358.[5]

The appearance of the Chionitae and the Hunnic Confederation altered the balance of power between Rome and Persia and presented a strategic dilemma to Shapur and his successors. Like Rome, Persia faced an established empire on one border and a series of hostile nomadic confederations on the other. Unlike the Romans, Shapur had no natural defensive terrain such as the Rhine and Danube on the Persian north-eastern frontier, and that frontier was longer and more porous than the Roman European *Limes*. The only solution to this dilemma was to make a lasting peace with one adversary.[6] Shapur eventually made peace with the Chionitae while his successors made peace with Rome.

The Chionitae had two avenues of approach into Persia. The first and most direct approach was along the main caravan route from Samarkand to Persia's eastern most outpost, the fortified City of Merv. The wall around the Merv oasis was almost 150kms in length. Strabo attributes construction of this wall to Antiochus I, son of Seleucus (who reigned circa 281 to 261 BCE). Persian King Chosroes I (531 to 579) most likely repaired these walls after the fourth century.[7] Even without the long walls, the fortifications at Merv would have been difficult for the Chionitae to contend with in their weakened state. Historian Tourai Daryaee argues that, based on a passage by al-Tabari that mentions Shapur establishing cities in Sind and Sistan that seems to confirm his rule over this region and Shapur campaigned in this region during this period.[8] Ammianus supports al-Tabari's statement when he lists the provinces of Persia as '...Scythia at the foot of Imaus [Himalayas], and beyond the same mountain, Serica, Aria, the Paropanisadae, Drangaiana, Arachosia, and Gedrosia'.[9] Daryaee's argument is also supported by numismatic evidence. A large percentage of gold coins produced during Shapur's reign came from eastern mints such as Merv, and a large number of his copper coins originated from Sakastan/Sistan and Kabul during the same period.[10] Finally, in most of Shapur's major battles and sieges with Rome, he relied on war elephants. To replace losses due to battle and disease Shapur would have needed a secure land route to India. As his battles of 363 demonstrated, his Royal cavalry was well trained to work with his elephants, which raises the inference that they had fought Indian armies or a Kushan successor state in addition to nomads between 351 and 357.

The second avenue of approach followed the Oxus River to the Caspian Sea and then turned south into the Persian settlements south of the Gorgan (aka Gurgaon) River. The Persians were heavily engaged against the various nomadic confederations on the Gorgan Steppes in the fourth through sixth centuries. Under Yazdegird II (438–457), forts were built to protect this region. His son, Peroz (459–484), continued fighting in the region, and it was recorded that he built a fortified town in the vicinity of Abiverd named Shahr-(ram)-Peroz.[11] Against this threat, in the late fifth or early sixth century, Persian kings constructed the Gorgan Wall (aka The Red Snake). This wall ran from the Caspian Sea to the modern town of Gumishan in the Elbarz Mountains. This massive brick fortification ran 195 kilometres and included a canal five metres wide that flowed along most of its length. This canal provided water to the brick kilns situated along the wall. There were over thirty forts spaced along the wall and a number of larger supporting forts south of the wall. The barracks capacity for the fortified zone has been estimated at 15,000 to 30,000.[12] The fact that later Persian kings committed massive resources of men and material to this stretch indicates that this was the gateway into the Persian heartland and may have been under constant threat from the mid-fourth century.

Unfortunately, few sources have survived for this period of Persian history. From the few references that have survived it can be concluded that Shapur successfully countered the nomad threat and a treaty was concluded. Based upon that treaty nomad auxiliaries appear in the Royal Army that marched against Rome in 359. In addition, Shapur's generals were actively undermining Roman authority in the Tran-Tigris Regions and in the area west of the Caspian Sea. After the fall of Amida, Shapur's brutal execution of Count Aelianus and the senior officers of the garrison may have had more to do with the unrecorded activities of the legions *Praeventores* and *Superventores* in the Trans-Tigris Regions than the death of Chionitae King Gumbates' son at the beginning of the siege.

Chapter 8

From the Hopeless Depths of Misery to the Height of Power: The Failure of Caesar Gallus

The purge of Constantine's male family members in 337 had unforeseen consequences. The premature death of two of his three sons, without having produced children, and Constantius' failure to provide an heir, left the House of Constantine bereft of direct male successors. With a major military campaign against the western usurper looming, Constantius was convinced that only a direct descendant could effectively represent his authority in the East. There were many competent military and civilian officials who could have been elevated to the rank of caesar. They could have been bonded to the House of Constantine through marriage to his sister Constantia. The gossipmongers at court, however, undermined Constantius' confidence in taking this course of action. With all the real and imagined threats to his throne from his circle of eastern supporters, Constantius was forced to look within his surviving male relations. This crises of succession resulted in Gallus being elevated to Caesar on 15 March 351 at the age of 25.

There was no adult ruler of the Late Roman Empire as ill-prepared for the responsibility of Caesar as Gallus.[1] Born Flavius Claudius Constantius Gallus, at Etruria in 326, he was the son of Constantius I and Galla. In 337, at the age of eleven, his life was spared during the purge because he was ill and not expected to survive. However, he did survive and, like his half-brother Julian, he was viewed as a threat to the throne and his life was monitored and controlled. He initially lived and went to school in Ephesus. In 344, at the age of nineteen, Gallus was moved to Macellum in Cappadocia.[2] It is clear from Gallus' later actions that he developed an affinity for the lower classes. He never learned to control his emotions, neither was he schooled in the fundamentals of government. Ammianus concludes that Gallus was raised from the hopeless depths of misery to the height of power and that his lack of proper training may have been the root cause of his cruelty and harshness.[3] Yet Ammianus, a member of the upper class of Antioch, may have been biased against Gallus for his political leaning and his harsh treatment of the upper classes.

Upon Constans' death and with the looming civil war, Constantius understood that ruling the Roman East was complicated; he was well aware that Gallus' lack of proper training had ill-prepared him for this appointed task. In his paranoid fashion, Constantius attempted to support Gallus while, at the same time, providing checks and balances against any threat of usurpation by Gallus.[4] As discussed in Chapter 8, Constantius married Gallus to his sister, Augusta Constantina, now between thirty-three and forty-three years of age. The marriage was to ensure Gallus' loyalty and officially recognized him as a member of the Constantinian Dynasty. The marriage helped Constantius build an executive team to rule the East. Augusta Constantia's experience with internal Imperial politics provided the firm hand to control the inexperienced and untrained new Caesar. It is also possible that Constantius did not trust his sister completely and that the marriage was a way to exclude Constantia from the Western Empire's unstable politics. As it turned out, she did more harm than good. She had a cruel nature and encouraged Gallus' ruthless actions. While the union was not a love match, the two autocrats were apparently somewhat compatible since, during their short marriage, Constantia had a daughter by Gallus.[5]

Constantius left military matters in the East to his *Magister Equitum* Ursicinus, who served in this position from 349 to 359. A member of Antioch society, he owned a house in Antioch. Ursicinus and Constantius must have served together for many years prior to the appointment, and he must have been a trusted companion to be left in command of the East when Constantius marched west. Ursicinus had several sons, most notable was Potentius who died at the battle of Adrianople.[6] Thus, while Ursicinus was a trusted companion, he was also a potential threat to the throne in the east, being a competent and popular soldier with sons to establish a prospective dynasty. Ursicinus' headquarters was located forward on the Persian front at the city of Nisibis.

Civil matters were placed in the capable hands of Thalassus. Thalassus was one of Constantius' counts in 345. Between 343 and 346, he was a leader of a delegation from Constantius to Constans at Poetovio. He was appointed praetorian prefect of the East in 351 (351 to 353) when Gallus became Caesar. Before the Battle of Mursa (28 September 351), Thalassus was still at the Imperial court. He arrived at Antioch after Gallus. The evidence suggests that he was connected with the Antioch upper class. He had two sons, Bassianus and Thalassius, and a daughter. He and/or his sons owned property in the Provinces of Phoenicia and Euphratensis.[7] Most probably his sympathies lay with the upper class.

Gallus arrived at Antioch in May 351 and found the Roman East in civil and military turmoil. In the aftermath of the 350 Persian invasion and siege of Nisibis, the region was faced with the spectre of famine, legal problems, and class unrest with the Usurper Magnentius' fifth column attempting to foment rebellion. In the approximately thirty-six months between his appointment and execution, Gallus was overwhelmed with problems of governance that would have taxed an experienced magistrate. The situation was complex and sources fail to establish a specific time line. It is not until the year 354, when Ammianus' history picks up, that events become clear. His regressions shed some light on Gallus' rule during the years 351 to 353.

Ammianus was a member of Antioch's upper class and was biased against Gallus for favouring the lower classes. Ammianus condemns Gallus for enjoying the bloody sport of boxing and horse racing. This condemnation is strange because, at the time, blood sports such as chariot racing and boxing were popular with the upper and lower classes until the end of Late Antiquity. Gallus probably encountered his upper class companions while attending these events. Early in Gallus' reign, Ammianus reports that he roamed the street at night undercover, asking all he encountered what they thought of Caesar. He continued this ruse until he was recognized. It is unlikely that he was alone, as Ammianus alleges, during these outings.[8] Tavern hopping is no fun alone. Ammianus fails to mention that Gallus was popular with a few members of the upper class who were above reproach, along with lower ranks in the army, and even church leaders.[9] The rowdier of these companions would have accompanied Gallus when he entered the city undercover. Who else would have manhandled those making negative remarks about Caesar?[10]

Prior to 354, Caesar Gallus and Augusta Constantia established themselves as rulers of the East with a ruthless hand. Cold War Journalist Ryszard Kapuscinski observed that all dictatorships take advantage of under classes by reaching out and giving them significance in life. By creating the appearance that the ruler relies upon them, the under classes are made to believe that they have a purpose often denied them by the upper classes. The man on the street that supports the dictator begins to feel at one with the authorities and to feel important. Since he most likely has been involved in minor crimes, he feels immunity for his transgressions. The dictator, meanwhile, gains an inexpensive, omnipresent intelligence agency.[11]

In retrospect, Kapuscinski's observations make the irrational acts of Gallus and Constantia appear coldly calculated to establish their authority. It is questionable, however, whether Gallus was sophisticated enough to have masterminded such an organization. Constantia, on the other hand, had first-hand experience with the darker side of her brother's use of Imperial power. Gallus' reign is characterized by a 'sinister web of informers' that seems to have been present from the beginning. The first reported victim was Clematius, whose only crime, as reported by Ammianus, was to spurn the advances of his mother-in-law. The unidentified woman was an intimate of Constantia. Without trial, she issued a death warrant for Clematius that was carried out by Count Honoratus.[12] In 354, an old, lower class woman reported to the empress's security force that there was a conspiracy against Gallus by some low ranking soldiers. Constantia rewarded the woman publicly by placing her in a royal carriage and driving through the main gate of Antioch with a town crier loudly proclaiming her service to Caesar.[13] Finally, Ammianus claims that the upper classes came to fear that their household slaves and other informers would report their conversations to the Imperial couple.[14] The establishment of a web of informers would have taken a short time to develop once the Imperial couple established themselves in Antioch.

The simplest problem facing Gallus upon arriving at Antioch was the revolt of the Jews in Palestine. In 351, he dispatched Ursicinus to restore order. It is unclear whether he accompanied the army into Galilee. The revolt was centred in the upper and lower Galilee district and may have been a response to the Christian domination of Palestine and Jewish opposition to church building in the region. The size of the revolt was beyond the capability of the Duke of Palestine to control and restore order. Ordered by Gallus to suppress the revolt and level Diocaesarea, Ursicinus led his troops into the region and burned Diocaesarea, Tiberias, and Diosopolis to the ground.[15] By 352, the revolt was suppressed.

While the initial military issue challenging Gallus was simple, the economy and famine were far more complicated matters to resolve.[16] The fact that Antioch was facing a famine in 354 should not have been surprising. In 350, the provinces of Osrhoene and Mesopotamia were put to the torch by Roman forces in order to deny the invading Persians food and fodder. Also, Persian raiders may have struck into Phoenicia sacking the town of Celseis, disrupting the harvest of this province as well.[17] To compound the problem, the region was struck by drought and, as the grain supply in Antioch decreased, its price started to rise.

The Antiochene Senate was comprised of rich landowners of the region who furnished food to the city. Foodstuffs could not be economically transported long distances over land. In the fourth century 100 miles [six days journey by ox cart] was a long distance. The realistic distance that food could be economically transported was less than twenty miles or one days travel by ox cart or wagon. Even without corruption, grain would be twice as expensive in Antioch as in the village it was grown. The destruction of the 350 harvest, the subsequent drought conditions in 351 to 353, and the massing of supplies for military operations on the border created a food shortage.[18] The rich Antiochene landowners' manipulation of food prices contributed to the problem. When Gallus ordered the landowners to lower prices they disobeyed. Gallus received no assistance from his senior advisors, as both Thalassus the praetorian prefect and *Magister Equitum* Ursicinus supported their own class and the Antiochene Senate.[19] These food shortages and price manipulations created a crisis that came to a head in the spring of 353.[20] Instead of being a stabilizing force, Thalassus, understanding Gallus' fiery temperament, provoked him to rash acts and then openly reported him to Constantius for mishandling the situation.[21] As the harvest was poor and famine imminent, Gallus ordered the leaders of the senate put to death for disobeying his edict on food pricing. At the last moment, Gallus was convinced by Count Honoratus to rescind the death sentence of these leading citizens. Gallus' actions would have been a warning to Constantius that he made a serious mistake.

The year 354 was pivotal in Gallus' reign. The harvest of 354 must have been poor again and, shortly before marching to Hierapolis in March 354 to counter Persian border incursions, Gallus was approached by the leaders of a mob requesting help in dealing with the impending famine. Ammianus attempted to shift the blame for the crisis onto the shoulders of the inexperienced Caesar for failing to provide grain from other provinces. Ammianus' charges are disingenuous. He would have been aware that the sea lanes would have been closed or just opening in March and the shipping of grain to Antioch would have taken months to arrange. This planning was beyond the capability of Gallus but should have been put into motion by his praetorian prefect due to the famine conditions of 353. The Governor of Syria, Theophilus, in 353, should have petitioned Gallus or the praetorian prefect to make arrangements for grain to be shipped to Antioch in 354. The record is clear that Theophilus did not make these arrangements because he and his supporters stood to gain from the inflated grain prices.

Gallus had good reason to publicly blame Theophilus for the famine. The mob, taking its cue from Gallus, lynched Theophilus and burned down the house of the wealthy merchant Eubulus. Both of these individuals are considered by historian Thompson to be the ringleaders who orchestrated the food shortage.[22] Constantius sent a commissioner named Musonianus to investigate Theophilus' death and then seemingly ignored the matter.[23]

Crop failure, Persian raids, and corruption were not the only cause of the famine that threatened the Roman East during Gallus' administration. Food distribution during Gallus' administration was also disrupted by banditry. Isauria was a poor mountainous region of western Anatolia occupied by a lawless people who repeatedly caused trouble over the centuries. The rich agricultural districts surrounding Isauria tempted its impoverished mountaineers into a culture of criminal activity. Isauria was far to the west of the Persian *Limes* but, due to its lawless nature, required a permanent garrison.

During the mid-fourth century the Isaurians were such a nuisance that a count and three legions permanently garrisoned the region and, as late as 395, this garrison still consisted of two legions.[24] In 353, the Isaurians became restless and started slipping out of their mountains and raiding their more affluent neighbours.

The cause of the Isaurians' unrest was the arrest of tribal members. Instead of punishing these criminals in the accepted manner they were thrown to the wild beasts during games in the amphitheatre at Iconium, a town in Pisidia. In revenge, the Isaurians went on the warpath and swept down from their mountains onto the coast in the vicinity of Sciron. With the help of a full moon they overwhelmed the sleeping crews of ships that had beached for the night and slaughtered the crews. They then carried off the ships' cargo back into the mountains. When the news of these attacks spread, ships bypassed Sciron and sailed directly to Cyprus.[25]

With the absence of victims on the coast, the Isaurians started raiding into Lycaonia, a district bordering Isauria. The raiders attacked travellers and inhabitants of the district and became such a problem that soldiers who were deployed in towns and forts along the border between the two districts were dispatched to neutralize the raiders. The soldiers patrolled daily engaging the raiders and pursuing them into their mountains. Once gaining the mountains, the Isaurians were able to lose their pursuers, often taunting them from cliffs and crags and showering the legionaries with missiles. The legionaries soon learned to break off pursuit before entering the badlands.[26]

The pressure from the Roman patrols caused the Isaurians to shift their hunting ground to the district of Pamphylia. The garrison of Pamphylia had been reduced to support counter-bandit operations in other districts, but the commander of the district was vigilant. Some legions were wintering near the town of Side. The district commander, detecting the Isaurians' approach, called upon the legions to set an ambush at a crossing of the swift and deep River Melas. As the bandits were crossing the Melas, the legions attacked pushing the forward tribesmen back into the river. The battle was not decisive because the River Melas prevented the legionaries from crossing the river and destroying the bandits. Reacting to this setback, the Isaurians quickly left the area and moved to the town of Laranda. Resting and recovering from their setback, the raiders started raiding wealthy towns in the region. Legionary cavalry were deployed in the area and they quickly forced the Isaurians back into the mountains.[27] Short of supplies and becoming desperate, the raiders descended upon the fortified coastal Imperial supply depot of Pelea. Unable to capture the supply depot by surprise, the raiders blockaded the fort for three days. Hungry and dispirited, the raiders lifted the siege and marched toward the city of Seleucia.[28]

Seleucia was defended by Count Castucius and legions I *Isauria sagittarii* [foot archers], II *Isauria,* and III *Isauria.* The legions would have been reduced in strength by infantry and cavalry detachments sent to other districts to counter the Isaurians' raids. The count deployed scouts along the avenues of approach to Seleucia. The scouts detected the Isaurians' approach but underestimated their strength. Planning to catch the bandits in the open, Castucius led his legions out of their fortifications, crossed the bridge over the deep and wide River Calicadnus, and formed battle lines. When the Isaurians appeared the legions started beating their spears on their shields to terrify the bandits. Their martial display caused the Isaurians consternation. But instead of joining battle, Castucius led his men back to the fortifications of Seleucia.[29]

To understand Castucius' decision not to engage the bandits in battle one must take into account the geography and forces deployed. If all three legions were present and at full strength, the Romans may have mustered up to 6,000 men but, due to detachments sent to counter bandit raids in other districts, the three legions together may only have mustered 2,000 men. They had no cavalry in support and had deployed for battle with an un-fordable river to their rear. We have not been provided the strength of the Isaurians but, since Castucius decided to decline battle, they must have been in greater numbers than the scouts' reported. The fact that the Romans returned to the city and prepared for an assault indicates that Castucius concluded that his soldiers were heavily outnumbered. Instead of assaulting the city, the bandits blockaded the city and fanned out to plunder the countryside.

The out-of-control Isaurian bandit activity disrupted the grain flow. Since the East was on the verge of famine, the situation had to be rectified quickly. Caesar Gallus dispatched Nebridius, Count of the East, to stabilize the situation. Nebridius created an ad hoc field army by collecting detachments from garrisons in the East and then marched to the relief of Seleucia. Upon hearing of Nebridius' approach, the Isaurians fled back into their mountains.[30] Since Ammianus only reported significant events, it can be assumed that the major raids were curtailed and that the Isaurians' lawless activity returned to normal levels. The lawless nature of the Isauria region would cause the empire problems for the remainder of the fourth century and, in 395, the legions II and III *Isauria* are listed at its garrison with I *Isauria sagittarii* being transferred to the regional field army.

During this same period, Gallus' spy network bore fruit and uncovered the usurper Magnentius' fifth column's attempt to foment rebellion. At about the time the mob lynched Theophilus, Serenian, former Duke of Phoenicia, came to trial. He was charged with treason for the inept defence of his province and allowing the city of Celseis to be sacked by the Persians. No historian clarifies when this event took place. It could have occurred as early as 350 during Shapur's last attack, or perhaps it was a separate incursion sometime between 351 and 353. Serenian was acquitted, which Ammianus attributes to forbidden magical spells. But well-placed bribes would have also gained his acquittal. Another newsworthy trial during the same period resulted in the conviction of a popular citizen named Theophilus. According to Ammianus, Theophilus was innocent and his conviction coming after Serenian's acquittal caused public unrest.[31] The lower class was presumably unconcerned with these trials involving wealthy citizens, so his reference to 'public unrest' probably referred to the upper class which, by now, was becoming more and more disenchanted with Gallus.

About this time, the Praetorian Prefect Thalassius died of natural causes. Upon receiving reports of all these events in 353, Constantius wrote to Gallus offering advice in mild terms while, at the same time, withdrawing the army units in the area on the pretence that they would be better employed elsewhere. Constantius contended that unemployed soldiers would become mutinous and could become a danger to Gallus and his administration. The troops under Gallus' direct command were reduced to his palace and personal guards and detachments from guard regiments *Scholae Scutarii* and *Gentiles*, a total force of not more than 1,500 men.[32] The redeployed units could have been sent to Isauria to suppress brigands, but the timing between these events, as reported by Ammianus, is unclear. The legions suppressing bandits on the southwest Anatolian highlands, under command of Count Nebridius, remained in theatre in case the Persians attacked but were no longer under Gallus' direct control. In these communications, Constantius also directed Gallus to join him in Italy.

Replacing Thalassius, Constantius promoted Domitianus from *questor* to praetorian prefect of the East and directed him to be respectful to Gallus while encouraging him to comply with the summons to join Constantius in Italy. Domitianus ignored his emperor's instructions, and his conduct could be considered treasonous from the first day he set foot in Antioch. Upon reflection, his disregard of Constantius' instruction and his efforts to incite rebellion against Gallus make it probable that he was an agent of the failed usurper Magnentius or an opportunist with knowledge of Constantius' weakening hold on the empire.

Instead of reporting to Caesar at the palace of Antioch, Domitianus ensconced himself at a villa in town and ignored the summons of Gallus while pleading illness. He remained in hiding plotting against Gallus' administration. He sent his son-in-law, Apollinaris, into Mesopotamia to sound out the troops to determine whether they supported Gallus and if Gallus was planning a rebellion. Eventually, Domitianus attended Gallus' consortium where, in front of its members, he ordered Gallus to depart at once for the west or he would cut off supplies to the palace. After he delivered his insulting ultimatum, he left the consortium. He ignored a summons to meet with Gallus during the next few days. Gallus was understandably enraged by Domitianus' disrespectful conduct and eventually ordered his guards to arrest the praetorian prefect.[33]

Upon hearing of Domitianus' arrest, the then aged *Questor* Montius, attempted to sway the leaders of the palace guard away from Gallus' course of action. Upon hearing of Montius' collusion Gallus, fearing for his life, called out all his loyal guards and ordered the arrest of Montius. The guards marched to Montius' house, arrested him, bound the old man, and dragged him through the streets to Gallus' headquarters. Domitianus was bound as well, and both men were dragged through the streets until dead and their bodies thrown into the river.[34]

Before dying, Montius shouted out the names Epigonus and Eusebius without further explanation. Suspecting rebellion, Gallus threw a wide net over possible suspects and had agents scour the countryside. Apollinaris was arrested as he fled to Armenia. In Tyre, agents discovered a partly woven purple royal robe, but it was never determined who had commissioned it. The governor of the province where Tyre was located was Apollinaris' father. He was arrested and brought to trial. Gallus was not particularly discerning in the rounding up of individuals allegedly plotting rebellion; as a result, many innocent people were arrested, brought to trial, and accused of treason and magic. Ammianus reports that trial results were clearly unjust resulting in execution (as well as confiscation of property) of the innocent along with the guilty.[35] Ursicinus was sucked into the maelstrom of injustice when he was summoned from Nisibis to preside over the treason and magic trials.[36] The verdicts were predetermined. The empress herself supervised the proceedings from behind a curtain periodically thrusting her head into the chamber to ensure the desired outcome.[37] While these Stalinist-type trials often resulted in unjust verdicts, Ammianus reports that the proceedings uncovered a real widespread conspiracy led by Domitianus and Apollinaris. It is clear that Montius was an active conspirator for he had arranged to arm the conspirators with weapons from the *fabricarum*.[38]

While these three years of instability disrupted the Roman East, the Persians were surprisingly inactive. John the Monk claims Gallus' aggressive and short-tempered nature, as well as his brutal suppression of the Jewish revolt, scared the Persians.[39] However, a more plausible explanation for Persian inactivity directed at Gallus was due to their military efforts in Central Asia against the nomads. In 354, the grandee Nohodares was tasked with continuing the war with Rome in the absence of the Persian king (who was with his army fighting nomads). He was given great latitude in how he carried out the war and was authorized to take advantage of a Roman weakness if and when the situation presented itself. Such an opportunity arose at the town of Batne in the region of Anthemusia in the Roman province of Osroene. Batne, located near the Euphrates River, was a rich trading centre that sponsored a yearly festival during the month of September. The market included valuable goods from India and China.[40] Because Persian deserters warned the Roman Army of an impending attack, Nohodares' planned raid was thwarted. Also during this period, Gallus made a visit to Hierapolis in March 354 with his troops and may have discouraged further Persian raids.

By late summer of 354, the civil tumult in the east had reached a dangerous peak and Constantius was ready to take decisive action.[41] His palace staff was making the situation worse by stirring the pot with rumours and innuendo. He first recalled Ursicinus on the pretext of conferring with him about the situation in the east. In Ursicinus' absence, Count Prosper assumed military command of the east. Like the dutiful soldier he was, Ursicinus and his protectors (staff officers) immediately set off west for Constantius' court.[42] Constantius next convinced Constantia to return to court. Fearing her brother's cruelty, but believing she might pacify him, she started the journey west, conveniently dying of a fever upon entering Bithynia. A number of messengers were sent to Gallus requesting his return to court. Finally, the Tribune Scudilo succeeded in convincing Gallus to return. When Gallus arrived in Poetovio in Noricum, Count Barbatio, commander of his own bodyguard, arrested him. He was taken to Pola, Istria (now Pula, Croatia) and interrogated by *Praepositus Cubiculi* Eusebius and *Agens in Rebus* Apodemius. While Gallus tried to blame his failures on Constantina, he was executed under the supervision of Count Barbatio.[43.] The irony of Gallus' execution is that there was no evidence that he ever plotted against Constantius. In actuality, the man who executed Gallus, Count Barbatio, was plotting against Constantius.

Ursicinus barely escaped execution. Despite the fact that he had sent warnings to Constantius of Gallus' misrule, he was charged with high treason. Constantius listened to the rumour-mongers and lies spun by Ursicinus' enemies. The Imperial staff, in a star-chamber hearing, convinced the emperor to deny Ursicinus a public trial and to execute him in secret. After the order of execution was given, Constantius had a change of heart. He first postponed the execution and subsequently suspended it.[44] Ursicinus and his staff remained at court in *Mediolanum* (Milan) under a cloud.

Despite contemporary historian vilification, primarily of Constantius' disposal of his male relatives, and based upon his experience as a teenage Caesar, he had a realistic expectation that Gallus would succeed in ruling the east. When Constantius was elevated to Caesar he had been properly trained and prepared. His father, Constantine I, dispatched him to the East surrounded by trusted advisors loyal to the House of Constantine who guided the young Caesar in the administration of his assigned region and command of the regional armies.[45] These advisors had a vested interest in ensuring that the House of Constantine succeeded in order to secure their own future and prevent civil war.

Constantius appointed men of proven loyalty as Gallus' administrators and generals. However, he failed to realize that these advisors were not motivated to ensure that the House of Constantine remained on the throne. To the contrary, based on their position and Constantius lacking an heir apparent, the advisors had a realistic expectation that at least one of them would be raised to Caesar if Gallus failed. The empire was simply too expansive and complicated for one ruler to maintain. If Gallus failed, it would only be a matter of time before events forced Constantius to appoint someone from the upper levels of the army or civil service to the throne of Caesar of the East. Gallus' nature and lack of preparation simply accelerated the process.

Gallus, unprepared for the responsibilities thrust upon him, made the mistake of alienating the ruling class of Antioch. In many ways, the failure of his administration falls squarely on Constantina's shoulders. Her failure to curb her husband's temperament and provide sage counsel undermined his development into an effective administrator. The only positive aspect of the Gallus debacle was that the Persians were so busy fighting barbarians on their northeast frontier that they could not take advantage of Rome's weakness in the East. The fall of Gallus instigated a purge of his court, supporters, and followers with a corresponding disruption of civil and military administration in the East.[46]

Chapter 9

Usurpation and Crisis:
Campaign in the West 350–355

In late summer or early fall of 350, Constantius shifted the centre of gravity of his *Praesental* Army from the East into north-western Anatolia and the eastern Balkans. The Persian threat had been neutralized for the 350 Campaign, and he now faced a complicated military and political crisis in the aftermath of his brother-emperor's murder. Until this point there had been no requirement for an eastern field army since Constantius' *Praesental* Army had been deployed with him in the East in 337. The assignment of his *Magister Equitum* Ursicinus to manage military affairs in the East implies that Constantius had actually detached a small force from his *Praesental* Army. This component would become the nucleus of the new Eastern Field Army.[1]

It is difficult to reconstruct the military operations during the Roman civil war of 350 to 353. Like all civil wars, political, economic, and religious issues were all involved.[2] Ammianus' books for this period have been lost and Zosimus' account is confusing. To clarify events, Zosimus' account can be supplemented with Julian's orations, ecclesiastical histories, numismatic evidence, map reconnaissance, and Roman logistic norms.

Flavius Magnus Magnentius (303 to 11 August 353) declared himself Emperor of the West on 18 January 350, at *Augustodunum Headuorum* (Autun) during a winter birthday party for his sons. At the time of his usurpation, Magnentius was the commander of the paired elite legions Herculian and Jovian. He was born in 303 at *Samarobriva* (Amiens) Gaul and was of Frankish decent. While little is known of his earlier military career, he would not have commanded these two legions had he not fought in Constans' Rhine and British campaigns.[3] Halfway through the party, with major military and civilian leaders of Gaul present, Magnentius disappeared and reappeared wearing garments of Imperial purple. Upon his reappearance, he was proclaimed emperor by those present. This well-directed melodrama had been planned for months and was the climax of a coup to depose the unpopular Constans.[4] While Constans' reign had started well, over time, his personal habits and administrative policies turned his army against him.

On 25 December 333, at Constantinople, Constans' father, Constantine I, elevated him to Caesar. Constans was ten years old at the time of his coronation. Upon his father's death four years later, Constans was elevated to Augustus of the central one-third of the Roman Empire. After political manoeuvring and dissatisfaction with the final division of the empire, the elder of the brotherly triumvirate, Constantine II (Flavius Claudius Constantinus, 316 to 340), died during a failed invasion of Italy attempting to enforce his rights as the elder son of Constantine. This left the now 17-year-old Constans master of two-thirds of the Roman Empire.[5] The young emperor and his supporters wasted little time in enforcing his authority in the Western Empire. Between 341 and 342, he successfully defeated Frankish incursions into Gaul and, in 343, he visited Britain, most likely to counter Pictish and Scottish raids.

In administering his portion of the empire, Constans was tolerant of Judaism but was biased against pagans, issuing an edict in 341 banning their sacrifices. He suppressed Donatism in North Africa and supported Nicene Orthodoxy against Arianism, which was supported by his brother Constantius. Constans tried to settle the conflict with his brother at the Council of Sardica in 343 but failed. Eventually, the two brothers reached an agreement that allowed each to support his own version of Christianity within his territories. Despite a positive and energetic start to Constans' reign, the sources indicate that the remainder of his rule was marred by cruelty and misrule. Dominated by favourites and preferring a select German bodyguard, as opposed to his elite legions (not to mention his overt homosexuality), alienated his power base: the Western Army.[6]

Church historians have condemned Constans' 'immoral' homosexual relationships with several of his German bodyguards. However, immoral conduct alone would have provided insufficient grounds for a coup. Other emperors led questionable private lives and remained on the throne. The army turned against Constans because of his administrative reforms that hit the pockets of junior officers and bureaucrats. The army and civil service were primarily paid in-kind, but officers believed they could justly extract money from the lower ranks in exchange for basic necessities. Constans' reforms sought to end this lucrative extortion. Resentment over reforms led to the formation of an anti-Constans faction in both the civil and military infrastructure within Gaul.[7] With the army and civil service supporting the coup, Constans fled south toward Spain but was overtaken by rebel cavalry at the end of February at a fortress near Helena close to the Pyrenees Mountains. Hiding in a pagan temple, Constans was dragged out into the open and murdered.[8]

To complicate matters for Constantius, other usurpers revolted shortly after Magnentius proclaimed himself emperor. On 1 March 350, in the city of Mursa, Vetranio (Contans' *magister peditum* and commanding General of the Army of Pannonia) declared himself emperor.[9] Vetranio was a commander under Constantine I and hailed from the Province of Moesia Superior. He was an elderly, well-connected, and experienced soldier approaching retirement. As a local from the Balkans, he was popular with the Army of Pannonia due to his long service, old-fashioned morality, and pleasant disposition. The courtly fops considered him devoid of all refinement, a dull witted, stupid rustic who only discovered literacy when he was an old man.[10]

Vetranio's motivation remains clouded by the passage of time. Philostorgius' account indicates that Constantina, on her authority as Augusta, appointed Vetranio Caesar to forestall Magnentius' revolt from expanding into Illyricum. Constantius apparently ratified this appointment when he sent Vetranio a diadem. While most modern historians discount Philostorgius' account, it is compelling when viewed in relation to Vetranio's actions upon being raised to the purple.[11] It was approximately six weeks between Magnentius' announced usurpation and Vetranio's elevation to the purple by his troops. Considering the time it would have taken for news to travel, especially during winter, Constantina probably acted without authority from her brother when she encouraged or convinced Vetranio to accept the elevation. Based upon the timing of Vetranio's action and the fact that Constantina lived close enough to Mursa to appreciate the situation, this politically astute woman likely encouraged Vetranio to revolt against Magnentius, thereby preventing the usurper from gaining control of the Army of Pannonia before she received instructions from her brother.[12]

Once elevated, custom required a new emperor to issue a donative in coin to the army. For any army paid primarily in-kind, donatives from an emperor were extremely important to the rank and file. Whereas Magnentius' coins declared him to be 'liberator', Vetranio's coins proclaimed him to be 'saviour of the state'.[13] Upon receiving news of Vetranio's accession, Constantius sent him a diadem, which not only ratified his elevation to emperor, but also bound the old soldier to Constantius' throne.

Both Constantius and Magnentius recognized that control of the Army of Pannonia would be decisive to the outcome of the coming civil war. Both sent agents to Vetranio's court to solicit his support, but Constantius' offer of legitimacy made it more likely than not that Vetranio would remain loyal to the ruling dynasty.[14]

Born sometime between 307 and 317, Constantina was the eldest daughter of Constantine I and Fausta making her an older sister of the three brother-emperors. Constantine I bestowed the title Augusta upon her, most likely an honorary title; however, she grew into a politically astute and formable woman. Her father arranged a political marriage between her and her kinsmen Hannibalianus in 335. She was widowed when her brother Constantius had Hannibalianus killed during the purge of 337. Afterward, she disappears from recorded history until 350 when she influenced Vetranio's actions. Even though Constantina worked with Vetranio to keep his army out of the usurper's order of battle, Constantius had other agents working behind Vetranio's back to undermine his authority, paying hefty bribes to key leaders of the Pannonia Army.

While the major players were busy with their political manoeuvrings, on 3 June 350, Flavius Julius Popillius Nepotianus Constantinus, son of Eurthropia, daughter of Constantius I, declared himself emperor in Italy. He rallied an army of gladiators and marched on Rome. On 30 June 350, Magnentius' *Magister Officiorum* Marcellinus defeated the gladiator army with the professional soldiers in Italy and killed Nepotianus and his mother. Nepotianus' misadventure underscores Vegetius' conclusion that committing untrained levies to battle only exposes them to slaughter.[15]

In September 350, Constantius advanced to Heraclea, just west of Constantinople on the European side of the Bosporus. Both Vetranio and Magnentius sent ambassadors to him. Magnentius sent Marcellinus,

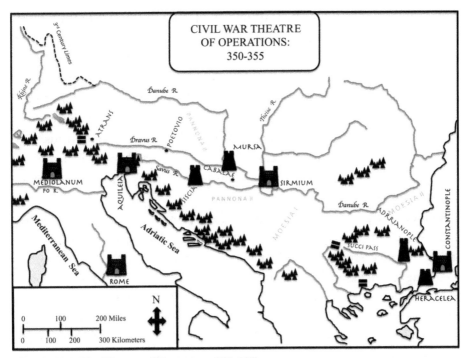

Map 9. Civil War Theatre of Operations 350–355.

Nunechius, and Maximus, while Vetranio sent his Praetorian Prefect Vulcacius Rufinus. By all appearances, Vetranio was in league with Constantius, and his ambassador may have been just a formality. Magnentius' objective was to stop the Imperial military build-up in Thrace. The offer presented to Constantius was that he would remain 'first among equals' and that Magnentius would bind himself to the Imperial regime with a marriage of his daughter to Constantius. The envoy, Nepotianus (leader of the pro-Magnentius senators in Rome), reiterated that since Constantius was now confronting two battle-hardened soldier-emperors he should seriously consider Magnentius' offer. Some sources indicate that Constantius had some anxiety following this attempt to intimidate him.[16] This anxiety was likely exacerbated by the logistical challenge of deploying his army to squelch the rebels in Thrace from Asia Minor in late fall and early winter.

Constantius responded the next day by arresting Magnentius' envoys but leaving Vetranio's envoy free. This act violated Roman standards of diplomatic procedure. Constantius justified his actions by his belief that he had received advice from his long-dead father in a dream.[17] Disregarding the supernatural intervention, there is a more practical explanation for Constantius' actions. First, Magnentius' envoys failed to comprehend that Constantius had already confirmed Vetranio's loyalty. Secondly, Marcellinus was Magnentius' *magister officiorum* and most likely one of the central conspirators and the 'money man' behind the revolt. Constantius and Constans were not particularly close, but they were brothers. Having one of the conspirators behind his brother's murder within his grasp was probably a great temptation.

Thrace was part of Constantius' original provinces and the base of his Thracian Field Army. This army may have included up to twenty legions and six cavalry regiments and mustered between 15,000 and 20,000, not including the *limitanei* legions and regiments in the region.[18] Thrace would have lacked the stockpiled grain to support Constantius' full military strength without some preparation. The usurper declared himself in January and Constantius arrived in Thrace in September of 350. The Imperial staff and court administrators would have had about six months to complete the logistical preparations for a campaign in Europe. Based upon modern conditions six months appears to be sufficient time to shift an army's logistics infrastructure. With near instantaneous communications, it took six months for the Coalition to build up enough combat power to allow them to take the offensive during the First Gulf War. In antiquity communication and movement of material took a much longer time. Between the time it took for news of the revolt to reach Constantius and considering the Persian attack on Nisibis and shipping schedules, grain would not have started to arrive in Thrace for the *Praesental* Army's redeployment until the spring sailing season of 351.[19] The controlling issue was when Constantius decided to transfer the *Praesental* Army west.

The Persian siege of Nisibis placed Constantius on the horns of a dilemma. The issue became whether to divert supplies from the eastern theatre to prepare for a western campaign in 351 or to handle the western political crisis with the Thracian Field Army and maintain the *Praesental* Army focused on the Persians in the east. The failure of the Persian siege in late summer or early autumn of 350, with the resulting Persian heavy casualties, eliminated the Persians as a threat in 351. It is not surprising that Constantius visited Nisibis after the siege before he rode west to confront the usurper. In the aftermath of the sieges of 338 and 345, and resulting heavy casualties from battle and disease, the Persians had refrained from invading, at least for the following three or four years. Constantius wanted to personally verify that the Persians had sustained heavy enough casualties to take them out of the fight for at least one or two years.

As events unfolded, it became clear that Constantius did not view the Persians as a viable threat after their failed siege of Nisibis. His decision to shift the Imperial main effort from the east to the west is not recorded. The majority of sources do not describe logistical preparations for the coming civil war, and Ammianus' account of events has not survived. Marching the *Praesental* Army into the Balkans would have been a simple manoeuvre. Providing food and fodder would have been a nightmare in late fall and winter. The grain supply would have most likely originated in Egypt. With the coming of fall and the end of the safe shipping season on the Mediterranean, shipping the gross tonnage of grain for 40,000 additional combat troops and tens of thousands of animals and servants would have been beyond the capability of the Imperial supply system. The specific preparatory movement of the *Praesental* Army is unknown. It is certain, however, that shifting the entire *Praesental* Army into the Balkans rather than spreading them into winter quarters in northwest Anatolia and the Constantinople region would have been folly.[20] Additionally, the strategic situation did not require the entire *Praesental* Army to be in the Balkans until the late summer of 351.

The circumstances indicate that Vetranio was in the Imperial camp; however, it is possible that he was playing a double game. Including 3,000 men of the guard regiments that must have ridden into Thrace with him, Constantius would have had 20,000 to 23,000 *comitatenses* soldiers to oppose any thrust by Vetranio's 20,000 men east through the Secci Pass toward Constantinople. The conference in Thrace demonstrated that Vetranio was, at least nominally, pro-Constantius or, at worst, neutral. The rebellion's overt threat of spreading to the East was temporarily negated by the presence of the reinforced Army of Thrace. With approximately 40,000 anti-Magnentius soldiers in Pannonia and Thrace, there was no reason to rush the *Praesental* Army's deployment before the logistics infrastructure was in place. Constantius' continued participation in stalled negotiations with the upstart emperors would have provided the time needed to prepare the logistics infrastructure for the *Praesental* Army's offensive.

Constantius' agents continued to subvert the Pannonia Army after the conference. On 25 December 350, the armies of Pannonia and Thrace were assembled near the city of Sirmium in Pannonia.[21] Both emperors were seated on thrones in front of the assembled legions. Constantius stood first as the senior emperor and spoke to the assembly. He reminded those assembled of his father Constantine's munificence and the oath they had taken to be loyal to his children. He charged Magnentius with the murder of his brother and proclaimed that Magnentius should not go unpunished for the murder of Constantine's rightful heir. Upon hearing Constantius' oration, the Army of Pannonia cried out they would not follow any mock emperor. Vetranio's own guards seized him, pulled him from his throne, and stripped him of his purple robe.[22] This apparently staged transfer of power from Vetranio back to Constantius ensured the support of the Army of Pannonia.[23]

Constantius demonstrated unusual leniency toward Vetranio. After the ceremony, Vetranio, now reduced to a private citizen, attended a banquet in honour of the merger and was, thereafter, retired at state expense to Prusa in Bithyma.[24] The friendly treatment of Vetranio was an unusual outcome for a presumed usurper compared to the arrest of Magnentius' envoy Marcellinus. But the increasingly paranoid Constantius ensured that Pannonia's favourite son was retired to a villa outside the Balkans where he lived out the remaining six years of his life peacefully. This benevolent treatment was not limited to the army leadership. Vetranio's civilian supporters were welcomed back into the fold. Julian points out that Constantius '…won over…a country that is extremely fertile…by winning over men who obeyed him of their own free will…[Constantius] deprived [Vetranio's] followers of nothing, but protected their privileges and gave many of them gifts'.[25]

With the Pannonia Army declaring for Constantius, he brought to arms against Magnentius the armies of Pannonia, Thrace, and his own *Praesental*. Zonaras, writing in the twelfth century, is the only source describing the strength of this combined Imperial army as mustering at 85,000 men.[26] These same armies in the *Notitia Dignitatum* in 395 would have numbered, at full strength, 81,500 men (65,000 infantry and 16,500 cavalry), close to Zonaras' estimate.[27] The *Notitia Dignitatum* field army estimates do not include the legions and auxiliary units commanded by the dukes along the Danube *Limes,* or contingents from Constantius' Armenian allies; all were present in unknown numbers.

According to Julian, the key to defeating the rebels was the Imperial heavy armoured *clibanarii/cataphractarii* and *sagittarii* (horse archers) regiments. Julian does not report the numbers of these types of cavalrymen included in the Imperial army but, out of the 16,500 cavalry listed in the *Notitia Dignitatum,* 3,500 would have been *clibanarii/cataphractarii* and 2,000 would have been *sagittarii* (horse archers). Based upon Constantius' reforms and his army's thirteen-year war with the Persians, these numbers are a reasonable estimate for the *clibanarii/cataphractarii* and *sagittarii* branches of his army. The rebel army, experienced at fighting Germanic infantry armies, was at a disadvantage in open terrain against the Imperial cavalry. While the Imperial forces in the region may have mustered as many as 85,000 men (as Zonaras alleges), it is unlikely that Constantius' field army outnumbered the rebels by any significant number. Based upon the disjointed sources, the Imperial army appears to have been broken down into a number of field and blocking forces. Julian writes that, when the two main bodies finally engaged, the Imperial army overlapped the rebel army.[28] A higher proportion of Imperial cavalry would have achieved this overlap. A thousand cavalry in combat formation would present a greater frontage than a formation of a thousand infantry. In addition, after a campaign of manoeuvre, Magnentius chose to give battle instead of attempting to retreat to rebel-controlled territory. If the rebels were outnumbered, they were still confident enough of victory to offer battle.

Magnentius was not idle after his usurpation in January 350. A year later, in January 351, he elevated his brother Magnus Decentius to the rank of Caesar and gave him command of the Rhine *limes.* Zonaras reported that Magnentius' army at Murse numbered only 36,000 men, but this was not the full manpower available to the rebel cause.[29] The *Notitia Dignitatum* fails to provide any information regarding the size and composition of the rebel army. The western portion of this document was drafted circa 420. At the time of its computation, the western army had been engaged in almost twenty years of attritional warfare against large and small Germanic war bands. Goldsworthy and Heather note that the Western *Notitia Dignitatum* revealed indications of losses and desperate improvisations in the organization of the field armies.[30] Significant portions of the field armies were *pseudocomitatenses* units stripped from the *limitanei* border armies or incorporated into the field armies after their province was overrun.

Unlike Constantius' eastern policy of not stripping the *limes*, the rebels formed at least two field armies by stripping the Rhine and British *limes* of units or by conscripting large drafts from the western *limitanei* armies to form new units. Earlier sources aid in the determination of the theoretical total forces available to Magnentius. According to the *Latin Panegyric* in 312, Constantine drew his army from approximately the same territory that Magnentius controlled in 351. During his Italian campaign, Constantine marched into the Po River Valley with only 40,000 troops despite the fact that he commanded a region garrisoned with more than 120,000 men.[31] The defensive requirements of the British and Rhine *Limes* required 80,000 men in 312. Constantine marched into Italy with the elite of his Gallic Army and, forty years later, Magnentius followed his example. Magnentius, however, had the added advantage of having Italy secured by local collaborators and garrisons that had declared for his cause. With his rear area secured by his brother in Gaul and his flank (eg Italy) secured by his collaborators, he was free to focus a field army of 40,000 men (supported by garrisons of over 80,000 men defending Britain, Gaul, the Rhine and upper Danube Rivers, the Alpine passes, and Italy) against Constantius.

To ensure loyalty, Magnentius arrested and executed the legion commanders who were not part of his conspiracy. As a result, discipline suffered in the rebel army. Magnentius enrolled Celts, Galatians, Franks, and Saxons into his army and stripped the Rhine legions, such as XXX *Ulipia*, of experienced men to create new legions as exemplified by the creation of the legions *Magnentius* and *Decentius*. Magnentius seems not to have had a field army of 40,000 readily available as Constantine did in 312. He had to build his army by stripping the legions along the Rhine of critical manpower. Critically important was Magnentius' failure to make peace with the Alamanni. This oversight had dire consequences for his rebellion in the short term and Rome's ability to rule Gaul in the long term.

There is no record of Constantius' or Magnentius' campaign plans for 351, but they can be reconstructed by analysing the events recorded by various sources. As Constantius demonstrated against Shapur, he was an operational artist. His handling of the Vetranio affair indicates that he understood the fickle nature of military, civilian, and religious officials. His Imperial agents infiltrated the rebel field army, and their activities would bear fruit during the final critical military manoeuvres. Operationally, the initial Imperial plan was to invade and confront the rebel army in the Po River Valley. Constantius' cavalry would have achieved freedom of manoeuvre to the significant disadvantage of the rebel army. The resultant foraging of both armies would have the added benefit of damaging the rebel Province of Italy.

Constantius understood the political advantage of the Constantine family connections. To ensure his continued support in the East, Constantius elevated Gallus to Caesar (on 15 March 351) and sent him to Antioch, further cementing relations by marrying him to his elder sister the Augusta Constantia (See Chapter 8). With the concentration of loyal armies in the Balkans, Constantius planned to steal a march on Magnentius by advancing one of his field armies toward Italy to secure the passes through the Julian Alps.[32]

Magnentius and his conspirators were not novices to the power politics of the empire. The disenchanted were always susceptible to bribery, extortion, blackmail, and espionage. Rebel agents worked to undermine the Imperial government in the East (see Chapter 8). His agents in the Balkans were extremely successful. They unravelled the Imperial campaign plan during the early months of 351. Not to be outmanoeuvred, Magnentius marched prior to the opening of the campaign season in June. He marched without a siege train, which would have hindered his speed of manoeuvre. He crossed the Julian Alps from Italy into Pannonia. His fifth column was useful in blinding the Imperial reconnaissance. Actus, Constantius' general holding the passes into Pannonia, was captured, along with his men, through treachery. With the passes safely in rebel hands, Magnentius' army marched undetected down the Dravus River Valley. The capture of Actus by rebel screening units seems to have gone unnoticed since the Imperial vanguard advancing from Sirmium up the Dravus River was ambushed and defeated with heavy losses near Atrans.[33] After the ambush, the Imperial vanguard

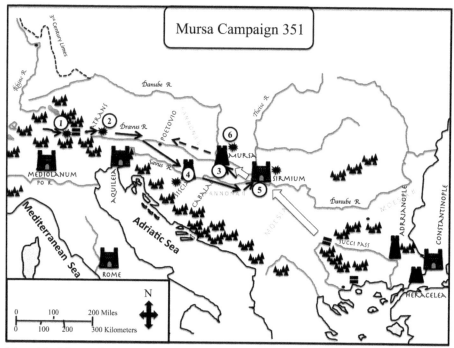

Map 10: Mursa Campaign, 351. 1. The rebels capture Imperial garrison defending passes through the Alps. 2. Imperial Vanguard Army is ambushed and conducts a fighting withdrawal down the Dravus and Savus Rivers Valleys. 2. Rebel army's advance is stopped by the defences of the city of Siscia. The Vanguard Army breaks contact and digs in near Cabalae. 4. After a period of short negotiation, the rebels storm Siscia and plunder their way toward Sirumium. 5. The assault of Sirmium fails and the rebels blockade the city. Upon detecting the approach of the *Praesental* Army, the rebels lift the siege of Sirmium, retreat up the Dravus River and assault Mursa. 6. The *Praesental* Army catches the rebels besieging Mursa. The *Praesental* Army decisively defeats the rebel army, but due to heavy casualties, the Imperial troops could not pursue the rebels.

retreated to Poetovio on the Dravus River. The rebels advanced on Poetovio, capturing it and forcing the Imperial vanguard south, back to the Savus River, fighting its way to the south bank. With the exception of the ambush, the fighting was mainly skirmishes up to this point. After the Imperial vanguard crossed the Savus River, a period of negotiations took place.

With the rebel army slipping into Pannonia undetected, defeating the Imperial vanguard and chasing it back to the Balkans, Constantius had to modify his plan. Unsurprisingly, he fell back onto his eastern strategy of a mobile defence based upon strong points while manoeuvring Magnentius onto ground favourable to his heavy cavalry. To delay the rebels, Constantius dispatched Flaius Philippus, a former praetorian prefect, as envoy. Philippus, one of Constantius' henchmen, had, in 350, disposed of Paul, Bishop of Constantinople, who had been a thorn in the emperor's side since 342. He was a well-connected bureaucrat, rising through the civil service until appointed consul with Flavius Salia in 348. He was escorted to Magnentius' camp (with Marcellinus, who was released from Imperial arrest). In an act of unbelievable stupidity, Magnentius allowed Philippus to address his army. In magnificent oration Philippus reminded the rebels that:

> ...Romans should not make war on Romans, especially when the emperor was the son of Constantine...as for Magnentius, he ought to remember Constantine's kindness to himself and [his father]... [and who] granted the highest honours. After recounting these facts, [Philippus] asked Magnentius to withdraw from Italy and be content to rule all of the provinces beyond the Alps.[34]

This oration unsettled the rebel army. Only the oldest tribunes and centurions would have served under Constantine I, but even the youngest soldiers would have heard the war stories and known about the rich rewards bestowed upon the troops by the Imperial family. Stalling for time, Magnentius announced his willingness to consider the emperor's terms. Ensuring the loyalty of his commanders over dinner that evening, Magnentius addressed his rebel army the next morning. Magnentius reminded his troops of Constantius' misrule and abuse of power. He then, unexpectedly arrested Philippus for allegedly abusing his authority as an envoy and spying on the rebel army.[35] Realizing that the negotiations were a ruse to stall for time, Magnentius resumed his march and attacked the town of Siscia.

The town of Siscia was located on the Savus River. The river valley was swampy. The only viable approach to the town was across a bridge that was well defended by the Imperial garrison. Siscia was an important Imperial mint and, due to its metalworking, most likely a weapons manufacturing centre. Due to the nature of the ground and the determination of the defenders, the first rebel assault failed. Magnentius, taking a page from the

Imperial playbook, presented Philippus as a ruse to convince the garrison commander he had Constantius' permission to cross the Savus to meet with the emperor. Once the rebels were across the river, they stormed Siscia, capturing the mint and most of the Imperil infrastructure intact. Shortly afterward, Magnentius issued bronze coins to commemorate the event and pay the rebel army a donative.[36]

With the breathing space gained by the negotiations, the Imperial vanguard established a strong defensive position at Cibalae.[37] The rebels marched down the Savus Valley plundering as they went. Rebel troops appropriated supplies from those who cooperated and looted the villas of those who did not. Fabius Titianus was sent as an envoy to the Imperial camp and delivered an insulting message, levelling absurd charges against Constantine and his sons and demanding Constantius step down as emperor. Despite the captivity of Philippus and personal insults, Constantius permitted Titianus to return to the rebel army.[38] No sources indicate where this meeting took place. Based upon the timing it could have been at Cibalae, Sirmium or at a local villa. But based upon the rebel actions after this meeting, the *Praesental* Army had not entered the area of operations.

When the rebel army reached the vicinity of Cibalae, an old veteran named Gratian welcomed them. Gratian was the father of future emperors Valentinian and Valens. He was born in the area of Cibalae of a humble family. Joining the army, he worked his way up to count and commanded the army in Africa and Britain. Upon discharge, he returned to Cibalae and established a villa and estate. He must have met Magnentius while serving together in Britain. Gratian provided food and fodder, along with hospitality, plus intelligence on the Imperial position nearby.[39] In return for his support, Magnentius may have taken fewer goods from Gratian and promised to advance the careers of Valentinian and Valens. Gratian's knowledge of the terrain and roads would have been extremely valuable to the rebel army.[40] Presumably relying upon Gratian's information to the effect that only the diminished Imperial vanguard was in Cibalae, the rebel army bypassed Cibalae. This manoeuvre also indicates that Constantius was not at Cibalae otherwise Magnentius would have attacked the Imperial position. The rebels marched on Sirmium seeking to take the region's capital and Imperial supply depot, and then locate and engage the *Praesental* Army.

Plate 1. Gold Coins of Constantius II and Shapur II. Coins, while important for commerce, also played an important role in the propaganda of both Rome and Persian. (*Photograph courtesy of www.ma-shops.com*)

Plate 2. Arch of Constantine, Siege of Verona. The Roman Army of the late third and fourth century were dressed and equipped significantly differently from the stereotypical Roman soldier depicted in mass media. The frieze of Constantine I's army besieging Verona provides a basic depiction of Roman military dress and armament during the fourth century. (*Photograph courtesy of Lisa Maish and Bill Storage*)

Plate 3. Soldiers from the Arch of Constantine in the field. The *testudo* or *fulcum* formation depicted here provided excellent protection against missiles. It was used in sieges and field battles allowing the Romans to advance on an enemy who was superior in archers. (*Miniatures from Armoraum & Aquila, Aventine, Gripping Beast, Footsore, Little Big Man Studios. Photography by LMarie Photo and Cyrus R Harrel*)

Plate 4. Recreation of the arms and equipment of a fourth-century Roman officer based on the Arch of Constantine. (*Photograph courtesy of the Britannia Society, http://www.durolitum.co.uk*)

Plate 5. Historian Dan Shadrake's recreation of an unarmoured Roman officer from the fourth century. Taken from the Arch of Constantine. (*Photograph courtesy of the Britannia Society*)

Plate 6. An unarmoured soldier armed with *archballista* or *manuballista* (early crossbow). The *ballistarii* that accompanied Julian on his first combat mission may have been armed with this type of weapon. (*Photograph courtesy of the Comitatus Society, http://www.comitatus.net*)

Plate 7. Arch of Galerius. A Roman medium cavalryman leading his horse through a city gate. (*Photographer Dr J C N Coulston, University of St. Andrews*)

Plate 8. Horse armour uncovered during the excavations at Dura-Europus. This discovery is the only example of horse body armour recovered from the third and fourth centuries. (*Courtesy of the Yale University Art Gallery, Dura-Europos Collection*)

Plate 9. Based upon archaeological and literary evidence the living history historians of the Comitatus Society have reconstructed a *Cataphractus Draconarius* arms and equipment. (*Photograph courtesy of the Comitatus Society*)

Plate 10. Battle of Ebenezer scenes 1 and 2. Painted by H Gute from the third century Synagogue battle mural uncovered during the excavation of Dura-Europos. Note the mounted fighters are holding their spears similarly to the equestrians in the rock carving at Firuzabad, Iran. (*Photograph courtesy of the Yale University Art Gallery, Dura-Europos Collection*)

Plate 11. The majority of Roman general purpose or medium cavalry would have been armed and equipped similarly to this equestrian. (*Photograph courtesy of the Comitatus Society*)

Plate 12. The combined arms formation described by Vegetius would have been at a disadvantage fighting Germanic infantry. Against Persian cavalry, the combination of steady shield wall (*fulcum*) of spear-armed infantry supported by assorted missile troops would have negated the Persian cavalry's missile and shock tactics. (*Miniatures from Aventine, Gripping Beast, Footsore, and Little Big Man Studios. Photography by LMarie Photo and Cyrus R Harrel*)

Plate 13. Drawing of French orientalist painter and traveller Eugene Flandin (1840): Sassanian King Ardachir Babakan's rock relief (Firuzabad 1), Scene showing an equestrian victory over Parthian King Artabanus V, province of Fars, Iran. (Voyage en Perse, *Itinéraire*, I.)

Plate 14. Centre figures from the Sassanian battle-scene at Firuzabad, Iran, which has been rendered by M Flandin. Sassanian Prince Shapur I pierce with his *kontos* (cavalry pike) the right side of an enemy, who is represented in the act of falling to the ground. (George Rawlinson. *The Seven Great Monarchies of the Ancient Eastern World, Volume VII*)

Plate 15. Persian Tactics. During the field battles of the Nisibis War, the Savaran mounted assault on Roman formations came in waves. The first wave of horse archers showered the Romans with arrows as the heavy Savaran charged home. If this attack failed, the first wave would disengage covered by the second wave's horse archers. Then the second wave's heavy Savaran would then charge home. During the June 363 battles elephants often were employed in the assault and support role. (*Miniatures from Armoraum & Aquila, Aventine, Gripping Beast, Little Big Man Studios, Photography by LMarie Photo and Cyrus R Harrel*)

Plate 16. Historian and actor Ardeshir Radpour portrays a medium Persian Savaran cavalryman. These elite cavalry fought with Suren's covering force against Julian's 363 Persian Expedition. (*Photograph by Holly Martin Photography*)

Plate 17. Historian and actor Ardeshir Radpour demonstrating the 'Parthian shot' used by the Persian Savaran cavalry. (*Photograph by Holly Martin Photography*)

Plate 18. The view looking south from the Roman fortress city of Marida (modern Mardin, Turkey). The Persian Royal Army's manoeuvres were under constant observation during the 359 Campaign once they entered the Mesopotamian steppes. (*Photograph by Linda Cohen Harrel*)

Plate 19. Dismounted Elite Savaran archer portrayed by historian and actor Ardeshir Radpour. A company of elite archers infiltrated through the unguarded water tunnel during the siege of Amida. (*Photograph by Holly Martin Photography*)

Plate 20. Ruins of the covered water tunnels of the Roman city of Cepha (modern Hasankeyf, Turkey). Covered and concealed tunnels at Amida and Cepha allowed the populace to draw water from the Tigris River in times of siege. A company of elite Persian archers infiltrated through a similar unguarded tunnel during the siege of Amida. (*Photograph by Linda Cohen Harrel*)

Plate 21. Recreation of a light ballista. This small torsion artillery piece would have been similar to the light ballista that shot down the elite Persian archers from the tower near the water tunnel during the siege of Amida. (*Photograph courtesy of the Comitatus Society*)

Plate 22. War Elephants were an integral part of the Persian war machine. They were present in the Royal Persian Army for the majority of Shapur II's battles and sieges. (*Aventine Miniatures. Photography by LMarie Photo and Cyrus R Harrel*)

Plate 23. The Triple Walls of Constantinople. The ultimate fortification of Late Antiquity. Repeatedly threatened and besieged by Persian and barbarian armies, now a reminder that Eastern Rome survived long after Western Rome's collapse. (*Photograph by Linda Cohen Harrel*)

While Zosimus alleges that the rebel assault on Sirmium was a total surprise to the garrison, it was not a surprise to the Imperial high command. The *Praesental* Army was not in the vicinity of Sirmium. The city garrison was small. Sirmium was the Imperial regional capital with arms factories and storehouses that were used to arm a hastily mustered militia to augment the garrison. With the large number of veterans settled in the region, this hastily mustered militia should not be viewed as consisting wholly of untrained civilians. Due to the small garrison, the addition of the militia to the garrison was critical to the defence of the city.[41] The surprise rebel assault failed and, lacking a siege train, the rebels could only blockade the city. In early autumn 351, having failed to take the city, the rebels were faced with a serious problem: they were in a trap. The Imperial vanguard was threatening their lines of communications, the *Praesental* Army was approaching, and they were running out of supplies. In order to evade the trap, the rebel army determined it had to march back north to the Dravus River and the plains around *Colonia Aelia Mursa* (modern Osijek and, hereafter, Mursa). Having his lines of communication cut, Magnentius attempted to re-establish communication by storming Mursa, the old Roman colony established by Hadrian. Fourth century Mursa had been reduced in size compared to the original colony by the unrest of the third and fourth centuries. The city's decurions had abandoned large sections of the city and surrounding lands, including the amphitheatre, applying the savings to maintain their fortifications in good repair.[42]

Rising above the leaves of the ancient sources and examining the forest rather than each leaf, the entire operational situation becomes clear. The *Praesental* Army, with its dominant cavalry, had failed to appear. The rebel army had been unable to locate and engage the *Praesental* Army. The rebels had stolen a march on the Imperial cause in the late spring or early summer but were unable to take advantage of that action. As in the war against the Persians, defended cities became critical to the revised Imperial battle plan. After initial setbacks, the Imperial battle plan was modified to entice Magnentius deeper into Imperial territory. The rebels advanced along the swampy (and not cavalry friendly) Savus Valley. By striking at the illusionary lightly defended Sirmium, the rebels were positioned deep in Imperial territory and, having ravaged the Savus Valley on their march against the city, had only one viable route of egress toward friendly territory. That route, the Dravus Valley, was blocked by the city of Mursa.

Since the ambush in the Alps, the rebels no longer considered the decimated vanguard army a threat. It remained a thorn in their side but did not pose a significant threat to the rebels entrenched around Sirmium. The failure of the rebel army at Sirmium was due to its gamble to forego their siege train in exchange for speed. Magnentius was forced from Sirmium due to a shortage of supplies and the detection by his scouts of the *Praesental* Army's approach.

The assault on Mursa did not go well for the rebels. Upon hearing of the rebel approach, the garrison closed and barred its gate and manned the walls. The rebel oversight in not bringing a siege train again limited their options to assault and/or blockade. Each rebel attempt to storm the walls was driven back by stones and darts from the walls. During one attack, a gate was set on fire but, before any damage was done, the civilians drowned the flames with water. Failing to catch the garrison by surprise, Magnentius was forced to blockade the city with the *Praesental* Army (now reinforced with the Imperial vanguard army) marching to its rescue.[43]

As the *Praesental* Army approached the city, one of the early skirmishes during the preliminary fighting involved an attempt by the rebels to ambush the Imperial advance guard as it marched to break the blockade of Mursa. The abandoned amphitheatre was just outside the city walls. The rebels concealed four regiments of Celtic *auxilia* within its walls hoping that as Constantius' army deployed to relieve the city, these regiments would conduct a surprise attack with the intent of disordering its manoeuvres.[44] While not mentioned by Zosimus, this plan must have included other units of the rebel army since four regiments, approximately 2,500 to 4,000 men, could not have hoped to destroy the entire Imperial army.

The garrison of Mursa detected the ambush and warned the approaching Imperial troops. The Tribunes Scolidos and Mandus, and their legions, were assigned the mission of neutralizing this rebel position. Selecting the best-armoured infantry and archers from their respective legions, undetected and presumably at night, they surrounded the stadium and blocked all of the exits. Then, part of this force, still undetected, infiltrated the amphitheatre and occupied the upper tiers. On a signal, the infiltrators attacked the Celts with darts and arrows. The startled Celts attempted to flee from the stadium but were halted by the blocking detachments. Unable to fight their way out of the stadium, the Celts rallied and formed into tortoise formation and attempted again to force a way through the gates. While some of the Imperial troops on the upper tiers continued to rain darts and arrows down upon the Celts, the majority closed with swords and cut the Celts down to a man.[45]

With the planned ambush thwarted, Constantius' advance once again placed Magnentius on the horns of a dilemma. He could maintain the siege of Mursa with a detachment, turn and engage Constantius with a significant numerical disadvantage; he could lift the siege and turn his entire army to engage Constantius, at only a slight numerical disadvantage or parity; or he could withdraw up the Dravus River toward the Alps.[46] The Dravus River Valley was perfect cavalry country, making a rebel withdrawal in the face of Imperial cavalry superiority difficult. Thus, the first two options were the only viable manoeuvre. Not surprisingly, Magnentius chose option two, which indicates he believed he had a reasonable chance of success and, therefore, was probably not outnumbered two to one as claimed by Zonaras. If the rebels defeated the Imperial army in an open field battle, the city of Mursa would become irrelevant.

At this critical point, Silvanus defected to Constantius with at least his regiment, the *Schola Armaturarum*. It is possible at this point that other legions and regiments joined him in defecting to the Imperial cause. The sources do not expound on the importance of this defection but, since Silvanus would be elevated to *magister* and given the task of restoring order in Gaul after the civil war, he must have provided important information about the military situation in Gaul and within the rebel army. Being commander of a guard regiment, he would have been privy to diplomatic and strategic information that could have undermined the rebel cause in the long term.

As dawn broke on 28 September 351, both armies deployed from their camps into battle formation. As novelist Q V Hunter observed, the Battle of Mursa was the day the Roman Army committed suicide.[47] The Imperial army deployed for battle with cavalry on both flanks and the infantry in the centre and with its right flank anchored on the River Mursa. The rebel army deployed in a similar traditional fashion, but with its left flank secured by the river. Based upon the battle descriptions for the fourth century, the

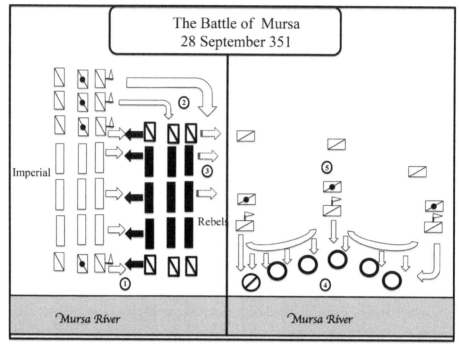

Map 11. The Battle of Mursa, 28 September 351. 1. The Imperial and rebel front lines engage. 2. The superior Imperial cavalry outflank the rebel army. 3. Detecting the danger Magnentius retreats with 12,000 men leaving the rest of his army to its fate. 4. Instead of routing or surrendering, the rebel army stabilizes the situation by tying in both flanks against the river. Imperial tactics change forcing the rebels into pockets that fight on until dark. At nightfall the rebel army was pushed into the river losing 24,000 men.

traditional infantry formation for an open field battle was three battle lines of legions and *auxilia* regiments. Archers, slingers, and other light infantry supported the frontline by launching missiles over the legionaries or dashing out between the centuries, maniples, and cohorts to counter enemy light forces. On the cavalry wings, the Imperial *cataphract* regiments formed the first line. Horse archers and lighter armoured cavalry formed a second line. The Imperial army slightly out-flanked the rebels on their unsecured right flank (left of the Imperial army). At least one source reports that Constantius was not present for the initial deployment and opening stages of the battle; rather, he was praying in a nearby chapel.[48] Since emperors travelled with a significant bodyguard, if these sources are accurate, a large portion of

Constantius' guard regiments would have been in the vicinity of the chapel, forming a significant Imperial reserve.[49]

Julian specifies that the core of the rebel army was its close order infantry, augmented with new recruits from Celts, Iberians, and Germans. This does not mean he relied on new *auxilia* units as these new recruits would augment seasoned regiments. The western legions would have recruited from these same nationalities – both those settled in Gaul and those from the Germanic lands east of the Rhine. *Auxilia* regiments from these same nationalities would have augmented the western legions since the reign of Constantine I. While Ammianus only mentions *auxilia* regiments conducting raids and other unconventional operations, in a formal battle both legions and *auxilia* regiments performed the function of close order infantry.[50] Despite being deficient in cavalry, Magnentius took no precautions to secure his open flank as Caesar did at Pharsalus by creating a fourth infantry line to support his outnumbered cavalry. On a signal, the legions of both sides clashed their shields and spears, and sang their war songs as they advanced into battle.[51] Missile storms of darts, arrows, and javelins were exchanged. When these were exhausted the infantry first lines charged each other and engaged in close combat with swords and shields.

Utilizing its superior armoured cavalry supported by horse archers, the left Imperial wing quickly defeated the right rebel wing. During the initial fighting, Menelaus, commander of the Armenian horse archers (who could allegedly shoot three arrows at once and hit three men) was killed by the rebel *Magister Pedium* Romulus, who likewise was killed in battle from an arrow fired by Menelaus.[52] The death of Romulus may have taken the fight out of the rebel cavalry. The demoralized rebel right wing broke and Magnentius, with approximately 12,000 rebels, escaped the field.

Instead of pursuing Magnentius, the Imperial armoured cavalry and horse archers rallied and turned on the unprotected rebel centre, throwing it into disorder and cutting off the rebel army's retreat.[53] With the usurper routed from the field, command of the rebel army fell to junior officers. Julian specifically notes that the rebel battle lines fell apart, not due to cowardice, but to the ignorance and inexperience of the rebel junior officers.[54] In other words, their attempt to shore up the open right flanks by pulling legions from the second and third lines failed. In most battles of antiquity, when an army's command structure falls apart, the army routs. At Mursa, instead of panicking and routing, the rebel centre regiments and legions rallied to their individual unit standards and continued to fight. The trapped rebels, well led by veteran tribunes, centurions, and chiefs, were determined to perish while killing their opponents.[55]

At this point in the battle, the rebel army closed its open right flank by tying it to the river. The rebel left wing cavalry dismounted and fought as legionaries, and the battle became a bloody stalemate with the rebels fighting with their backs to the river in legionary and regimental pockets while the Imperial infantry attempted to break their cohesion.[56] To break the stalemate, the Imperial generals changed their approach and employed tactics learned from fighting Persians: combining horse archer arrow storms with *cataphract* charges.

Contrary to popular modern notion, horses are not very intelligent, but they are not stupid. Unlike humans, they will not charge into four ranks of closely packed men holding bayonets, spears, or a formed shield wall. If the obstruction is small, like a legion or cohort in a square, horses on the run will flow around the formation like water. If the obstruction is a shield wall, a galloping horse will most often come to an abrupt stop, throwing the rider. Horse survival instincts were well known to ancient cavalrymen. Well-trained infantry that maintains its cohesion will stop a cavalry charge every time. This is why Constantius incorporated *cataphracts*, armed with *kontos*, and horse-archers as a fighting force. The *kontos* was a cavalry pike that required two hands to employ, but it was longer than the infantry spears of the legionaries. Under the covering fire of the horse-archers, the *cataphracts* would trot up to the shield wall and use their long cavalry pikes to strike the legionaries who could not reach the *cataphracts*. Once the forward momentum of the *cataphracts* was halted, the shield wall would open gaps and the younger and more agile defending infantry would charge into halted armoured horsemen attempting to hamstring the horses and pull the armoured riders out of their saddles. On a signal, the armoured cavalry pulled back and the horse-archers would move to the front attempting to inflict casualties before the skirmishing infantry regained the shield wall. The process is then repeated. Imperial armoured cavalry could break formations where rebel legions and regiments lost heart, became disordered, or were slow to react. These tactics pushed the rebel defensive formations back toward the river.[57] If they could have maintained cohesion, with an adequate water supply, the cavalry would have eventually been driven off. Constantius' cavalry attack supported the infantry slugfest that took place in the centre. The Imperial cavalry kept the rebel flanks pinned. As individual legions and regiments were ground down, the rebel army broke into isolated pockets against the river.

Constantius understood that a bloody civil war victory would weaken Rome's ability to defeat the barbarians. He offered terms to the fighting pockets of rebels; but neither his officers, nor the rebel officers, would heed his pleas to stop the fighting. In the confusion, as night fell some rebels escaped toward the plains, the rest were pushed into the river.[58] Approximately 12,000 rebels made it out of the death trap.

The *Praesental* Army was in no shape to take advantage of their pyrrhic victory. The only recorded numbers for the battle indicate that the rebel losses were 24,000 of 36,000 engaged and the Imperial losses were 30,000 of 80,000 engaged. These figures would be much too high for the victor in a single battle and probably represent the Imperial losses for the entire campaign, including battle deaths, disease, and injuries. Since the wounded rebels would all have been killed (and those pushed into the river left to drown), the reported 24,000 rebels killed in action would be within the realm of possibilities. Since it is unlikely that Constantius had 80,000 men at Mursa and more probable that he mustered 40,000 to 50,000, it is clear from the sources that his casualties during the entire 351 Campaign were serious enough to stop the Imperial advance into Italy during the remaining two months of the campaign season.

More significant than the overall general body count was the number of veteran leaders lost. The Roman Army's Achilles' heel was the time it took to train replacements for decimated units and replace destroyed legions. Contemporary military leaders understood this fact as exemplified by Ammianus' routine listing of casualities in terms of tribunes killed or wounded, even when he provides a total casualty figure. As an example, at the disaster of Adrianople, thirty-five tribunes (both command and staff) were killed while, at the Battle of Strasbourg, there were four killed.[59] Only the Tribune Arcadius, commander of the Imperial legion *Abulei*, is identified as being lost at Mursa.[60] Caesars' *War Commentaries* reports that in hard fought victories or defeats, the centurions and other veterans took a disproportionate percentage of the casualties.[61] Without these veteran officers and 'chosen men', training replacements and maintaining discipline become extremely difficult. The only positive aspect of this pyrrhic victory was the recovery and repair of armour and weapons left on the battlefield. The Imperial authorities were spared the expensive proposition of rearming new legions and replacements with brand new equipment that would have taken years.[62]

Despite the immobilization of his army for the rest of the campaign season due to casualties, Constantius was not idle. Realizing the rebels still had manpower reserves of up to 80,000 men in Gaul, an additional 20,000 in Italy, and possibly another 40,000 men in Africa, he shifted to a diplomatic offensive. Zosimus asserts that Constantius entered negotiations with Chnodomar of the Alamanni and enticed him to attack Gaul in 352.[63]

During the winter of 351 to 352, Constantius offered amnesty to the low ranking members of the rebellion while the rebel army entered winter quarters at an unidentified coastal Italian town near Aquilea, protected by mountains.[64] The mountains acted as a defensive rampart while the seaward approaches were protected from naval attack by marshes and shoals. As the snow in the passes melted, and as the campaign season opened, the Imperial scouts located an unguarded path over the mountains. Constantius personally led his legions along the path at night and caught the rebel army by a surprise dawn attack. Magnentius and his rebel leaders, over-confident in the security of their position, had failed to secure all the approaches to their winter quarters. The rebel army was defeated in detail in Magnentius' absence. That morning, the usurper and his companions had travelled to a nearby town to attend a horse race and local festival. Magnentius' luck held and he escaped the destruction of his second army by fleeing to the southern provinces of Gaul.[65] As Constantius was disposing of one rebel army, Chnodomar lead the Alamanni across the Rhine into Gaul defeating Decentius' army on the way to looting and settling the west bank of the Rhine.[66] Chnodomar's assault may have been coordinated with Constantius' storming the passes of the Julian Alps, marching into Italy, and then capturing the former Imperial court, depot and communications hub at *Mediolanum* (Milan).

With Constantius in *Mediolanum* and Chnodomar on the west bank of the Rhine, Decentius and Magnentius had to rebuild their armies. They could not join forces without providing one of their two opponents uncontested access to their bases of support in Gaul. Their indecision in this regard was their undoing. Constantius' only aim was the destruction of his enemies and securing his throne. He was willing to unleash barbarians on disloyal provinces to achieve his goals. Decentius and Magnentius employed half measures and failed to mass against Constantius, their primary opponent. If left unchecked, Chnodomar could only ravage the countryside since capturing fortified cities without a prolonged siege was beyond his military capabilities. Chnodomar's gains could have been reduced once Constantius was defeated. Stripping the *limes* was the only way to rebuild the rebel armies after their repeated defeats, making the *limes* collapse inevitable. With both rebel armies defeated, impotent, and rebuilding for the remaining 352 campaign season, the Alamanni and other Germanic war bands went unchecked in the Roman provinces west of the Rhine. Constantius re-established Imperial control of Italy, and his deputies organized a naval force and landed armies in Spain and Africa, securing these important provinces for the emperor.[67]

The 353 Campaign season opened in July as Constantius marched north from *Mediolanum* to finish off the rebellion. The rebels had apparently decided to join forces, but were sluggish in execution. Magnentius was cornered at Mons Seleucus in the Isere Valley where his army was defeated a third time. Magnentius once again escaped, this time deeper into Gaul. Finding the situation hopeless, he committed suicide on 11 August 353. On 18 August 353, Decentius, on his way to reinforce Magnentius, was informed of the usurper's death and hanged himself at Senonae. With the defeat of the rebels, Constantius sent agents to locate and arrest rebel supporters and establish control in the breakaway provinces.

Constantius secured his throne and preserved the East but seriously damaged the West. His short-sighted policy to squelch the rebellion included encouraging the Alamanni and Franks along the Rhine to attack into the Gallic Provinces. This strategy resulted in the collapse of the Rhine *Limes*.[68] The Gallic *limitanei* legions *I Minerva*, *XXX Ulpia*, *XXII Primigenia*, and *VIII August*, reduced by drafts to form five *comitatenses* legions for the usurper's army, could not hold the Rhine *Limes* and may have been destroyed when Decentius was defeated in 352 or in some unrecorded battle between 352 and 355.[69] The Rhine *limitanei* armies were shattered, and the cities of *Argentorate* (Strasbourg), *Brotomagum* (Brumath), *Tabernae* (Rheinzabern), *Saliso* (Seltz), *Nemetae* (Speyer), *Vangiones* (Wroms), and *Monguntiacum* (Mainz) were taken along with *Colonia Agrippina* (Cologne), the last to fall in 355, after a ten-month siege.[70] By the end of 355, the Franks and Alamanni were well established west of the Rhine, having captured and destroyed over forty cities on the west bank of the Rhine.[71] Constantius' action validates Isaac's argument that the emperor's primary interest was safeguarding his throne rather than preserving peace and prosperity for his subjects.[72]

The 354 Campaign season saw Constantius' army attempting to push the Alamanni back across the Rhine by attacking them in the spring and summer in the vicinity of *Augusta Raurica* (Augst). He rewarded Silvanus' loyalty by elevating him to *magister peditum* and giving him command in the Gallic Provinces. Silvanus' Gallic Field Army, mustering about 8,000 to 13,000 men, was not recorded as making any headway against the Germanic war bands operating on the west side of the Rhine. The soldiers from the *limitanei* legions, auxiliaries, and cavalry *alae* that survived the collapse of the *limes*, had disappeared into the cities west of the Rhine. This state of affairs should not be surprising since the reconstituted Gallic Field Army was comprised of legions and *auxilia* that had survived three major defeats at the hands of the Imperial forces and one at the hands of the Alamanni; consequently, it was only a shadow of its former self. Based upon a passage from Ammianus, until Julian lead them to victory in 357, these Roman units were routinely defeated in skirmishes with the Germanic war bands.

Constantius continued to fight the Alamanni in the campaign season of 355. He defeated an Alamanni force near *Lacus Brigantinus* (Lake Constance/Bodensee) in early summer 355. The Franks crossed the Rhine and began their ten month siege of *Colonia Agrippina*. *Magister Peditum* Silvanus, distracted from his duties by court intrigue, accomplished nothing against the rampaging war bands in the Gallic Provinces; neither did he attempt to lift the siege of *Colonia Agrippina*. Silvanus, a dutiful soldier, son of a Frank general of Constantine I, was driven to revolt on 11 August 355 due to false treasonous accusations against him being circulated at court. To counter this revolt, Constantius sent *Magister Equitum* Ursicinus to negotiate with Silvanus. Ursicinus had barely escaped execution and was at court under a cloud in the aftermath of the execution of Caesar Gallus and the purges associated with his fall (See Chapter 8). But instead of negotiating, Ursicinus and his staff had secret orders to ride to Gaul to kill Silvanus. Ursicinus reached Gaul and carried out his orders to arrange for Silvanus' death by 7 September 355. The timing of this event indicates that Constantius' agents must have detected Silvanus' intent before he revolted. The fact that he selected Ursicinus to eliminate Silvanus shortly after he was almost executed due to the Gallus affair is revealing.

First, the East was stable in 355 and lower military officials could supervise the military situation. Second, Constantius must have developed a close personal bond with Ursicinus between 337 and 350 when they fought together in the East. Despite Constantius' paranoia and Ursicinus' enemies at court, they may have maintained a friendship. Finally, in August 355, there was no one left at court who Constantius considered loyal enough to get the job done.

While the East remained calm during the civil war, Constantius knew it could flare up at any time. He knew that he would have to eventually send Ursicinus back to the East, but he needed a family member to oversee the defeat of the Germanic tribes overrunning the west bank of the Rhine and to restore order and loyalty in the Gallic provinces. His solution was to elevate his sole remaining male relation, Flavius Claudius Julianus to Caesar on 6 November 355. Known to history as Julian the Apostate, Constantius sent him to Gaul in December 355 in the midst of a crisis without the tools for a solution.

Chapter 10

Caesar Julian: 'An Emperor in Strategy, a Commander in Tactics, a Hero in Combat'

L ibanius describes Julian's military traits as '… an emperor in strategy, a commander in tactics, [and] a hero in combat'.[1] This is a fair summary of the positive military traits of the young emperor who modelled himself on the heroes of the Hellenistic and Heroic Ages. Thanks to Ursicinus' posting to Gaul, with Ammianus included as a protector and staff officer in his entourage, we have a detailed account of Julian's first years in Gaul as caesar. Julian, in his Letter to the Athenians, also provides complementary information to Ammianus' account. Before he was raised to caesar, Julian was interested in a Classical and Hellenistic education that developed the mind as well as the body. Ammianus describes Julian as of medium height, thick neck, large and broad shoulders, head to foot perfectly built, and a strong runner.[2] He did not develop these physical qualities lifting scrolls in a library or sitting under a tree arguing philosophy. Therefore, it should be no surprise that his education included military training.[3] The fact that he exhibited, at times, the reckless bravery of a Homeric hero in battle indicates that he was as skilled as Constantius at the Roman martial arts of horsemanship, swordsmanship, and possibly wrestling. If not skilled in these arts, his repeated exhibitions of reckless bravery in battle would have indicated that he was a fool.

No matter that near contemporary Christian writers considered him a fool for trying to turn the tide of Christianity and reinstate paganism, his skills at governance refute such shallow assessments of his character and abilities.[4] Unlike his brother Gallus, Julian's studies prepared him for his new responsibilities as caesar. While this study focuses on Julian as a military leader, it should not be overlooked that he exhibited the cardinal virtues of self-control, wisdom, justice, courage, dignity, and generosity. He was an excellent administrator and judge though often inflexible in judgments.[5]

This new 23-year-old caesar of unknown and unlimited potential arrived in Vienne (on the Rhone River) at the head of a bodyguard of 360 men, under the same type of shadow as one of Stalin's World War II generals released from the gulag in Siberia.[6] Julian was elevated to caesar, but was guarded and advised by potential assassins. He was nominally in command of the Army of Gaul but responsible for rectifying the situation, all the while with the sword of Damocles hanging over his head.

The military situation Julian faced was daunting. The *limes* had been pushed back to the Rhone and Seine Rivers (See map). The region between the Mosel River and the Rhone-Seine *limes* was a no-man's land where Germanic war bands could materialize without warning, enhancing their mobility by travelling along the Romans' roads.[7] Ammianus considers war bands smaller than 500 insignificant and does not record their marauding activities. But smaller war bands were certainly present and, while not a threat to formed Roman Army units, would have been lethal to the civilian landowners and their small bodyguards. While we envision these bands raiding for gold and silver objects, these items would have been rare. Raiders were often looking for material objects as mundane as cauldrons, bowls, and ladles. A rare find dating from an Alamanni raid of the third century uncovered the household goods of a single Roman villa packed into three carts that were being rafted to the east bank of the Rhine. The raft was probably sunk by a Roman patrol boat. The only items missing were the gold and silver items that the villa would have been expected to contain. The Germanic world was not as developed as that of the Romans, but the tribes along the Rhine were more sophisticated than their ancestors who fought Augustus Caesar. As a result, Roman household domestic goods would have had great value in Germanic villages.[8]

Julian was faced with opposition in his own camp, which, at the expense of the suffering Roman citizens of Gaul, was not supportive of his success or the re-establishment of Roman law and order. In the winter of 355 to 356, Julian was sent to Gaul with 360 men, not as commander but as a figurehead and subordinate to the generals at the front.[9] In June 356, he was allowed to join the army.[10] At the time, the Army of Gaul mustered approximately 13,000 men and was still in winter quarters spread throughout the Roman-controlled territory in small field forces. The Roman strategy in the winter

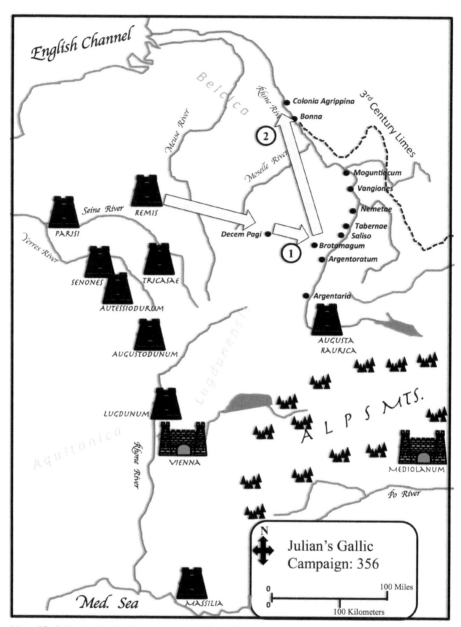

Map 12. Julian's Gallic Campaign, 356.[11] 1. The Army of Gaul attacks into Alamanni and then into (2) Frank controlled territory. At the time the main Alamanni and Frank war parties were absent raiding the Roman provinces.

was to divide the Army of Gaul into smaller field forces to defend as many cities and towns as possible from Germanic raids and to spread the logistics burden of supporting the army over a wide area. The standard operating procedure for the army was to mass at *Remis* (Reims) in June and then start operations against the Germanic tribes.

As the Army of Gaul was proceeding to the assembly area at *Remis* from its dispersed winter quarters, Julian received word that a barbarian force had conducted a surprise attack on *Augustodunum* (Autun). The city's defences had been reduced by neglect. The local soldiers were not prepared for the attack, and the city was only saved by the swift reaction of a band of local discharged veterans. Mustering the available troops at Vienne, Julian marched to the relief of *Augustodunum*, arriving on 24 June 356, without incident.

A council of war was quickly convened at *Augustodunum* to consider the safest route to *Remis*. The most direct route – and the most dangerous – was the road through *Autessiodurum* (Auxerre) and *Tricasae* (Troyes), which traversed extensive dark woods not controlled by Roman forces. This route had been used the year before by Silvanus and then only with a force of 8,000 *auxilia*.[12] Julian decided to take this route accompanied by a force of *cataphracts* and *ballistarii* (crossbow-armed infantry).[13]

This force was an inadequate escort for a caesar and, at first blush, Julian's ride appears to be a rash move and a reckless replication of the exploits of the young Alexander the Great. But it should be remembered that, up to this point in his life, Julian had no experience as a soldier or a military commander. To earn the respect of the soldiers and generals, he had to slip his handlers and gain some combat experience. It is an interesting historical parallel to that of Shapur who began his legendary reign as a young king leading 1,000 knights to redress the wrongs the Saracens inflicted upon the Persians Julian's first independent command was to lead Roman knights to right the wrongs the Germanic tribes had inflicted against the Roman Gallic citizens. Both military operations shaped the two leaders' characters and would foreshadow the outcome of their confrontation. Shapur's well-planned and executed campaign under supervision of trusted advisors and generals versus the impromptu glory ride during which Julian's generals were hoping he would die.

By taking the shorter, more dangerous, route Julian carved a small independent command from the force at *Augustodunum* and eluded his handlers. Undoubtedly, there were informants watching his every move, but he was free to prove himself in battle. The force that he selected was uniquely tailored for the task. The *cataphracts* and *ballistarii* at first appear ill-suited for the mission. Yet the rampaging barbarian war bands were mostly on foot and had little to counter heavily armoured soldiers on armoured horses. Vegetius mentions handheld weapons named *archballista* and *manuballista*. These weapons were similar to medieval crossbows. While the soldiers of the legion *ballistarii* may have been siege artillerists, for this mission they would operate as missile and skirmisher support for the *cataphracts*, using a hand weapon that, while slow to fire, could penetrate the Germanic shield wall.

Julian's small brigade reached *Autessiodurum* (Auxerre), a distance of about eighty miles, in two to four days without incident, and halted for a short time. The forty mile march to *Tricasae* (Troyes) was more challenging. This stretch of the march turned into a running fight between various small barbarian warbands and the Roman cavalry brigade. In a series of engagements, Julian varied his tactics based upon the terrain. In close terrain, he sent scouts ahead and watched his flanks as he fought his way through. In open terrain, he rode down the plundering warriors and trampled them underfoot scattering the survivors. Due to the heavy armour of his *cataphracts*, once broken, the Germanic warriors were able to break contact when they reached the dense forest or rough ground. After fighting a number of skirmishes, Julian reached *Tricasae*. His appearance was so unexpected that the garrison of the city did not initially open the gates upon the appearance of Caesar and his standards.

With the Roman army massed at *Remis*, the command of the army was given to Marcellus, Ursicinus' successor. Ursicinus was ordered to remain in the vicinity until the campaign season concluded. It seems that Constantius did not trust Julian or Marcellus enough to leave them unsupervised. It is most likely, at this time, that Ammianus met Julian for the first time. While Ammianus gave Julian credit for planning the 356 campaign, this would have been unrealistic given the presence of two senior veteran *magisters* (Marcellus and Ursicinus) and the inexperienced Julian, who was not familiar with the

terrain or Germanic fighting methods. In a number of unrecorded staff
meetings, courses of action were considered; it was finally decided to attack
the Alamanni in the direction of *Decem Pagi*. Despite the presence of the
experienced senior leadership and veteran soldiers, the Alamanni were more
familiar with the terrain and weather than were the Romans. As the Roman
Army marched rapidly into Alamanni controlled territory, they failed to take
sufficient security precautions. An Alamanni warband, taking advantage of
lateral roads to the Roman advance, ambushed the rear guard of two legions.
These legions would have been annihilated had not *auxilia* from the main
body heard the battle and returned to save them.

After the near disaster, the Roman army advanced with more caution to
seize the unoccupied former Roman town of *Brotomagum* (Brumath). Before
reaching the town, an Alamanni war band contested the Roman army's
advance in open battle. The Romans formed for battle in crescent formation,
outflanking the warband on both flanks. The Germans were broken with a
few prisoners taken while the rest fled the field. After this demonstration
against the Alamanni, the army counter-marched to strike the Franks in the
vicinity of *Colonia Agrippina* (Cologne).

The Franks had not occupied *Colonia Agrippina* after its fall in 355.
The Roman army marched into the city unopposed and reoccupied it.
The Romans remained in the city until the Frankish kings asked for terms.
While not mentioned in the historical accounts, the Roman Army must have
been foraging in the area for supplies and raiding Frankish settlements in
the vicinity. Ammianus does not provide details of the terms given to the
Franks, but the terms must have required the Franks to provide supplies.
The Roman army did not remain in the vicinity over the winter.

It is significant to note that both the Alamanni and Franks were targeted
for punitive expeditions, not re-conquest. Julian and the *magisters*, with
limited resources, were targeting both groups nearly simultaneously. From
the limited evidence, the Franks and Alamanni warbands were not present
in their newly conquered western Rhineland territory and must have been
raiding along the new Roman *limes*. Based upon the events of 357, the 356
punitive operations were intended to force the Alamanni and Franks to
mass their warriors to defend their new western Rhineland conquests. With
Julian's first campaign as a figurehead a great success, and with the approach

of winter, the Gallic army broke down into small field forces and entered winter quarters. Julian, and a detachment under his command, wintered in *Senones* (Sens). At the request of neighbouring towns, Julian sent his *Scholae Scutarii* and *Gentiles* cavalry squadrons to protect them during the winter.[14]

Hearing from deserters of the weakened garrison at *Senones*, a large Frankish warband attacked the region and blockaded the city. Due to his small force, Julian could not sally from *Senones* and engage the raiders. Marcellus was garrisoned with a large force at the nearby city but failed to march to the aide of his Caesar. After a month ravaging the region and blockading the city, the warband withdrew from the region. Ammianus alleges that the barbarian warlords concluded that besieging a walled city was foolish.

Julian and the Army of Gaul spent the rest of the winter resting, recruiting, and gathering supplies. The region was devastated with little food and fodder able to be obtained from the countryside. While Ammianus simply states that Julian's energy overcame this obstacle, in reality, the only way to gather food and supplies for his army was to import it from *Aquitanica*, which had not been devastated.[15]

The fact that Marcellus did not march to the aide of Julian was not missed at court and came to the notice of Constantius and the grand chamberlain, Eutherius. Constantius relieved Marcellus of his position and ordered him to court. In an attempt to defend his conduct and regain his position, Marcellus attempted to shift blame for the misfortune in Gaul onto Julian. Marcellus reached the court at Milan and was called to address Constantius and his council. While ranting and raving, Marcellus accused Julian of arrogance and planning for a higher position. These allegations indicated that Julian had his eye on Constantius' throne. During Marcellus' heated oration against Julian, Eutherius asked permission to enter the chamber. Asked to speak his mind, Eutherius in moderate and respectful tones indicted that Marcellus had procrastinated and intentionally failed to aid Julian and lift the siege. Eutherius then vouched for Julian's loyalty with his life. Constantius accepted Eutherius' defence of Julian, dismissed Marcellus, and sent him home to Serdica.[16]

With Marcellus dismissed, and Julian proving his worth with the help of friends at court, Constantius no longer considered him a figurehead and gave him full command of the Gallic Field Army. With the Sarmatians raiding across the Danube River, on 29 May 357, Constantius marched his army from Rome toward the Balkans. He recalled Ursicinus to join him and detached the veteran commander Severus when the *Praesental* Army reached *Tridentium* (Trent) to replace Marcellus. Severus was an excellent choice for *magister peditum*. He was neither factious nor arrogant and turned out to be the model executive officer and coach for the young and inexperienced Caesar. Ursicinus remained with Constantius for a short time before being ordered back to the East as a commander. Ursicinus' older staff members were given commands and his younger staff, including Ammianus, returned to the East with him. Barbatio, promoted to *magister peditum praesentalis*, was detached with 25,000 soldiers to help counter the Alamanni threat.[17]

Ammianus did not record the planning details of the 357 Campaign. Based upon Ammianus' description of its execution, the 357 Campaign plan was instigated by Constantius and envisioned a pincer movement to trap the Alamanni massed warbands between Julian's 13,000-man Gallic Army marching to the Rhine from the north and Barbatio's 25,000-man army marching from Italy toward the Rhine.[18] While the exact movements of Ursicinus, Severus, and Barbatio cannot be accurately tracked, they all were with Constantius at about the time the plan was developed. In fact, Severus may have actually carried the operational plan north to Julian.

According to the plan, Barbatio would march his army from Italy to *Rauraci* (Augst) on the upper Rhine.[19] Julian, departing from *Remis*, was to march southeast toward Alamanni-controlled Gaul. The intent of the manoeuvre was to trap the Alamanni main body between the two converging Roman armies. Before the Roman forces could block the roads, however, small *Laeti* tribal war parties slipped between the jaws of the pincer movement and raided the *Lugdunum* (Lyons) region.[20]

The *Laeti* were Germanic tribes and clans allowed to settle on Imperial lands in tribal groups. These *Laeti* communities were required to provide young men for the army. The system existed before the Tetrarchy and continued until the end of the Western Empire. Ammianus does not identify the tribal affiliation of this warband. But since it appears that they operated from Alamanni-conquered lands west of the Rhine it is probable that its members were related to that tribal confederation before settling within the empire.[21]

Unable to take *Lugdunum* (Lyons), the warband broke down into war parties and raided the area and then started to withdraw back to Alamanni territory. Julian, with an understanding of the terrain and road network, dispatched three cavalry regiments to block the raiders' routes of egress. While the invading war band could infiltrate past the Roman armies, the plunder-laden war parties would have been confined to routes where wagons and livestock could be driven. Along the two routes nearest Julian, two of the *Laeti* war parties were ambushed and destroyed with the plunder recovered by two of the cavalry regiments. The third route passed near Barbatio's camp, most likely enraging his officers because Julian's Tribunes Bainobaudes and Valentinian's (the future emperor) *Equites Cornuti* Regiment were operating in his area. Julian's cavalry was prevented from establishing an ambush site in the area by Barbatio's colleague the Tribune Cella (commander of the *Scholae Scutarii*). With the route unguarded, one *Laeti* war party slipped through the cordon and returned safely to Alamanni territory. To cover the failure, Cella forwarded a report to Constantius alleging that both tribunes had been sent by Julian to disrupt his command. After reading this report, Constantius cashiered both men and sent them home.[22] Due to the time it would have taken the messages to travel and the short time between events in Gaul, Valentinian would have commanded the *Equites Cornuti* at the Battle of Strossberg. The first contact between the two converging Roman forces resulted in a failure to cooperate.

Putting Julian's and Barbatio's personalities aside, one commander operating in a friendly commander's zone causes problems for modern military forces even in the twenty-first century. Today, a modern Julian sending combat forces, even in hot pursuit, would not be tolerated without being approved and coordinated with the commander of the violated zone. With modern communications, such coordination can be accomplished in a matter of minutes. A modern Cella would have been justified in sending a protest to the mutual higher commander if such coordination was not established. So, while Ammianus considers the interference with Julian's manoeuvre and the resulting failure to intercept the third war party to be Cella's responsibility, the fact that Julian was operating in the vicinity of

Bainobaudes' and Valentinian's ambush site might have derailed Cella's unrecorded plans to intercept the third war party.

Three under-strength cavalry regiments, divided into three ambush sites, with the mission of destroying three *Laeti* war parties, was not a significant event. The purpose for Ammianus including this series of skirmishes in his narrative was to emphasize the animosity between Julian and Barbatio. The two had good reason to hate each other and hinder each other's military operations. Barbatio was Caesar Gallus' guard commander and was instrumental in undermining his authority and his eventual fall. Barbatio wanted to be emperor and was involved in plots against Constantius for which he and his wife would be eventually executed. He had a vested interest in seeing Caesar Julian fail.[23]

The Germanic tribes occupying the former Roman territory west of the Rhine were not idle. Those tribes not part of the Alamanni Confederation defended their new homes by blocking the roads at choke points with felled trees. These tribes distracted Julian from his main objective of driving the Alamanni Confederation back across the Rhine. Some of these tribes were small and disorganized and sought refuge on islands in the Rhine. Julian attempted to negotiate with Barbatio for seven boats but, not only did Barbatio fail to cooperate, he burned the boats. Since it was now high summer, the boats turned out to be unnecessary as captured tribal scouts revealed that the Rhine's low level would allow the Romans to reach the islands by fords. Julian sent Tribune Bainobaudes and his lightly armed *auxilia* regiment *Cornuti* to clear these islands. Wading through the shallows and swimming, using their shields to support themselves, the *Cornuti* surprised the first island and slaughtered those sheltering on it. Capturing boats, Bainobaudes used them to surprise the other islands and destroy the German opposition. The *Cornuti* returned to camp with a rich haul of loot. Hearing of this successful raid against their island refuges, the other small Germanic bands fled to the east side of the Rhine.[24] While these small operations were taking place, Julian's main body was repairing the fort at *Tres Tabernae* (Saverne). This fort became a main supply base for Julian's army. His men had plundered the enemy crops and stocked the fort with a year's provisions for the garrison and twenty days' supply for the rest of the army.

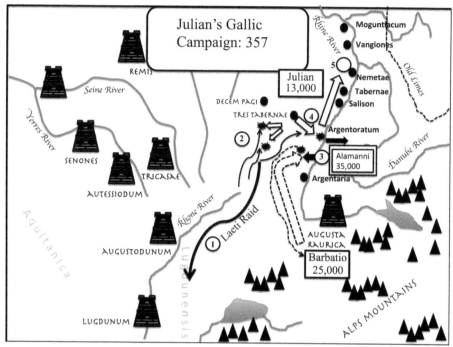

Map 13. Julian's Gallic Campaign: 357.[25] 1. The Laeti raid slipped through the gap between the two converging Roman armies. 2. Julian's attempt to ambush the three returning Laeti war parties interfered with Baratio's operations. 3. Barbatio is defeated and burns his and Julian's supplies as he retreats. 4. The Alamanni Tribal Confederation is caught by Julian fleeing to the east bank of the Rhine.

While the Army of Gaul was busy rebuilding the fort and foraging for supplies, the Alamanni conducted a surprise assault on Barbatio's army defeating it and pursuing it back to Augst. Barbatio's baggage train was also captured. During the retreat, Barbatio's men plundered and then burned a supply train destined for the Army of Gaul. Ammianus sees ulterior motives for the burning of Julian's supplies. He ignores the fact that the larger Roman army had been defeated and was in full retreat. A failure to burn the supplies would have allowed them to be captured by the rampaging Alamanni. Ammianus alleges that, after his defeat, Barbatio regrouped his army and then, instead of re-entering the campaign, broke his army into detachments and sent them into winter quarters while he returned to court.[26]

The Alamanni tribal confederation that had repeatedly humbled the Roman Army in the early 350s was led by seven kings of whom Chnodomar is reportedly mentioned as the primary king in Roman sources. The other kings, Vestralp, Urius, Ursicinus, Serapio, Suomar, and Hortar each lead a canton or sub-tribe in the Alamanni host. It would be a mistake to picture these warriors as the half-naked Gallic and Germanic warriors that Julius Caesar fought in the first century BCE. The Alamanni were well armed and armoured by barbarian standards, with many having served in the Roman army. Chnodomar had defeated the usurper Decentius in open battle and sacked many towns in Gaul, and his warriors had defeated most of Julian's legions and *auxilia* regiments in the countless skirmishes that were not recorded. The Alamanni warriors easily recognized these unlucky legions and regiments by their shield devices. A deserter from Barbatio's army informed the kings that Julian only mustered half of Barbatio's force. With Barbatio routed from the field, Julian now allegedly faced 35,000 confident and well-armed warriors with only 13,000 Roman soldiers. The Alamanni kings were so confident of victory that they sent an envoy demanding Julian retreat from the territory they had won by the sword.[27]

While there are problems with Ammianus' narrative due to his bias up to this point, they become glaring leading up to Julian's victory at *Argentorate* (Strasbourg).[28] There is a good indication that Barbatio's defeat and Julian's victory at *Argentorate* took place within thirty days of each other. Julian issued his men twenty days rations when he left *Tres Tabenae* and Barbatio plundered and burned his resupply convoy; however, Ammianus does not state that the Army of Gaul suffered from lack of supplies during the manoeuvres before and after the battle. King Chnodomar, an experienced and successful warlord, did not march out and force a battle with the outnumbered Army of Gaul. Instead, he established a defensive position with the River Rhine to his back. Only a fool would occupy a defensive position with an unfordable river to his back. Yet Chnodomar had repeatedly demonstrated he was militarily no fool. The only logical conclusion is that, while Barbatio's army was defeated by Chnodomar's warriors, it was not routed. The Romans were able to retreat destroying anything useful, including Julian's supplies, as they fell back toward *Rauraci*. Even in victory, the Alamanni would have suffered a large number of casualties, particularly wounded. In addition, the Alamanni had settled the west bank of the Rhine and their families were in danger. With a fresh Roman army bearing down on the Alamanni, the only logical conclusion for Chnodomar was to cross the Rhine and allow his warriors and their families to recover from their 'victory' before seeking battle with the fresh Army of Gaul. The real reason that Barbatio had burned the boats Julian requested may have been to prevent them from falling into enemy hands after his defeat. This reconstruction is supported by the fact that Barbatio was not cashiered for his conduct in 357 and, in 358, would lead a Roman army to victory against the Juthungi.[29] This also explains Julian's rush to engage the Alamanni. If they were not trying to escape, there would have been no reason for him and his generals to consciously violate a number of Roman principles of war.

When viewing an emerging operational or tactical situation, Ammianus reports that Julian held a war council of his generals on the field of battle in the presence of the enemy. During his operations in Gaul, Ammianus rarely mentions Julian calling such meetings. When the unrecorded messenger arrives in his camp announcing Barbatio's defeat, it is inconceivable that Julian would not call a meeting with Florentius, his praetorian prefect, and Severus, his senior *magister,* the night before the battle. The subject matter of this meeting is recorded, not as notes of the meeting but as orations given as the Army of Gaul is deploying from tactical march column to line of battle for dramatic effect.[30] Florentius outlines the key points requiring the Army of Gaul to attack the Alamanni from march column. First Florentius emphasizes that they need to accept risk and attack the Alamanni while they are massed. The previous year's army-size raids were conducted to force the Alamanni and Franks to stop raiding and mass to defend their newly conquered territory west of the Rhine. Despite the defeat of Barbatio, they were now massed but appeared to be ready to disperse. Second, Florentius emphasises that the army may mutiny if Julian does not force an engagement since the men are frustrated after years of chasing small war bands of raiders to no effect.[31]

The morning after the decision was made to force an engagement, the Army of Gaul force-marched twenty-one miles and confronted the Alamanni. With the Roman cavalry providing the van and flank guards, the army covered the distance by midday. If starting at sun up, the Roman army had to march at about 4mph to reach the vicinity of the Alamanni camp in approximately five hours. The speed of the march assumes that the Roman infantry were carrying no more than 60lbs of weapons, armour, a few biscuits, and watered vinegar. The lumbering army trains would have been left far behind the infantry and cavalry.

Julian and Florentius staged a disagreement in front of the army in the presence of the enemy. Julian argued that the army should build a camp, rest, and attack the warriors in the morning, refreshed. Florentius argued that they should throw caution to the wind and immediately attack the barbarians. The result was that the soldiers clamoured for battle but knew that Caesar had their welfare at heart. For dramatic effect, Ammianus reports that a standard-bearer stepped forward and shouted: 'Follow Caesar, the guidance of your luck star. You are fortune's darling, and in you we see valour and judgment combined…With heaven's blessing you shall see what your men can do under a warlike general…when their blood is up.'[32] This illusionary impromptu event, staged with great oratory, was nonetheless, a dramatic attempt to motivate the tired troops, worthy of Julius Caesar and Alexander the Great.

The Roman security screen surprised three barbarian scouts on a hill overlooking the Rhine and captured one scout. When the command group and standard bearers reached the hill, they observed the Alamanni crossing the Rhine. The prisoner informed the Romans that his fellow tribesmen had been crossing the river for three days and nights. It was clear to Julian and his senior officers that if they did not engage the Alamanni immediately, they would slip across the Rhine. The vanguard and command group then formed a covering force to allow the Roman army to deploy from march column into battle formation while staging their little drama referred to above. 10,000 men in march column would have covered two miles of road space and required about one hour to deploy. Julian, observing the prospective battleground from the hill, deployed his infantry into the traditional Roman three-line battle formation but, instead of splitting his cavalry between the two flanks, he massed them on his right wing. As the Roman army deployed, the Alamanni formed into their warbands around their kings. Noticing that the Roman cavalry was massed on their right wing, the Alamanni deployed their cavalry opposite the Roman cavalry. They also noticed that the Roman cavalry's main strike force was its two *cataphract* regiments and, thus, they reinforced the Alamanni lighter cavalry with light infantry.

As pointed out by Florentius, the Army of Gaul was reduced in strength due to the drafts during the civil war and years of attrition warfare with the Germanic tribes. Traditionally, a Roman deployment placed the best legionary unit on the right of the first battle line as a point of honour. The reason for this was that the unit's unshielded side was exposed to enemy missile and flank attack. Julian had a serious problem when considering Roman norms of deployment. His legions were woefully under strength due

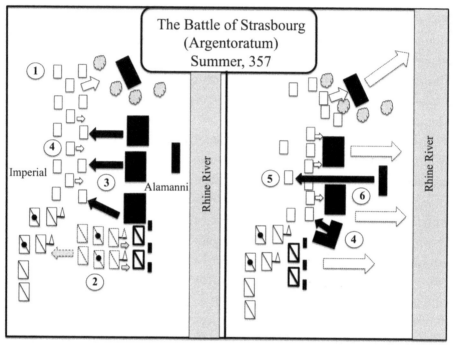

Map 14. The Battle of Strasbourg (Argentoratum), summer 357. 1. Sereverus, detecting the Alamanni in the woods, deploys the Roman left wing to counter the threat. 2. The Roman cavalry attacks the Alamanni cavalry. The Alamanni cavalry supported by light infantry defeat the Roman cavalry forcing them to retreat. 3. The withdrawal of the Roman cavalry exposes the right flank of the first Roman battle line. The Alamanni attack the Roman infantry right flank, but the *Cornuti* and *Bracchiati* prevent the line from being routed. The second Alamanni attack engages the entire first line. 4. The intensity of the Alamanni attack nearly overwhelms the Roman first line, and the second line is committed to battle. The *Batavians* and *Reges* prevent a penetration of the Roman line and stabilize the situation. 5. The third and final Alamanni attack breaks through the Roman first and second line but is halted and routed by the fresh elite legion *Primani*.

to casualties and desertion and could probably muster only a few hundred men instead of their full strength complement of 1,000. It is, therefore, not surprising, based upon Ammianus' narrative, that the *auxilia* comprised the first two battle lines and Julian's best infantry unit, the veteran legion *Primani*, was deployed in the centre of the third line.

The position of honour, on the right of the first line, was not assigned to a legion but to the *auxilia* regiments *Cornuti* and *Bracchiati*. Julian's battle plan is simple to deduce and very Alexandrian. His army would advance onto the Alamanni position with his infantry pinning their main body in place while his cavalry drove the Germanic cavalry off. Then Roman light cavalry would pursue the Germanic cavalry and prevent it from reforming. Julian's *cataphracts* and horse archers, after defeating the Germanic cavalry, would then wheel left and attack the German centre. A sound simple plan, but it did not take into account the weather and it underestimated King Chnodomar and his veteran warriors.

Command of the Roman left was delegated to Severus while Julian commanded the centre and either the *cataphract* Tribune Laipso or Innocentius commanded the cavalry. The future emperor Valentinian and his *Equistes Cornuti* would have been with Julian's cavalry wing. Since Ammianus does not mention Valentinian or his regiment in the narrative, they must not have distinguished themselves during the engagement and Valentinian was too junior to command Julian's cavalry. The Roman infantry lines would have occupied a little more than a 300m frontage and, from his central position, Julian would have been able to observe his whole army. Since the battlefield was so small, if there was any sign of trouble Julian could quickly ride with his 200 guards to reinforce any hard pressed unit. After deployment, and an unrecorded short rest, the Roman army advanced on the Alamanni. Severus, suspecting an ambush from some trenches, halted and faced the threat. Julian observing this threat and that Severus had it contained, continued the advance of the centre and right wing.

As the Roman infantry approached the Alamanni, both sides started throwing darts and launching missiles while the Roman and Germanic cavalry charged each other. At the moment of contact, one of the *cataphract* tribunes was wounded and one armoured horse collapsed throwing its rider. The twenty mile march during the hot humid weather in full armour followed by a charge at a fast trot into battle was too much for some *cataphract* horses. The Roman charge was stopped and became disordered. The Alamanni light infantry joined the battle and hamstrung the armoured horses. The Roman cavalry wing lost heart and started to retreat uncovering the Roman first line's right flank. Seeing the success of their cavalry, the Alamanni attacked all along the front line. The *auxilia* regiments *Cornuti* and *Bracchiati* with their right flank exposed, locked shields and grimly held their ground.

Julian, seeing the disaster unfolding, rode with his bodyguard and rallied the cavalry, getting them reorganized and back into battle to guard the infantry's flank. With the situation stabilized, there appears to have been a lull in the battle. While the details are not fully understood, the Roman army had a practical system of passage of lines and preferred to reinforce or replace tired units with fresh ones, rather than maximizing the depth of the fighting line.[33] Ammianus' description appears to indicate that the combat was continuous. When reviewed closely, and stripped of its artistic language, Ammianus is describing three different Alamanni infantry attacks and the Romans' execution of two passages of the lines.[34] The Alamanni's first attack's main focus was on the Roman open right flank while the second Alamanni attack closed with the whole Roman front line. The second line, including the *auxilia* regiments *Batavians* and *Reges,* moved forward, replaced the first line and stabilized the situation by halting the first and second attacks. A third and final Alamanni attack, led by their nobles, crashed into the centre of the Roman front. Before a second passage of lines could be executed, the Alamanni chiefs broke through the second line and the tired nobles were confronted by the fresh veteran legion *Primani.* The warriors repeatedly attacked the Roman battle line looking for weaknesses, but tired warriors were no match for fresh armoured and disciplined troops.[35]

These last attacks did not squander the lives of the Alamanni since the warriors were selling their lives as a rear guard to allow their tribe and families to finish crossing the Rhine to safety. While Ammianus does not mention the presence of the tribe's non-combatants, the fact that the tribe spent three days and nights before the battle crossing to the Rhine's east bank indicates that the evacuation of the whole tribe, and not just the warriors, was underway. Ammianus reports that there were 35,000 Alamanni warriors present and that they fought with their backs to the Rhine. When the Alamanni finally broke, the majority rushed to the river and attempted to swim to safety. Only 6,000 warriors were found dead on the field and Ammianus reports that many more of the dead were carried off by the river. Chnodomar with 200 followers, unable to cross the Rhine, was captured during the pursuit. The Romans lost 243 killed and unreported numbers wounded. Despite assertions to the contrary, the cavalry did not sit out the fight after its near rout. Both *cataphract* Tribunes, Laipso and Innocentius, were killed after they re-entered the fray. Bainobaude, Tribune of the *Cornuti*, also died most likely holding the Roman right flank when the cavalry panicked.

Tactically, the Battle of Strasbourg was an unqualified success. It was, however, a gamble that was nearly lost by ignoring basic principles of war. Julian did not take into account the effects of the weather and the long hard march on his armoured horses. While speeches can revitalize exhausted men to do battle, exhausted horses simply die. While the Roman battle plan was simple and Alexandrian in concept, it ignored Chnodomar's battle experience. Chnodomar had defeated two Roman armies in open field battles. *Cataphractus* were not new to him, and it appears that he had faced them in prior battles. He negated their effectiveness by mixing light infantry with his cavalry, a time-honoured Germanic tactic dating back to the first century BCE. Operationally, Julian achieved a draw. The campaign plans for 356 and 357 succeeded in reducing Alamanni raids by forcing them to mass their warriors to defend their newly conquered territories. The attempt to destroy the Alamanni as a threat to the empire failed because Barbatio and Julian hated each other and refused to cooperate while Chnodomar realized, at the last moment, that his tribe was sitting in a trap. As a result of his and the other kings' foresight, the majority of the tribe escaped to the east bank of the Rhine.

With the Alamanni temporarily no longer a threat, Julian turned the Army of Gaul against the Franks. After the battle, Julian marched his army to *Saverne*, sending the booty and prisoners to *Mediomatrici* (Metz). He next convinced his troops to raid into Germania and marched them to *Maozamalcha* where a bridge was quickly thrown across the Rhine. The Roman army won a decisive battle with local tribes who then sued for peace. Julian re-established a fort on the east bank of the Rhine that the defeated tribes agreed to supply with food throughout the winter and then retired to the west bank. On his way to winter quarters, Julian broke his army into detachments so they could be billeted in various towns for supply purposes and to provide the towns with protection from raiders. One of these detachments destroyed 600 Frankish marauders that had occupied two abandoned forts.

Julian wintered in *Parisii*. Due to the devastation in eastern Gaul, supplies for the army had to be imported from *Aquitania* (western Gaul). The weather and regional late harvest prevented the Roman army from taking the field until July 358. Worrying about the Alamanni massing to attack into Gaul made Julian march before the harvest. Taking food supplies from his shipments for the winter camps, he had a twenty-day supply of biscuits prepared for his army. The 358 Campaign plan had two objectives. The first was to defeat the Frankish sub-tribes of *Salii* and *Chamavi*. He first struck the *Salii* who had settled the area around *Tungii* (Tongres). Using a combination of diplomacy and swift attacks, the *Salii*, and then the *Chamavii*, were subdued. Julian then marched to the Meuse River and repaired and garrisoned three forts at strategic locations along the river. His army was still loaded down with seventeen days' rations and, to enhance his mobility, he left part of his army's rations in the forts planning to supply his army by foraging in the lands of the *Chamavi*. The crops that the army marched through turned out not to be ripe and ready for harvest. Once their biscuits were exhausted, the troops became mutinous. While Julian's tactical error left them without food, their real grievance was the fact that they had not been paid and had received no donative since Julian arrived in Gaul. While not mentioned by Ammianus, the success of Julian against the Germans had the effect of bringing the soldiers scattered across Gaul back to their standards. The fact that the Army of Gaul had not been paid was not as critical as it appears. The Roman Army at this time was paid 'in-kind'. Most of the coin received by the army came in the form of donatives from the Caesars and Augustus at various times and celebrations. Constantius had not released funds to Julian and, as a result, Julian could not pay a donative to his army. Using persuasion, not force, and assuming that he would find supplies to feed them, Julian convinced his army to march against the Alamanni. Julian bridged the Rhine and forced Alamanni Kings Sumar and Hortar to make peace on Roman terms. The Army of Gaul then crossed back into Gaul and dispersed into winter quarters.

While not mentioned by Ammianus, Constantius ordered Julian to provide reinforcements to the East at about this time. Julian's recruitment efforts had been successful and the Army of Gaul was rising in strength both from soldiers returning to their units and new *auxilia* regiments. In accordance with Constantius' summons, Julian dispatched seven legions and two cavalry regiments to the East.[36] If dispatched late in 358, these legions would have arrived in the East in the spring 359 in time for Shapur's late spring offensive in 359.[37] It is probable that the march brigade of the Gallic legions *Magnentius*, *Decentius*, and XXX *Ulpia Victrix*, and two Illyrian cavalry regiments that Ammianus discovered in the Amida region, were some of the units dispatched by Julian as reinforcements for the East late in 358.[38]

The campaigns for the years 358 and 359 continued to hammer the Germanic tribes and forced them to accept peace on Julian's terms. As the military situation stabilized, Julian was able to focus on the administration of Gaul. Early in 359, while still in winter quarters, he reviewed the tax situation for the provinces that had borne the brunt of the Germanic incursions. Florentius, the *Praetorian Prefect of Gaul*, wanted to levy a special tax on these devastated provinces. After reviewing the data Julian, by detailed and accurate calculation, discovered that the current taxes exceeded the necessary public expenditures. Florentius protested Julian's interference in his duties, but Julian held firm. Constantius attempted to intercede on Florentius' behalf and warned Julian not to undermine his *praetorian prefect*. Julian countered that the provincials should be congratulated, not punished with added taxes. Despite being plundered, they still provided the standard taxes and to punish them with a supplemental levy would ruin them. Constantius backed off and allowed Julian to implement his policies.[39]

A review of Julian's time in Gaul from 356 to 359 demonstrates that he was a very talented novice who learned quickly how to lead and motivate soldiers and provincials. He overcame the road blocks put in place by the emperor and established himself initially as a valuable asset to Constantius. As a military commander, Julian had developed into a traditional Roman general by learning on the job. He discovered that a traditional Roman victory was gained by marching into the middle of the enemy territory, ravaging it until the barbarians were forced to fight, and then defeating the warriors in battle. At that point, he would continue plundering and destroying their fields until they were forced into an unconditional surrender. He learned the hard lesson that a campaign needed to take into consideration the time of year and when the harvest came due. He learned the importance of selecting the correct personalities to command separate armies when they were required to coordinate their manoeuvres to a command campaign objective. He learned that planning campaign logistics around living off the enemy's harvest has pitfalls that can demoralize an army and lead to a mutiny. Based upon fighting Germanic tribes, Libanius' statement that Julian was an emperor in strategy, a commander in tactics, and a hero in combat was an accurate assessment. With his journeyman skills, Julian would alter the Roman Eastern strategy of his predecessor and march east to face the master of war, Shapur.

Chapter 11

Roman Passive Defence 358–361

U pon Shapur's return to the Roman front, it became evident that he had matured as a general. Thanks to the records of Ammianus, we have sufficient details of Shapur's 359 to 361 campaigns to deduce his strategy. Warmington argues that, in 359, Shapur's intent was to force a decisive field battle on Constantius by marching through the Mesopotamian fortified zone, crossing the Euphrates, and striking into the Province of Syria.[1] This, however, may be an over-simplification of Shapur's true intent.

Historians continually ponder the eternal question of whether history makes great people or whether great people make history and how individuals can determine the course of history, as well as the role of unexpected fortune. In 358, Shapur and the Persian war effort received critical assistance from an unexpected source, Antoninus, the financial officer of the Duke of Mesopotamia. Antoninus was a staff officer, but he was also a merchant. Through his dealings with some questionable persons he had acquired a large debt that was coming due. Fearing for his life, he decided to defect to the Persians. To ensure he would be well received, he compiled details of the Roman defence in the East, including troop dispositions, war plans, location, and status of military supplies throughout the region. To avoid the *limitanei* border patrols, Antoninus bought an estate on the Tigris River and moved his household to the border. He contacted the Persians and, with their assistance, crossed the river in the dead of night.[2]

Roman misfortunes were compounded by their own palace politics. Ursicinus was recalled from the East to take the position of *magister peditum in praesentalis* and Sabinianus, '…an elderly man of culture and wealth, but no soldier…' and popular with the palace eunuchs was appointed *magister peditum* in the East. Ammianus' assessment however, may have been biased. Sabinianus was Duke of Mesopotamia before being appointed to *magister peditum* and, therefore, would have had military and administrative experience.³ Meanwhile, Antoninus was escorted to Shapur at his winter palace and the traitor's information was incorporated into the Persian war plan.⁴

Ursicinus and his personal staff, including Ammianus, were in the Province of Thrace when he received a letter from the Emperor ordering him to return to the East. When Ursicinus was recalled to court, he would have been aware of the deteriorating situation along the Tigris River but did not travel west with due haste. He returned to the East with haste. Upon his return to Syria, Ursicinus met with Sabinianus but the two men could not agree on a course of action to fight the Persians. Since the Persians had started raiding across the Tigris River as far as Nisibis, Ursicinus and his small personal staff rode for Nisibis.⁵

Ammianus does not clearly describe the command relationship between Ursicinus and Sabinianus. Sabinianus had taken over command as *magister peditum* east. Ursicinus, despite his experience at senior command, was still *magister equitum* east and therefore the junior general. Based upon the conflict between the two senior Roman commanders, it is evident that the letter recalling Ursicinus did not clearly return him to command of the East. As events unfolded, Ursicinus became the 'de facto' commanding general of the *Limitanei* armies of Mesopotamia and Osrhoene, while Sabinianus continued as commander of the small Field (*Comitatus*) Army of the East. This arrangement violated a principle of war referred to as 'unity of command'. To ensure unity of effort, there must be one responsible commander.⁶ The Romans repeatedly violated this rule in late antiquity, but it was normally mitigated through cooperation between the appointed commanders. In this case, however, the command relationship failed.

Ursicinus was left to counter Shapur's campaign without support from Sabinianus. Ursicinus was a resident of Antioch and held his position of *magister equitum* of the East since 349. He probably participated in the fighting during the 340s.⁷ He would have been well informed about Shapur's prior methods of operation. The pattern Shapur developed during the 340s was to cross the Tigris just north of the Great Zab River in the vicinity of Nineveh, then march along the Roman road to Singara and strike north along the Roman roads to attack and besiege Nisibis. However, during these campaigns, Singara was either taken or blockaded to prevent its garrison from attacking the Persian army supply and lines of communication.[8] In the previous three sieges, Nisibis had been able, just barely, to withstand the Persian attack without the intervention of the Field Army of the East.

Ursicinus had a small manoeuvre force in the Province of Mesopotamia. The Gallic legions *Magnentius, Decentius,* and XXX *Ulpia Victrix* were in the region but had not been assigned to any specific fortress.[9] These three legions were part of the six legions and two cavalry regiments dispatched from Gaul by Julian late in 358. There were two newly arrived *Equites* Illyrian regiments with a combined strength of 700 and an element of the *Comites Sagittarii* cavalry regiment (an elite field army barbarian horse-archer unit).[10] Finally, Count Aelianus and his light legions *Superventores* (Catchers) and *Praeventires* (Preventers) were in the region but unassigned to any specific city.[11] Count Aelianus' two legions of 'Catchers' and 'Preventers' may have been the field army of the Trans-Tigris Regions and had been ordered to Amida by Ursicinus. When Ursicinus arrived at Amida he had a mixed *comitatus* and *limitanei* manoeuvre force of three heavy legions, two light legions, and three cavalry regiments in the fortified zone.[12] Ursicinus did not have the combat strength to oppose Shapur's main army in the field or even engage a large raiding party, but he did have sufficient reserves to reinforce a fortress that was projected to be attacked by Shapur or to harass the Royal Army's supply and lines of communication while it besieged a fortress. Amida was a strong fortified town and the Nisibis-Mardin-Amida road passed through mountainous terrain in which a small Roman force could block and hold at bay a larger Persian force.

Ursicinus had good intelligence throughout the Province of Mesopotamia. From the Roman headquarters at Nisibis observers could see the signal beacon of Singara on top of Sinjar Ridge, a distance of seventy-five miles. From Mardin, the entire Khabur River Valley could be observed.[13] Obviously, details of small groups could not be distinguished without modern optics, but the dust cloud of the movement of 30,000 to 50,000 men and tens of thousands of animals moving as a group, as well as their camp fires at night, could easily be distinguished. While some enemy movement could be detected, the main Persian Royal Army had not been located. Persian cavalry was raiding up to the gates of Nisibis and scouts and spies had penetrated as far west as the Euphrates River. Due to the Persian cavalry's activities the *limitanei* patrols could no longer maintain observation posts in the vicinity of the crossing point on the Tigris River.

In this uncertain situation, Ursicinus decides to shift his small headquarters and escort to Amida. Immediately upon riding out of Nisibis, a Persian raiding party observes his party leaving the city. Ammianus, detached in the confusion to return a child to the safety of Nisibis, rides by the Persian patrol avoiding capture. The Persians were torturing a tribune's servant in an attempt to determine who the important official was that they observed leaving the city. When they discovered that the official was Ursicinus, they killed the servant and pursued Ammianus. Ammianus' horse was fleet of foot and remained ahead of the Persians as he reached Ursicinus' escort where they planned to camp. He, signalling 'enemy was upon them' with his cloak, found that, by the time he reached Ursicinus' party they were mounted and ready to ride. The Persians chased them into the moonlit night until they were tricked to follow a pack animal with a lantern tied to its back.[14]

After giving the Persian patrol the slip, the Romans rested at a deserted village named *Meiacarire* where they uncovered a former Roman deserter turned Persian spy. During interrogation it was uncovered that he had been sent by the Persian Generals Tamsapor and Nohodares and was returning to them to report what he had discovered during his scouting mission. The spy was put to death but his information heightened Ursicinus' anxiety and he pushed his party to greater speed toward Amida. Upon reaching Amida, Roman scouts brought in a parchment from Procopius, a member of Count Lucillian's peace delegation to the Persians. When the message was decoded it gave a warning of Persian intentions and Antoninus' treason, but failed to provide any operational details that would have allowed Ursicinus to derail Shapur's plans.[15]

In an attempt to locate the Persian main body, Ammianus (escorted by a centurion) was sent to Jovinianus, the semi-independent governor of Corduene and a friend of Ursicinus. Corduene was one of the Trans-Tigris areas ceded to Rome by the Treaty of 298 but, in 359, was falling under Persian influence. The Roman cavalry regiment, *Ala quintadecima Flavia Carduenorum*, was most likely recruited from this region. Jovinianus sent Ammianus to a lofty observation post where he could observe fifty miles south along the Tigris River. On the third day, he spied the Royal Army marching north. Ammianus provided a detailed description of the Persian array. While he would not have been able to see specific details, he did observe the Royal Army's dust cloud and campfires. Ammianus observed the Royal Army as it began to cross the Tigris at Nineveh and estimated it would take three days for the army to cross. Ammianus returned to Jovinianus and quickly reported to Ursicinus.[16]

Based on the intelligence supplied by Ammianus, Ursicinus apparently concluded that Shapur planned to attack Nisibis. The fact that he shifted his command post from Nisibis to Amida supports this conclusion. During the three previous sieges of the city, Constantius left the tactical defence of the city to a trusted subordinate. This allowed Constantius' *Praesental* Army to harass the Persian lines of communication and supply, forcing Shapur to deploy considerable forces to establish a cordon to protect his siege lines from Roman raids. In this case, Ursicinus planned to use Amida as his base of operations against Shapur's line of communications.

At a steady rate of advance of fifteen miles a day, the Persian main army required ten days to reach the Khabur River from the Tigris. From Amida, Ursicinus dispatched orders to Duke Cassianus and Governor Euphronius of Mesopotamia to move their peasants with their households and flocks to safer quarters, to abandon the weakly fortified city of Carrhae, and to set fire to the fields and grasslands to prevent the enemy from foraging for fodder. Military units were sent to the fords on the Euphrates to defend with field fortifications supported by artillery.[17] The grain was reportedly dry enough to be consumed by fire, which indicates that it was late May or early June when Shapur attacked. Sabinianus and his army did not take part in the preparation of defences east of the Euphrates River but he was reported to have been in Edessa drilling his army. Edessa would have offered a perfect fortified blocking position from which to defend the approaches to the main crossing of the Euphrates at Zeugma.[18] The fact that Ursicinus did not order the fields near Amida burned indicates that he did not expect the Persians to attack the city and that he may have been planning to use the fortress for a base of operations.

Shapur advanced up the Roman road from Singara to the base of the mountains in the vicinity of the town of Bebase, a twelve-day march from the Tigris. Shapur paused while his scouts reconnoitred the routes to the

Euphrates.[19] Bebase was near a major road junction on the Khabur River. It was 160 miles east of the bridge crossing the Euphrates at Zeugma/Apamea and about thirty miles west of Nisibis. From that location Shapur had three options. His first option was to turn east and attack Nisibis. This was his standard campaign plan during the 340s. Ursicinus' actions in burning the nearby fields rendered this option difficult. In any event, this option would not have resulted in a decisive defeat of the Roman Eastern Field Army. It had not resulted in luring the Roman Army into taking the field in the past and, even if the siege was successful, the Roman fortresses of Singara, Amida, Bezabde, and Castra Maurorum still commanded the lines of communication back to Persia. Shapur's second option was to take the

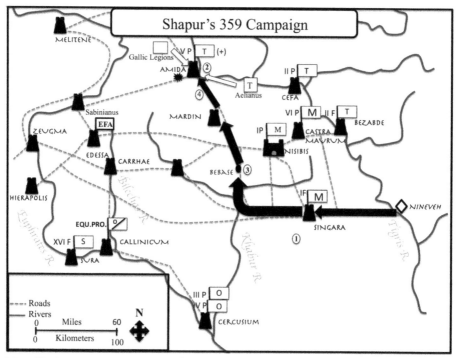

Map 15. Shapur's 359 Campaign.[20] 1. The Persian Royal Army crossed the Tigris and blockaded or stormed Singara. 2. Count Aelianus with two local legions and the three Gallic legions reinforce the garrison of Amida. 3. Shapur halts at Bebase to consider his options based upon his scouts' reports. 4. Tamsapur, with 20,000 cavalry, conducts a surprise night attack from Bebase, blockading and isolating Amida. The main Royal Army arrives at Amida, capturing nearby forts and storms Amida after a seventy-three day siege.

bridge over the Euphrates at Zeugma/Apamea and attack into Syria. Despite the flooding, Ammianus indicates that the bridge was still up; however, the Eastern Field Army blocked this route. Ursicinus had not yet ordered this bridge demolished. To capture the bridge, the Persians had to contend with a small Roman force at Zeugma on the west bank and the relatively small Eastern Field Army at Edessa. The Eastern Field Army could have quickly withdrawn to Zeugma had Shapur marched west. Capturing the bridge by surprise was unlikely since the Romans were on the alert due to the Persian raiders rampaging over the countryside. Fighting to cross a major river was not the type of field battle that Shapur was seeking.

Shapur's third option was to march north along the Roman road to Amida into the Province of Cappadocia. Ammianus records that Shapur chose this course of action when the scouts reported the Euphrates was in flood and impassable.[21] Antoninus, the traitor, with his insider knowledge, apparently advised Shapur that this option would allow the Persians to march through regions that had not been burned which would provide sufficient supplies for an extended period.[22]

Ursicinus must not have deduced Shapur's change of course or his scouts failed to report the Persian reaction to the flooded river. Ammianus does not report where Ursicinus' manoeuvre force was before it mysteriously appeared at Amida. It is too much of a coincidence that five legions just happened to be in the vicinity of Amida, with a battle-hardened count, when the Persians unexpectedly attacked north. This is especially odd given that Ursicinus initially believed that Nisibis was Shapur's target. These five legions and three cavalry regiments were most likely massed at Amida to serve as a field army to harass the Persian siege of Nisibis and not as a reinforcement to Amida's garrison. Ursicinus deployed the two *Equites* Illyrian regiments as a screen along the Nisibis road to provide early warning and to block Persian raiding parties from using the Nisibis-Amida Road.[23]

Despite the proper security deployment of the Roman cavalry the two *Equites* Illyrian regiments, 700 strong, failed to detect and report to Ursicinus the Persian vanguard, reportedly 20,000 strong, under the Persian General Tamsapor and guided by the traitor Antoninus, riding toward Amida. These two regiments most likely were two of the three cavalry units dispatched by Julian to the East late in 358. They were given a mission within their capabilities as light or general purpose cavalry along a route passing though mountainous terrain. Their conduct makes it clear that they were not familiar with the terrain and were incompetently led. Instead of posting pickets to provide early warning in case of being attacked in the dark, the regiments pulled off the road to camp and, as a large force of Persian cavalry passed them in the night, failed to send warning of the Persian approach to Amida. Ursicinus and his staff first learned of the Persians' presence when they rode out of Amida in the early morning twilight heading toward Zeugma and Capersana to ensure the bridges over the Euphrates had been broken down. They rode straight into the lead cavalry regiment of Tamsapor's vanguard. Ursicinus' escort, now reinforced with additional cavalry, engaged the point of the Persian advance guard. Ammianus does not inform us of the size of Ursicinus' escort, but it was large enough to fight the Persian vanguard regiment to a standstill for half an hour. During a lull in the skirmish Ursicinus exchanged words with the traitor Antoninus. Antonius explains to Ursicinus that he was forced into treason and that even if he had come to Ursicinus for help he would not have been saved from the unscrupulous men he was in debt to.[24] As more Persians joined the ensuing melee, Ursicinus' escort was scattered with Ammianus barely making it back with a wounded comrade to Amida. The surviving Romans were pursued to the banks of the Tigris, Ursicinus escaping with a tribune and a single groom.[25]

Tamsapor's vanguard established a cordon around Amida trapping Ursicinus' only significant mobile reserve in the city. The Persian main body marched up and captured the Roman forts of *Reman* and *Busan* before proceeding to Amida. Shapur paused to take these forts because of the wealth abandoned by the fleeing population and the presence of a beautiful woman, who was the wife of Carugasius, a leading citizen of Nisibis. Upon storming the forts, he captured the lady along with her small daughter and a group of Christian nuns. He treated these upper class and religious women honourably.[26] As the siege of Amida unfolded, he used the lady as leverage to turn Carugasius against Rome.[27]

A few days after Tamsapor isolated Amida, Shapur and the main Persian army arrived. Allegedly, Shapur did not intend to besiege Amida but, rather, to bypass it. In full armour Shapur and his escort rode within hailing distance of the main gate of Amida to demand its surrender. The Roman response came in the form of arrows and bolts from the walls. Shapur's royal trappings did not impress Count Aelianus. Based upon the conduct of these two commanders before, during and after the siege, Count Aelianus and his 'Preventers' and 'Catchers' may have been a thorn in the Persians' side for the past ten years. Shapur was enraged by this display of disrespect but was eventually calmed down by his generals and he was convinced to summon the Romans to surrender again the next day. The next morning the Persian ally King Grumbates, of the Chionite, and his son boldly approached the walls of Amida to demand the Roman surrender. The defenders loosed a *ballista* bolt killing Grumbates' son. A general exchange of arrows and bolts continued until sundown.

Ammianus reports that Persian traditions of honour required Shapur to take Amida to appease King Grumbates' thirst for vengeance.[28] The Persians and their allies mourned the death of the prince for seven days. A war council was held and during that meeting it was decided to change the campaign plan and besiege Amida.

Yet Ammianus' explanation is too simplistic. According to Ammianus Shapur intended to penetrate into or beyond the fortified zone to bring the under-strength Eastern Field Army to a decisive battle. Constantinus' *Praesental* Army was tied down in Europe and the Eastern Field Army was only a shadow of the army that confronted the Persians between 337 and 350. Failing to force the decisive engagement, the Persians planned to plunder the rich province of Syria; however, the flooded Euphrates required a change of plan.

Historians overlook the fact that the first major Persian attack in the war was the destruction of Amida in 336/7. Shapur, like all kings and generals of Late Antiquity, was interested in plunder, but he knew that plundering Cappadocia or Syria would not have won the war. Such action would have placed his army deep in Roman territory with all exit routes controlled by *limitanei* fortresses. As many invaders of Rome's border provinces discovered, breaking into a province to plunder was one thing, leaving the province with plunder was more difficult. Amida was the gateway into Armenia for the Romans and the northern gateway for the Persians into Roman Mesopotamia. Plunder does not appear to have been the Persian objective. Shapur was well aware of Amida's importance and, by besieging the city, he had a realistic expectation that the Romans would march out and contest the siege.[29]

With stripping the fortresses of their garrisons, Sabinianus realistically mustered no more than 20,000 men in the Eastern Field Army. Ursicinus unsuccessfully tried to convince Sabinianus to actively campaign against the Persians besieging Amida. Since Ursicinus unintentionally had committed his small field army to the defence of Amida, he wanted light troops from the Eastern Field Army to harass the Persian besiegers. It is probable that Sabinianus was operating on instructions from the emperor not to risk an open battle.[30] If Ursicinus had been in command, the Eastern Field Army would have marched to relieve Amida and Shapur would have achieved a field battle on favourable terms.

The normal garrison of Amida consisted of the legion V Parthia supported by an unidentified cavalry regiment. A detachment from X Fortenses, the *limitaneus* legion of Palestine, was also present during the siege. This detachment was over 300 miles from its home base at Aila in *Palestina Salutaris* and may have only numbered 300 men.[31] The small garrison was unintentionally reinforced with Ursicinus small five-legion field army. Ammianus claims this army 'had forestalled the approach of the Persian host by force marches.'[32] Ursicinus was surprised by the Persian attack toward Amida. Which means Count Aelianus and his army of the legions *Magnentius, Decentius,* XXX *Ulpia Victrix, Superventores* and *Praeventires* and *Comites Sagittarii* were initially ordered to Amida for a different purpose than reinforcing the garrison. With the addition of these five legions the garrison was increased from approximately 1,300 to 5,300 soldiers and 16,000 civilians arrayed against the initial Persian vanguard of 20,000, eventually (allegedly) reinforced with a main army of up to 80,000 men.[33] With Count Aelianus and his men, the Romans had a good chance of holding Amida against a determined Persian Royal Army.

After the seven day mourning period for the Chionite prince, the Persians spent the next two days plundering the region for supplies and material for the siege. On the third day the Persian Royal Army surrounded the city five ranks deep and tried to erode the Roman legions' morale by a display of military might until nightfall. Early next morning the Persians again surrounded the city but upon signal from the king, assaulted the walls from three sides. Both sides launched clouds of arrows, bolts and rocks inflicting casualties on both attackers and defenders. The Persians employed siege engines, captured at the sack of Singara, to great effect. Because of the garrison's reinforcements the defenders were able to fight in relays. At night the Persians halted their assault and resumed it the next morning. The assaults continued for a number of days and the defenders had problems properly disposing of their dead bodies. The humid heat and rotting bodies soon caused pestilence to break out in the city which only subsided on day ten after a slight rain washed the city clean and dispelled the stifling air.

The Persians, realizing that they could not carry the city by assault, began a formal siege by constructing mantelets to protect archers, mines, penthouses to protect rams and siege towers to mount artillery to drive the defenders from the walls. The defenders constructed defensive works to counter the Persian efforts and used their artillery to great effect. Skirmishing between the slingers and archers on both sides continued without pause. The Gallic legions *Magnentius*, *Decentius* and XXX *Ulpia Victrix* were comprised of strong active men use to fighting in open country and useless in the work required during a prolonged siege. Instead they conducted unauthorized sallies with great boldness taking unnecessary casualties while achieving no important result. They became disgruntled when their officers barred the gates to prevent future unauthorized sallies.

In a remote tower on the southern wall sited on a cliff overlooking the Tigris River, was an underground passage which cut through the rock down to the river. The passage was so steep that it was left unguarded. A renegade civilian defected to the Persians and lead a company of seventy elite Persian archers at midnight though the passage and captured the tower undetected. At sunrise they displayed a red cloak from the tower, which was the signal for another Persian assault. As the Persian ladders reached the wall, the archers from the tower started launching arrows at the Romans defending the walls. Faced with incoming arrows from the tower and assault upon the walls, the Romans quickly adapted to the situation. They moved five light *ballistae* to fire upon the archers in the tower. The crews quickly killed the Persians in the tower and then repositioned their engines to repulse the assault. By noon the Persians had realized their plan had failed and halted their assault after suffering heavy casualties.[34]

At dawn the next day, the Persians paraded past the defenders of Amida a host of captives take with the fall of the Roman fortress of Ziata. Ziata was a major fortress with defensive walls forming a perimeter of over a mile. Persian detachments had taken Ziata and other Roman forts that made up the Amida *limes*. The Persians not only took the defenders of these forts captive but also the civilian population that took refuge within the forts. When the old and infirmed could not keep up with the column of captives they were hamstringed and left to die on the side of the road. The Gallic legionaries seeing the mistreatment of the captives clamoured for action. They threatened their officers with harm if they were not allowed to take revenge on the Persian. To placate their aggressive spirit, Count Aelianus authorized a raid on the Persian outposts.

To take the Persians unaware, the raid was planned for a few days after the column of captives passed Amida. Count Aelianus authorized the raiding force to attack the Persian outpost line, which was just outside of missile range. If the legionaries were successful in breaching the outpost line they were authorized to continue their attack and create as much havoc as possible. It should be remembered that Count Aelianus had made a name for himself as a young staff officer leading such a raid during the siege of the fortress of Singara in 348. While the Gallic legionaries were preparing for the raid, the remainder of the garrison was manning the defences exchanging arrows and bolts with the Persians. When the Persians erected two great earth works, the Romans built two great earth works to counter the Persian effort.

Then on the night of the new moon, the Gallic legionaries, led by their *campidoctors* (drill instructors) emerged from a postern gate in close order and charged into the Persian picket lines, killing the sleeping sentries, and continued their attack into the Persian camp. The sentries within the camp hearing the Roman attack on the camp sounded the alarm. The Persians came pouring out of their tents and immediately attacked the Romans in a disordered angry mob. This mob forced the Romans into close formation and back out of the camp while other Persians started falling into their companies and battalions. Understanding the danger the two *campidoctors* conducted a fighting withdrawal backing toward Amida. As the Persian trumpets were sounding all over their camp, the Romans sounded their trumpets and opened the gates to allow the raiding legions back into the city. The Roman artillery started operating without projectiles. In the dark, the Persians could not observe whether stones and bolts were falling around them but hearing the engines operate discouraged them from cutting off the retreat of the raiders. Employing these tactics, the legionaries were able to break contact with the Persians and re-enter the city.

The raiding force lost 400 Gallic legionaries. While a number of grandees were slain leading the defence of the camp, no serious damage was done to the Persian siege works. A three-day truce was agreed to between the parties allowing the Romans breathing space and the Persians time to bury their nobles. Despite the fact that Constantius would later erect two statues in Edessa honouring the *campidoctors* that lead the raid, the raid itself was a failure. Almost twenty-five per cent of the three legions involved in the raid fell which resulted in killing only a few Persian nobles. The Gallic legionaries achieved a pyrrhic victory at best.

After the truce the siege continued with fury. Over the days and weeks the Persians deployed siege towers, which were disabled by Roman artillery before they were decisive. Attempts to breach the walls of Amida failed. During one of the hotly contested fights Shapur advanced within missile range of the walls in full regalia and was targeted by Roman artillery. He escaped without a scratch. When all else failed Shapur ordered a siege ramp constructed to tower over the Roman walls. The Roman engineers easily matched this construction and on the dawn of the seventy-third-day of the siege it appeared that Shapur's efforts were in vain. But as the day wore on, the Roman mound suddenly fell forward and filled the gap between the wall and the Persian siege ramp.

The cause of the collapse is not reported, but it was most likely caused by a Persian mine. The rubble from the mound filled the gap between the city wall and the Persian ramp and presented the Persians an unobstructed bridge into the city. The Persian assault troops immediately crossed over the wall before the Romans could stop them and the garrison was overwhelmed. The immediate follow-on assault indicates that the collapsed mound was a pre-planned event by Persian engineers.[35] Count Aelianus' skill at defending the city resulted in high Persian Army casualties (allegedly 30,000). After sacking and destroying the city, the Persian campaign culminated with the fall of Amida. Count Aelianus and his senior officers were executed and the survivors were led across the Tigris River into slavery.[36]

As the siege unfolded Shapur continued his intelligence gathering and planning for future operations. As mentioned above Carugasius was a leading citizen of Nisibis. His wife and family were reported missing after Shapur's Royal Army advanced past Nisibis on its way to Amida. Shortly after their capture, Shapur informed Carugasius' wife (a noble woman) that if she could not entice her husband to join her when the Royal Army marched back to Persia, she would be forced into marriage with a Persian noble. As the fates dictated the two were very much in love, the lady could not bear the thought of being separated from her husband. She secretly sent one of her slaves to infiltrate the city of Nisibis. Using the cover story that he had escaped Persian captivity Roman guards allowed him passage and sent him on to his master. Carugasius decided to defect in order to reunite with his wife and sent the slave back to the Persian camp. Upon receiving her husband's reply the lady begged her captor, Tamsapor, to intercede with Shapur so that Persian patrols would search for and protect her husband as he attempted to join her.[37]

The sudden disappearance of Carugasius' slave caused Duke Cassianus and the officials of Nisibis to fear that Carugasius might attempt to defect. Carugasius knew that any attempt at defection would be dealt with severely. Understanding the dire consequences, but longing for his wife, he kept the fact that she was alive and being well treated a secret. Over the seventy day siege, Carugasius mourned the loss of his wife and as a ruse made arrangements to marry a highborn maiden. In preparation for the wedding feast he went to his villa eight miles north of Nisibis. While at his villa, Carugasius heard of a Persian patrol in the vicinity. He mounted his fastest horse and joined the patrol. Being warned to expect him, the patrol escorted him to Tamsapor. Carugasius was reunited with his wife and treated with honour by the Persians.[38] Ammianus failed to appreciate the value of the information Carugasius was able to provide to Shapur. Ammianus generally focused on the tactical aspect of Roman traitors and deserters as part of the Persian campaign plan, while at the same time generally ignoring their strategic implications on Persian long-term objectives. Shapur made great use of deserters, traitors, and disgruntled civilians to unhinge the Roman defence of Amida. Carugasius' knowledge of Nisibis' defences and population would have been valuable intelligence had Shapur made a fourth attempt on Nisibis.

Ammianus escaped the sack of the city. After a number of adventures and evading Persian patrols he rejoined Ursicinus at the town of Melitene, in Lesser Armenia. Ammianus rejoined the general's staff as it rode to Antioch. From Antioch, Ursicinus and his staff proceeded to court where he took up the office of *magister peditum praesentalis* in succession of Barbatio who had been relieved and executed for treason.

According to Ammianus, upon arriving at court Ursicinus' handling of the defence of the East became the subject of malicious gossip and false charges were laid against him. Constantius appointed Count Arbitio and Florentius, the *magister officiorum*, to conduct an inquiry into the causes of the fall of Amida. It should be no surprise that Ammianus and Ursicinus considered the inquiry unfair, admitting evidence unfavourable to Ursicinus and ignoring evidence that would have exonerated him. Finally frustrated by the proceedings, Ursicinus declared the officials conducting the inquiry had no authority to sit in judgment of him and the matter was of such importance that only Constantius himself could judge his actions. Upon hearing this, Contantius dismissed Ursicinus from his command and ordered him into private life without looking into the matter.[39]

While Ammianus defends his patron's conduct of the campaign, it was not Ursicinus' finest moment. Even though he did not have the cooperation of the *magister peditum* of the East, Ursicinus failed to anticipate Shapur's attack north to Amida. He did not order the fields around Amida burned as he did in the vicinity of Nisibis which raises the inference that he was planning to use Amida as a base of operations against the rear of an expected Persian thrust toward Nisibis or Edessa. He deployed two newly arrived cavalry regiments, that did not know the terrain, to defend the Nisibis-Mardin-Amida Road against expected Persian raiding parties. Instead of a raiding party the cavalry screen was faced with Tamsapor's 20,000 cavalry and the 700 Romans quickly scattered. The fact that Ursicinus did not post one of his protectors, like Ammianus, with the screen to ensure a messenger was dispatched upon detecting the Persians was a critical error.

Because Shapur out-manoeuvred Ursicinus, the Roman small field army of five legions was trapped and destroyed in Amida. On the balance sheet the Persians are reported to have lost up to 30,000 men but the Romans lost the major portions of seven legions and two cavalry regiments, one major city (possibly a second city if Singara was taken) and a majority of the forts along the Amida *limes*. In addition, the Romans lost thousands of other soldiers killed in the countless unreported skirmishes. The Roman losses were so severe that Constantius ordered Julian to provide him massive reinforcements. The Persian losses were not severe enough to prevent the Royal Army from taking the field in 360.

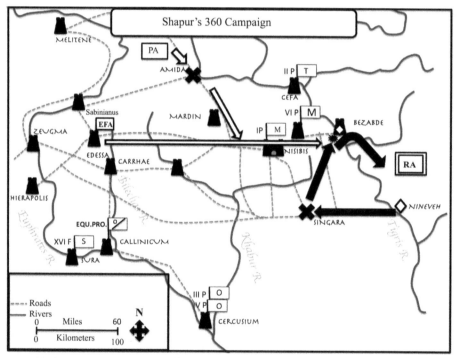

Map 16: Shapur's 360 Campaign.[40] 1. Shapur captures and destroys Singara then counter marches and captures and occupies Bezabde. After capturing some additional minor forts Shapur crosses the Tigris and waits for the Roman response. Constantius marches the *Praesental* Army into Mesopotamia late in the campaign season. His attempt to recapture Bezabde fails.

With the withdrawal of the Persian Royal Army and the closure of the 359 Campaign, it first appeared that the Persians had accomplished little. They caused havoc among the peasants of the region, disrupted trade, and sacked, but did not occupy, one of the key fortress cities. The loss of a large part of the 359 harvest would have been hard on the peasants, but the Roman government could import supplies from Egypt to feed the army. Unnoticed by Ammianus and modern historians was Shapur's transformation in strategy from the direct approach (attacking Nisibis) to the indirect approach of isolating Nisibis.

The exact moment of Shapur's strategy transformation is not recorded. Ammianus unknowingly provides a hint when he notes: '(T)here was at the time in Corduene, which was subject to Persian power, a satrap called Jovinianus...to him I was sent... for the purpose of getting better information....'[41] Corduene was one of the Trans-Tigris regions within the Roman sphere of influence. This note indicates that by 359 the region was already drifting back to the Persian sphere of influence. In addition, the Persian Army not only included the king of the Chionitae but also the King of the Albani.[42] Albani, according to the Treaty of 298, was in the Roman sphere of influence. Shapur's emissaries and agents had been busy undermining Roman authority west of the Caspian Sea and severing the northern trade route. It is debatable whether Shapur developed his indirect strategy during the planning phase of the 359 Campaign or as the 360 Campaign unfolded, but it is clear that it was fully developed by the early summer 360.

As to Roman military operations during this campaign, the evidence indicates that Constantius did not understand the nature of the new threat in the Roman East. He remained in Europe and wintered in Constantinople.[43] He ordered Julian to provide massive reinforcements in the form of specific legions and *auxilia* units and 300-man detachments from each of his remaining regiments and legions.[44] In the spring of 360, Constantius moved to Caesarea in Cappadocia where he learned that Julian had been proclaimed Augustus by his army.[45] It is significant that, at this point, Constantius considered Shapur a bigger threat than Julian. Constantius moved in late spring or early summer to Edessa.[46] By deploying his army to Edessa at the beginning of the campaign season, Constantius was ready to intercept an anticipated attack by Shapur on Nisibis. His operational plan for 360 was reactive and based upon the assumption that Shapur would follow his operational pattern from the campaigns of the 340s.

Shapur opened his 360 Campaign late in the summer with an attack on Singara. The Roman Army could not march to the relief of the city because the timing of the attack coincided with the drying up of the water sources on the roads leading from Edessa and Nisibis.[47] Singara was defended by legions or legionary detachments from I Flavian, I Parthia, and cavalry that had taken refuge within the city from the quick Persian advance.[48] The siege raged for several days until a large battering ram was brought up and, despite the defenders' countermeasures, it was used to collapse a tower that may have been damaged in 359. After the initial assault into the breach, the defenders surrendered and the captured Roman soldiers were transported to remote parts of Persia.[49]

Instead of marching toward the Khabur River, as the Persians did in 359, Shapur unexpectedly counter-marched his army to besiege Bezabde. Bezabde was a strong fortress defended by II Flavian, II Armenia, a detachment of II Parthia, Zabdiceni militia archers, and possibly the infantry regiment *Cohors quartodecima Valeria Zabenorum* (Zabdiceni). Shapur attempted to entice the garrison to surrender but was driven back by *ballistae* bolts. The Persians assaulted the city for a number of days. As casualties mounted, the Persians deployed their great battering ram and broke into the city. A large part of the garrison escaped capture.[50] After taking the city, Shapur rebuilt the defences, stocked the city with supplies, installed a garrison, and moved on, taking a number of forts but unsuccessfully attacking the fortress of Virta. He then pulled back to the eastern side of the Tigris to await the Roman reaction.[51]

Shapur's 359 and 360 campaigns demonstrated his evolved knowledge of the art of war and the indirect approach to manoeuvre and siege warfare. Missed by western sources were the combined impacts of the loss and destruction of Amida in 359 and the loss of Singara and occupation of Bezabde in 360. These attacks isolated the Trans-Tigris region and its forts gained by Rome in the Treaty of 298. They also secured lines of communications for an attack on Nisibis from the north, east, and south and provided the Persians a forward logistics base at Bezabde. Also, by taking Bezabde late in the 360 campaign season, repairing its defence, and garrisoning it quickly, Shapur denied Constantius the time required to recapture it before winter. Rome's prestige suffered from the loss of Bezabde, and Constantius was personally humiliated by his inability to quickly recover the city.

The Campaign of 361 was equally disastrous for Constantius. Initially, the Persians' mere presence on the east side of the Tigris prevented Constantius from besieging and retaking Bezabde. Julian's unexpected revolt caused Constantius to march west and Shapur stood down his army, winning the campaign without expending a single arrow. Ammianus records that Shapur's failure to cross the Tigris was due to bad omens.[52] The facts, however, suggest that Shapur succeeded because Constantius failed to recapture Bezabde, which undermined his ability to rule the area. When Constantius marched west to confront Julian, after two years of Persian military successes, the Trans-Tigris regions, as well as the Kingdoms of Albania and Iberia, returned to the Persian sphere of influence. Armenia alone remained free from Persian dominance.[53]

When Julian decided to follow the road to Augustus is not clear. But his recruitment of *auxilia* was part of his plan. As early as 355, *auxilia* comprised a substantial component of the Army of Gaul. There were at least 8,000 *auxilia* in the Army of Gaul when Silvanus was *magister peditum*. With the field army only mustering 13,000 men, it is no wonder that *auxilia* regiments are mentioned by Ammianus' narrative more frequently than legions. Unlike the legions, *auxilia*, even if mauled by the civil war battles, did not have to be trained to legionary standards. *Auxilia* units that fought for the usurper during the civil war could bring their strength up quickly by recruiting fellow tribesmen from east of the Rhine and new regiments could be quickly formed from defeated tribes. They were equipped similarly to the legions and yet served as line infantry and light infantry. Their primary drawback was their lack of discipline and dislike of the fatigue duties that accompanied building marching camps and repairing damaged Roman infrastructure. When marching through friendly territory, *auxilia* had a tendency to plunder as they marched. It, therefore, should be no surprise that they were at the centre of the conspiracy to raise Julian to Augustus.

Ammianus and Julian both allege that the *auxilia* enrolled upon the condition that they would not serve 'beyond the Alps'.[54] Like the previous year, and due to the Roman defeats in the East in 359 with the complete loss or mauling of nine legions, it should have been no surprise that Constantius ordered Julian to provide him with significant reinforcements. The deployment order specified the *auxilia* regiments *Aeruli, Batavi, Celts,* and *Petulantes* and 300 men from each remaining unit (*numeris*). Finally, Julian's guard was reduced with his most fit guardsmen from the *Scutariis* and *Gentiles* ordered east. The guards were ordered to leave for the East immediately under the command of Tribune Stintula, the head stable-master.[55]

At that time Julian's primary advisors were not in Paris with him. Lupicinus, his *magister equitum,* was in Britain with a force consisting of the *auxilia* regiments *Aeruli, Batavians* and two *numeris* of the legion *Moesians* to fight the Scots and Picts. Florentius was in Vienne arranging supplies. Florentius, fearing a mutiny, refused to return to Paris when summoned. In the absence of his advisors, Julian issued the orders to start the troops drafted moving east. In response, in the camp of the *Petulantes*, an anonymous letter was discovered on the parade ground, which among other things said: 'We verily are driven to the ends of the earth like condemned criminals, and our dear ones, whom we freed from their former captivity after mortal battles, will again be slaves of the Alamanni.'[56] When the note was brought to Julian's headquarters, he found the soldiers' complaints reasonable and authorized them to use government wagons of the courier service to move their families to the East.[57] The *Petulantes'* route from their winter quarters in Gaul to the east ran through Paris. Julian was still present in the city when the regiment arrived. Julian met the regiment at the edge of the city, praised them for their accomplishments, and invited their officers to dinner. While Ammianus and Julian do not admit it, this dinner was most likely where the mutiny was planned.

The events Constantius put in motion looked similar to the events leading to Gallus' arrest and execution. Julian had disagreed with the administration of the Prefecture of Gaul, and Constantius had sent Julian a letter directing him not to undermine the praetorian prefect's authority. Despite the warning, Julian continued with his tax reforms and became very popular with the provincials. Silvanus was bullied into revolt by the rumour-mongers at court on lesser grounds. Julian was well aware that, when his brother Gallus was undermined at court, various reasons were found to first transfer his troops from his control and then reduce his bodyguard before the commander of his bodyguard arrested him. Here, with the Emperor's military defeat and the effective loss of nine legions in the East, Julian's success and popularity in the West could have been perceived by a paranoid Constantius as a threat to his throne. Conversely, the transfer of almost forty per cent of his army to the East appears to have been viewed by Julian as the preliminary steps to his arrest and execution.[58] Constantius' track record would not have given Julian much confidence that the massive deployment of his troops was due to the Roman defeats in the East and not to Constantius' loss of confidence in him.

Based upon these facts, it should be no surprise that shortly after the dinner party broke up, the soldiers of the *Petulantes* mutinied. The soldiers marched on the palace and hailed Julian as Augustus. They remained outside the palace until morning when Julian appeared. At first he appeared annoyed, and declined the offer, but told them he would take their grievances about serving beyond the Alps to Constantius. The soldiers would not take no for an answer, and Julian was compelled to consent. He was raised upon an infantry shield and declared Augustus. Looking for a diadem, the soldiers called for an ornament from Julian's wife. He refused and insisted that women's jewellery was not fitting. They then looked for a horse's trapping, but that was also rejected. Then the standard bearer of the *Petulantes* took off the neck chain he wore as the carrier of the Draco standard and stepped forward to place the chain upon Julian's head. Julian promised a donative to each member of the *Petulantes* of five gold coins and a pound of silver.[59] While Ammianus claims the mutiny was a spontaneous action of *auxilia* soldiers, an examination of the facts shows it was a well-staged event. Constantius saw through the farce instantly. The political and military manoeuvring of the confrontation are, however, irrelevant to an examination of the Nisibis War. The timely death of Constantius averted yet another bloody civil war. Constantius died on 3 November 361 of natural causes at Mopsucrenae in Cilicia as he marched to confront Julian.

Criticisms of Constantius' strategy are numerous in the near contemporaneous sources. As early as 363, Libanius attacked Constantius' strategy as cowardly, both in the failure to fight battles and to relieve besieged cities.[60] A decade later, Eutropius summarized Constantius' reign, concluding that he failed against the Persians and only succeeded in civil wars. While this was also Ammianus' opinion, he at least moderated his harsh judgment by including a statement attributed to Sabinus, citizen of Nisibis, that 'Constantius… up to his last day he had lost nothing, whereas Jovian…had abandoned the defences of provinces whose bulwarks had remained unshaken…'[61]

Chapter 12

Roman Strategic Offence, 362–363

W hen Julian ascended to the throne in 361, he capitalized on Constantius' preparations for a major Persian offensive. Julian invaded Persia in March 363, just eighteen months after assuming the mantle of sole emperor. A Roman emperor's first priority was to maintain power rather than defend the empire.[1] Julian had to earn and retain the army's loyalty in order to retain power. Peace meant boredom to the Roman Army with its accompanying low pay and limited advancement. Battle resulted in wealth and promotion.[2] Julian was young and tired of inactivity, eager for glory and an opportunity to avenge past wrongs committed by the Persians. He advanced preparations for a 363 campaign and ignored advice to the contrary.[3]

Blockley points out that Julian had enjoyed success in Gaul with a policy of confrontation, pursuit, and devastation against the Germanic confederations.[4] Twenty-five years of war had convinced Julian that a decisive victory could not be achieved in the Northern Mesopotamian or Armenian Theatres. Campaigning in these fortified zones resulted in costly, fruitless sieges and indecisive battles. As evidenced by Constantius' running the war for twenty-five years, Julian was well aware that winning defensive battles did not lead to victory but, rather, a long war of attrition. As a scholar, Julian would have studied earlier attacks on the city of Ctesiphon and would have been well aware of the manpower and logistics requirements for such an endeavour. He would have known that prior emperors had achieved victory by achieving two objectives: sacking Ctesiphon and defeating any Parthian or Persian army that tried to intervene. But Julian had a third objective, one that had eluded all previous successful Romans fighting Parthia or Persia. To obtain a decisive victory, Julian had to break into the Iranian Plateau and/or replace Shapur with a client king.

While Julian's intent to lead the attack on Persia was understood by his contemporaries, his strategic goals were unclear. The sources disagree as to whether Julian's intended operation was a larger version of his Gallic campaigns, which were actually raids across the Rhine against the Germans, or a serious attempt to overthrow Shapur and subjugate Persia to Rome. In the fifth century, the Christian Socrates suggested that Julian actually believed he was Alexander reincarnated, destined to extend the empire to India.[5] The Persian Prince Hormizda was one of Julian's commanders.[6] The option of replacing Shapur, as Constantine had planned in 337, was a viable course of action. There is a reference to Hormizda in a letter from Libanius implying that Julian planned to place the exiled prince on the Persian throne.[7] Despite his Christian enemies' wild claims, Julian had an achievable goal to end the war and that was to turn western Persia into a client kingdom under Prince Hormizda. In all probability the great Persian families would have revolted and torn the eastern kingdom apart destroying the Persian Empire.

Julian's army, in June 363, marched north to the Diyala (Douros) River, which placed him in position to advance toward the Persian heartland. The main Silk Road followed the Diyala River onto the Iranian Plateau and, by June, the passes in the Zagros Mountains should have been passable. This was the axis of advance that Muslim armies used to break onto the Iranian Plateau and destroy Persia in the seventh century.[8] After Julian's arrival at this strategic avenue of approach into the Persian heartland, it should have been no surprise that on or about 17 June 363, Persian and Roman main armies clashed on the banks of the Diyala River.

While his strategic goals are cloudy, Julian's operational plan was surprisingly modern in concept and very similar to Constantine's plan in 337.[9] Julian envisioned two armies attacking along separate axes, each initially threatening a key Persian region and eventually converging on the kingdom's capital: Ctesiphon. His forces would then mass and capture Ctesiphon. With the Royal Persian Army defeated, the second phase would commence with the Roman army breaking onto the Iranian Plateau, and ultimately replacing Shapur. It was projected that the *Praesental* Army and the Army of Mesopotamia independently would have a reasonable chance of defeating the Persian Army in open battle. The main effort, under Julian, would attack down the Euphrates River to take the Persian capital. The supporting attack would cross the Tigris River, march through the Trans-Tigris regions, re-establish Roman rule and alliances, then move into Persian territory, marching east of the Tigris, and south toward Ctesiphon.

The composition and size of Julian's *Praesental* Army is unclear. Zosimus was the only historian to reference the size of the army noting that when Julian reviewed the army in March 363 it mustered 65,000. Gibbon accepted this figure and added the Army of Mesopotamia's 20,000 to 30,000 men to the force for a total of between 85,000 and 95,000 soldiers committed to the offence.[10] A number of historians subtract the Army of Mesopotamia from Zosimus' 65,000, reducing the *Praesental* Army to between 30,000 and 45,000, depending on which source they accept for the size of the Army of Mesopotamia.[11] If these numbers were accurate, Julian's army would have numbered between 35,000 and 47,000 in strength, and would have been insufficient to accomplish the campaign objectives. The problem with this small figure for the *Praesental* Army is that most historians overlook the fact that 20,000 men from Julian's army were engaged in manning and providing security for the supporting fleet, leaving only 15,000 to 27,000 for land operations.

Assuming Vegetius' ratio of one horseman to four infantry, the 65,000-man *Praesental* Army would have contained 13,000 cavalry and 52,000 infantry. The infantry consisted of Roman legions from Gaul, the Balkans, and the East, as well as *auxilia* regiments of Gauls and Germans from the Rhine River Valley. The core of Julian's infantry was his loyal *auxilia* from the Army of Gaul who had declared him Augustus. Of the fourteen infantry units named by the sources, eight units were *auxilia* regiments from Gaul, four were elite legions (two from Gaul), one *comitatenses* legion from an unknown home region (possibly Thrace), and one *limitanei* legion from the East.[12]

Julian's cavalry consisted of regular Roman regiments supported by Goth and Saracen *federates*, Armenian allies, and rebel Persians.[13] Ammianus refers to the Goths as Scythians; that could cause confusion until one remembers that the Roman Province of Scythia was located where the Danube River enters the Black Sea and across the River from the Gothic homeland. The only regular cavalry regiments named by the sources are the *Promoti* and *Tertaci* with the guard units *Scutarrii* and *Domestici Protectores*.[14] The renegade Persian Prince Hormizda would have had a contingent of followers

Units Named in Sources

Comitatenses Legion	*Comitateses Auxilia	Limitanei Legions	Cavalry
Herculiani*	Bracchiatii	II Armenia	Scutarri
Ioviani*	Celtae		Domestici-
Lanciarii*	Cornuti		Protestroes
Mattiari*	Eruli/Heruli/Aeruli		Tertaci
Zianni	Victores		Promoti
	Petulates		Gothic Federates
	Reges		Saracen Federates
	Victores		Persian Rebels
			Armenian Allies

Army Estimated Strength: 52,000 Infantry, 13,000 Cavalry   (until April 363)

*After 364, these elite units were classified as *Palantini*

Julian's *Praesental* Army
Late March 363

at least as a bodyguard if not a full cavalry unit. The Armenian General Zawray commanded 7,000 of his country's horsemen and was probably present at the initial March 363 mustering of the invasion force.[15]

Ammianus provides some details about the logistics build-up for the invasion but little analysis about the logistics plan for the invasion. The cities of Mesopotamia were transformed into massive supply depots. A large fleet of over 1,000 supply boats and barges was built to support the main effort down the Euphrates River. These boats and barges carried the army's siege train, replacement weapons, and armour, but the vast majority carried the expedition's rations. While vast quantities of sour wine and other foodstuffs were carried, the majority of the weight would have been grain. A large percentage of grain was baked into biscuits for the army's rations thus reducing the amount of wood needed for the campaign.[16] Fifty war ships protected the fleet and fifty pontoon boats were included to build bridges.

On land the army was supported by a massive baggage train and, while not mentioned by the sources, must have included a large herd of horses for cavalry remounts and cattle for rations. Mules were required to carry the *contubernium* daily camping equipment (tents, cooking utensils, entrenching tools, rations, etc.). It took 1,200 mules to support 5.000 men which could have been replaced by 350 ox wagons; 50,000 infantry would have required 12,000 mules or 3,500 wagons. Light artillery and other equipment and supplies needed to establish a camp would have required wagons. The exact number is impossible to calculate, but the supply train for an army of 60,000 would have been massive.[17]

The water requirements for this force dictated the Romans' axis of advance and confined it to rivers or major canals. In the temperate climate of Europe, 2 litres of water per person were required per day. Cavalry mounts and pack animals required approximately 15 litres to 20 litres or quarts of water per day. Spring and summer operations in Mesopotamia doubled that requirement. The daily water requirement for 60,000 men was 120,000 litres or 40,000 gallons, and water for the army's animals exceeded 600,000 litres or 158,000 gallons.[18] There was no way that the army could transport one day's water rations, and the location of a campsite with an adequate water source was a primary task of the Roman scouts and outriders. Moving this massive force was difficult. While well organized, the Romans set no speed records. When compared to march rates of early industrial armies the Romans made comparable daily marches. Both forces, centuries apart, averaged 15mpd/20kpd.[19]

It is clear from Julian's march down river that he did not plan to use the Euphrates River as a supply line or even as a line of communication. He started the advance south in March 363, three months before June harvest, in the vicinity of Ctesiphon. He bypassed key Persian fortresses guarding the Euphrates. These fortresses were no direct threat to his army but were a significant threat to any river traffic between the last major Roman fortress of Ciresium and Julian's invading army. These key facts indicate that as Julian's army marched south along the Euphrates he intended to feed his army from the supplies on his riverboats supplemented from stores captured en route to Ctesiphon. Once in the vicinity of the Persian capital, the Roman army's primary source of supply would be the region's June harvest.

Until the *Praesental* Army marched south of Ciresium, its manoeuvres created a dilemma for Shapur: should he protect the Persian homeland or Ctesiphon and prevent economic ruin. Until Julian marched south of Ciresium, there was the possibility that he could have turned east along the Singara road and invaded the Persian heartland. It would have been novel (and very un-Roman) had the Romans marched onto the Iranian Plateau without first sacking Ctesiphon. Yet the Romans striking directly onto the Iranian Plateau was the most dangerous course of action. The only source indicating Shapur's location in March 363 is Magnus, who places the Persian Royal Army in Persian Armenia not near Ctesiphon. Shapur, no longer a novice at operations, had placed himself and the Royal Army in a central position from which he could defend Bezabde and block the northern route onto the Iranian Plateau, or march to support the garrison of Ctesiphon.

Historians ignore the character and reputation of the two men selected to lead the Army of Mesopotamia: Procopius and Sebastianus. In 363,

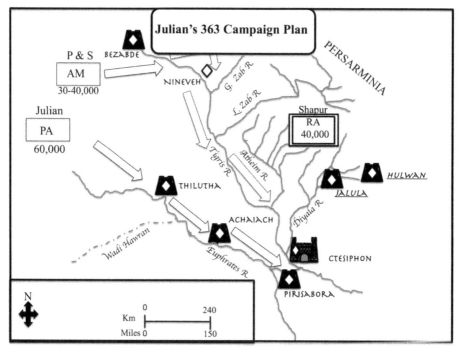

Map 17. Julian's 363 Campaign Plan. Julian planned to attack Persia along two converging axis. The *Praesental* Army, the main effort, attacked down the Euphrates with the objective of capturing Ctesiphon. The Army of Mesopotamia, was to defend Mesopotamia from a Persian counter attack and then attack down the Tigris in support of the *Praesental* Army.

Procopius would have been 37-years-old and had gone through life 'innocent of bloodshed'.[20] He had risen to the rank of count through family connections to Constantius and Julian but, prior to 363, held no field command mentioned by Ammianus or any other historian. While politically loyal to Julian, he lacked experience.

The key to Julian's plan was not his kinsman Procopius, but the seasoned eastern soldier Sebastianus. By the time Sebastianus was selected co-commander of the Army of Mesopotamia, he had been Duke of Egypt.[21] The mid-fourth century list of Dukes of Egypt identifies Sebastianus of Thrace as Duke of Egypt in 353 to 354.[22] During his tenure, Constantius, an Arian Christian, was in conflict with the Alexandrian Christian Church. Duke Sebastianus and his soldiers enforced the Emperor's edicts.[23] According to Athanasius (circa 296 to 373), Bishop of Alexandria, and foremost opponent of Arianism[24] Duke Sebastianus was a '...profligate young man'.[25] The key phrase is 'young man'. Romans considered men young until age 30.[26] To be appointed Duke of Egypt when he was in his twenties indicates that Sebastianus was either well connected, had proven himself in the field, or both. In historian Ramsay MacMullen's opinion Count Sebastianus was '[A] true soldier, then: solicitous for his men; an aggressive officer, model of integrity, everything a military leader should be; therefore, rewarded with high commands by Constantius II, Julian, and Valentinian [I]....' and finally Valens.[27] There is no record of his activities between 354 and 363, but the fact that Julian gave him co-command of the Army of Mesopotamia indicated that the emperor had great confidence in him.[28] The appointment of Julian's kinsman, Procopius, assured that the ruling family would receive credit for Count Sebastianus' deeds.

Shapur would have been aware of the massing of 85,000 to 95,000 soldiers, 1,100 boats, and thousands of tons of supplies moving in the Roman East.[29] By 363, Shapur would have had two years to consolidate his power over the Trans-Tigris princes.[30] He would have been very aware of Persia's strength and weaknesses. The political centre of gravity for Sassanian Persia was Mesopotamia and its capital Ctesiphon, but its military centre of gravity was the Iranian highlands where its military manpower was located. The main arteries for trade and military movement followed the Tigris and Euphrates rivers south to Ctesiphon, then east across the Zagros Mountains into the

Persian heartland. There are no records indicating whether the eastern Persian regiments wintered in Mesopotamia or whether they joined Shapur after the snow in the passes of the Zagros Mountains melted in June. Since the confrontation between the main Persian and Roman armies did not take place until June 363, it is most likely the eastern regiments did not winter in Mesopotamia.

As mentioned above, the assembly area for Shapur's Royal Army during the 363 Campaign remains unidentified but, based upon the timing of Shapur's appearance in the vicinity of Ctesiphon in June, it must have been in the vicinity of the junction of the Tigris and the Greater Zab River. Initial Persian regiments originated from the Iranian highlands west of the passes in the Zagros Mountains. Their assembly areas would have been in Persian Armenia and near Nineveh.[31] Support for this proposition comes from Magnus of Carrhae, a veteran of the expedition who recorded the following: 'King [Shapur], thinking Julian...was coming via [Nisibis], hastened against him with his whole force. Then he was informed that Julian...was behind him...and a large [Roman] force was coming against him from the front; realizing he was in the middle, he fled to [Persian Armenia].'[32] Whether he fled through the snowbound mountains into Persian Armenia is debatable. It is clear, however, that he declined to cross the Tigris to engage the Army of Mesopotamia and left the opposition of Julian's advance to his general, Surena, and his small border cavalry army.

The paladin, Surena, commanded the small Persian border army opposing Julian's advance down the Euphrates. The 'Surena' was an official second only to the King of Kings. The unidentified grandee and general headed the second most powerful family of the seven main noble houses in the Persian Kingdom. The office was a holdover from the Parthian Kingdom. In 36 BCE, the fourth century Surena's predecessor was given the task of opposing Crassus with his 9,000 horse archers from his own estates' retainers and 1,000 *cataphract* cavalry from the Parthian Royal Army.[33] In the fourth century, instead of under-equipped retainers, Surena commanded well equipped Persian Savaran cavalry armoured with helmets and coats of mail who were experts in archery. *Phylarch* (Emir) Podosaces' Assanitic Saracens supported the Persian defenders.[34] The sources do not estimate the size of this Persian delaying army, but its successful delaying action for almost sixty days, including defeating three Roman cavalry regiments in one engagement, indicates that Surena led an army of at least 3,000 to 5,000 cavalrymen. These Persian cavalry and Saracen brigands following Surena were only border garrison units and desert tribesmen, not the elite Savaran cavalry and the steppe allies of the main Persian Royal Army. Surena, however, demonstrated that he was a superior cavalry commander understanding the details of hit–and–run tactics, which he may have learned fighting against the eastern nomads during the 350s.

Chapter 13

The March Down River

On 18 March 363, Julian joined his massed army at Carrhae.[1] At Carrhae the Army of Mesopotamia detached from the *Praesental* Army and marched east toward Nisibis. The *Praesental* Army trailed the Army of Mesopotamia until it reached the Belias River and then followed the river road reaching Callinicum on 27 March 363. At Callinicum, he granted an audience to a delegation of Saracen chieftains who presented Julian with a gold crown and swore allegiance to Julian. Since they were skilled at scouting and the hit-and-run tactics of desert warfare, they were a valued addition to the army as *federates*.[2] Ammianus does not identify the Saracen *phylae* (tribes) that pledged loyalty to Julian. As *federates*/mercenaries, these Saracens remained loyal as long as they were paid and rewarded.[3] There were twelve *phylae* divided into two groups. The Lakhmid tribal confederation was generally pro-Roman. In contrast, the Assanitic Saracens, associated with the Ghassanids tribal confederation, were generally pro-Persians.[4]

Count Lucillianus, with the fleet, joined the army at this point, and the army was now ready to proceed with the invasion. Julian marched south on the east bank of the Euphrates River to the fortress city of Circesium at the junction of the Euphrates and Khabur River. While at Circesium, Julian received a message from Sallustius, Prefect of Gaul, requesting him to call off the invasion based upon omens. Ammianus goes into some detail about divinations and omens at this point of the narrative foreshadowing, with 20/20 hindsight, the impending defeat. While divinations and oracles were important to pagans like Ammianus and a large section of the army, that may not have been the primary reason for Sallustius' dispatch. The majority of the Army of Gaul had marched east for the Persian War. Gaul was severely undermanned again. It is probable that Sallustius' message about the omens included a report that the tribes across the Rhine were becoming restless again.

The garrison of Circesium mustered 6,000 men. Julian detached 4,000 men and the commanders Accameus and Maurus to reinforce the garrison.[5] Magnus of Carrhae hints that this detachment was to reinforce the garrison. These men were more likely the sick and lame of Julian's army.[6] Throughout Ammianus' account, he fails to mention the fate of those soldiers too wounded or sick to keep up with the army. Unlike Caesar's Gallic campaigns, there was not a main depot to evacuate the sick and wounded and allow them to recover in safety. Throwing a pontoon bridge across the Khabur River, the *Praesental* Army marched south along the east bank of the Euphrates passing Zaitha on 9 April 363.

Upon crossing the Khabur River, the Romans were officially in Persian Assyria and their column deployed into tactical formation. Fifteen hundred mounted scouts preceded the army followed by an advance guard of 1,500 infantry from the legions *Lanciarii* and *Mattiarii*.[7] The main body of infantry was led by Julian in two columns with the baggage train massed between the columns. Nevitta, with several legions, formed the right flank guard skirting the bank of the Euphrates. The left wing cavalry, under Arintheus and Hormizdas, guarded the army's left riding in close order through the fields. Dagalaifus and Victor commanded the rear division and Duke Secundinus of Osdruena commanded the rear guard. The column stretched ten miles from the head of the infantry columns to Secundinus' rear guard. Ammianus tells us that Julian extended the interval between units so the army would appear larger to the Persians than it was. At first, this statement appears strange. His audience would have been aware that a Roman army of 60,000 men would create a tactical march column ten miles long. What Ammianus fails to mention at this point in his narrative is that 20,000 soldiers were occupied with working and guarding the ships for the entire campaign until they were burnt in June.[8] With only 40,000 men marching in the main body, with the infantry in two columns, the army would have occupied considerably less than ten miles. With only 40,000 men readily available for combat, it was wise of the Romans to extend their column to make their army appear larger. In this march formation, it would take three to four hours for the rear guard to close with the head of the column.

On 6 April 363, the *Praesental* Army passed the deserted city of Dura-Europos situated on a bluff on the west bank of the Euphrates. At sundown

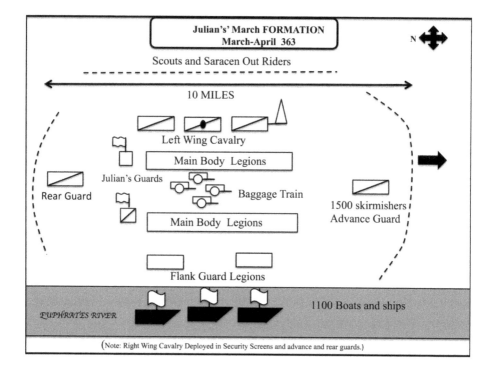

the next day, a thunderstorm passed over the army and lightning killed a soldier named Julian and the two warhorses he was leading up from the river. After consulting with his philosophers and soothsayers about this omen, Julian decided to give a pep talk to the army. On 8 April 363, Julian ascended a hill with his army deployed around him and his men formed in their centuries, maniples, and cohorts and started his oration. He reminded his men of the past victories of Roman arms against their enemies, the omens, and that if the men did their duty they would be victorious. The speech was well received by the *Praesental* Army and especially the Gallic troops who showed their enthusiasm with joyous shouts.[9] This passage is important because it confirms the maniple as a standard tactical unit in the fourth century Roman Army and that Julian's Gallic troops were the core of the *Praesental* army and his key supporters.

On 12 April 363, after a four day march, the Romans arrived in the vicinity of the Persian island fortress city of Anatha. Count Lucillianus, with 1,500 light troops, at sundown, embarked on ships and, undetected, blockaded the city. At sunrise, the Romans were detected and the city manned its defensive walls. Julian, with Hormizdas and ships armed with siege engines, reinforced Lucillianus' blockade. Negotiations were opened with Hormizdas playing a key part and, on 13 April 363, the garrison surrendered on terms. Pusaeus, the Persian commander was given the rank of tribune and would later rise to the position of Duke of Egypt. The remainder of the garrison and the civilian population were transported and settled in the city of Chalcis, Syria. An old Roman soldier, left behind when Maximian invaded Persia, was instrumental in the city's surrender. He was estimated to be nearly 100 years old and had been left behind when he was a teenager. He had married multiple wives and was surrounded by many descendants. While not mentioned by the sources, Pusaeus, the Persian commander, may have been one of his grandsons, which would explain Pusaeus' commission into Julian's service and the relocation of the city's population into Roman Syria. Other Persian garrison commanders did not receive such lenient treatment.

On 14 April 363, Saracen outriders captured Persian scouts belonging to Surena. These Saracens were rewarded before being sent back on picket duty. As the day progressed, another thunderstorm and possible tornado struck the Roman encampment causing havoc, sinking a number of boats and possibly covering the Persian sabotage of sluice-gates, which resulted in flooding the area around the Roman camp and its route of advance.

The *Praesental* Army continued its march south with foraging parties plundering the countryside and burning what was not required to supply the army. On or about 15 April 363, the Romans camped in the vicinity of the Persian fortress city of Thilutha. Thilutha was situated on an island and built on a lofty peak. This natural fortress was reinforced with man-made fortifications that made the city nearly impregnable and would have required that Julian spend considerable time to capture it. Julian opened negotiations with the garrison commander. Unlike the commander of Anatha, this grandee refused to surrender but claimed the garrison would remain neutral. Shortly after bypassing Thilutha, the Romans were confronted with the fortress city of Acaiacala which was also built on an island, and reducing it would have been time consuming. This commander also refused to surrender his fortress and claimed he would remain neutral. At this time, Persian patrols were detected shadowing the *Praesental* Army on the opposite bank of the river, picking off stragglers.[10]

As the Romans advanced, the Persians abandoned the fortress of Diacria due to its weak defences. The Romans looted Diacria and continued their advance. On 22 April 363, the army reached the town of Ozogardana where the Romans rested for two days. During this rest period, the renegade Persian Prince Hormizdas, while leading a reconnaissance party, was ambushed by Persians and Saracens under Surena and Podosaces. The prince and his party were only saved because the ambushing Persians fired an arrow storm from the opposite bank of the river and the river was too deep and swift at that point for them cross and ride down the prince's party.[11] Since the ambush site did not allow the Persians to close to sword point with Hormizdas' men, it was more likely a chance encounter than a planned ambush based on the reports of Persian spies in the Roman camp as Ammianus alleges.

The next morning the Persians contested the Roman advance. The sources provide very little information about this first major skirmish. The 3,000 men of the Roman vanguard most likely fought this engagement as they left camp before the main body trooped out of the camp. The quick advance of the 1,500 infantry of the vanguard in support of the 1,500 cavalry scouts likely encouraged the Persians to withdraw. No casualties on either side are reported, and this skirmish set the pattern of the hit-and-run tactics that Surena would employ as the Romans marched deeper into Persia.

From this point forward there were two campaigns being fought. The Romans fought in their traditional manner: marching straight toward the enemy capital fighting any army or besieging any fortress blocking their approach to their objective. In this case, that objective was the Persian capital Ctesiphon. The Persians were fighting a delaying action and also fighting a counter-reconnaissance battle that Ammianus and the Roman command staff were not aware of and failed to understand. The counter-reconnaissance campaign is a modern term for standard nomadic tactics. To beat a civilized army, a nomad chief had to prevent the civilized army from finding his main encampment where the tribe's families and flocks were located. To accomplish this objective, the chief had to blind the civilized army's reconnaissance and lead the army into terrain where he could destroy them in detail. Whether Shapur and his generals were aware of this strategy before 350 when they marched east to fight the nomads is debatable. It is clear that earlier and later generations of Persian kings did not understand this strategy and Persian armies marched to their doom in the Asian steppes.[12] As events unfolded, it became clear that Shapur's generals did understand these unchivalrous tactics and were professional enough to employ them against the Romans.

On 26 April 363, the Romans reached Macepracta north of the Naarmalcha (Royal) Canal and a pontoon bridge was thrown across the canal. While the infantry crossed the bridge, the cavalry in full armour and the baggage animals attempted to swim the canal. The far bank had not been secured properly and Persian raiders showered the crossing with arrows. In the confusion, some of the cavalry and baggage animals were carried off in the current and drowned. The situation was restored when lightly armed *auxilia* sallied from the bridgehead and forced the Persians to withdraw. With the canal behind them, the Romans marched on and arrived at Pirisabora on 27 April 363.

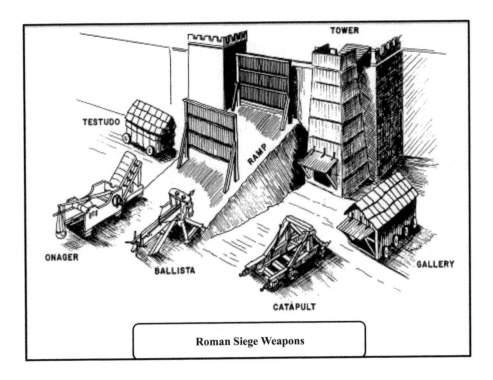

TOWER

TESTUDO

RAMP

ONAGER

BALLISTA

CATAPULT

GALLERY

Roman Siege Weapons

Pirisabora was the key fortress guarding the canal approach from the Euphrates to Ctesiphon on the Tigris and had to be taken for the Romans to continue their march to Ctesiphon. The siege lasted from 27 April to 9 May 363. Hormizdas' attempts to entice the garrison to surrender were meet with insults with the defenders calling him a traitor and deserter. The Romans were forced to unpack and assemble and deploy their heavy siege engines. Romans used engines to try to breach the walls. Julian personally led an attempt to breach a gate but was driven back by missiles from the towers and walls. Finally, in desperation, Julian ordered the *helepolis* unloaded and assembled. This massive siege tower on wheels, known as the 'Taker of Cities', was a multi-storied tower with a battering ram at ground level. The height of the tower allowed the attacker to shoot arrows and throw other missiles down on the defenders of the city walls and towers. Before the *helepolis* could be pushed against the city walls, Mamersides, the garrison commander asked for terms. After a meeting with Julian, the fortress was surrendered. Only 2,500 prisoners were taken, since the civilian population escaped before the siege started. Within the citadel a large supply of arms and provisions was discovered.[14]

10 May 363 was spent repacking the siege engines, resting the army, and attending the many wounded. At sunrise, the cavalry screen and foragers would have gone into the countryside to search for supplies and enemy patrols. One reconnaissance party, consisting of three cavalry regiments, rode into an ambush set by Surena's cavalry. A large number of Romans were killed, including one tribune, and a regimental standard was captured. The Emperor's bodyguard riding to their rescue saved the remaining Romans. The two surviving tribunes were cashiered and ten soldiers, the first to flee the fight, were executed.[15]

Julian sent word to the soldiers promising them 100 denarii each for their participation in the siege. This caused some grumbling because the gift was so small. To put the gift in perspective, a new pair of military boots cost 100 denarii, a pint of good wine cost thirty denarii, ordinary wine cost eight denarii and beer cost between four and eight denarii.[16] From a soldier's perspective, this award was barely sufficient for one night on the town. Upon hearing the grumbling Julian addressed the assembled troops and berated them for their ingratitude. Through various oratory techniques, he berated them for their greed at the expense of a tottering empire while promising them riches and glory if they stayed on task. This placated the soldiers, and they returned to their work.[17]

The *Praesental* Army marched east on the south side of the canal past the town of Phissenia. The advance was slowed due to the Persians breaching the dams and turning the fields into swamps. On 13 May 363, after plundering abandoned villages and investigating ruins, the Romans established a fortified camp near the fortress of Maiozamalcha. Julian took extra precautions against the Persian cavalry. Their daring and valour in the skirmishes and small battles up to this point in the expedition had caused the Romans to fear and respect their abilities.[18]

Julian, with a small party, conducted a dismounted reconnaissance of Maiozamalcha's defences. While scouting along the city's walls, a squad of Persians noticed Julian's small party. Ten Persians exited a sally port in the walls and attacked Julian's small patrol. In a short, violent skirmish, Julian killed one Persian soldier while his followers killed a second. The surviving Persians were put to flight. After this escapade, the Romans developed a plan to take the city. The Romans threw a bridge across the canal and established a fortified camp with a double palisade. The double palisade was to protect the Roman camp from the Persian cavalry. This passage is not clear, but the double palisade may have been built around the whole city in a method similar to that Caesar used at Alesia. There is no reason to build a double palisade around a Roman camp to defend the Roman camp. A double palisade around the city cuts the city off from the outside while, at the same time, protecting the besieging troops from being attacked by bands of roving enemy cavalry. After completing these defensive arrangements, the Romans began the siege of the city. Despite these defensive arrangements, the animals still needed to be let out of the camp to graze. When the pack animals were herded to a palm grove to graze, Surena's raiders struck. They were driven off by the reaction of cohorts deployed to scout and secure the area.[19]

Maiozamalcha was a major fortress with a double wall and towers that reinforced the natural high cliffs defending the city. Ditches blocked the approaches to the city's walls. The towers of the walls reached the same elevation as the natural rock that formed the citadel. The sloping plateau upon which the rest of the fortress was built sloped down to the canal and was fortified with strong battlements. This natural fortress must have been relatively small since the Roman infantry deployed in a formation three ranks deep and surrounded the city demanding its surrender. Nabdates, the Persian garrison commander, was unimpressed by this martial display and declined the invitation to surrender.[20]

The plan for the siege developed by Julian and his generals called for the Roman infantry to conduct the siege while the cavalry broke down into regiments and detachments to plunder the countryside for supplies and keep the Persian cavalry at bay. Nevitta and Dagalaifus were assigned supervision of digging the mines and construction of mantelets to cover the assaulting infantry. Julian personally supervised the rest of the siege works' construction. Victor was assigned the task of reconnoitring the road to Ctesiphon. While not mentioned by Ammianus, Victor's mission must have been to determine whether there was a Persian relief force marching from the capital to the relief of Maiozamalcha.[21]

The work on the Roman siege works progressed rapidly. Siege mounds were built and the ditches defending the approaches to the fortress walls were filled in. The miners ran their tunnels undetected toward the foundations of the fortress walls. The artillery was assembled and mounted on the siege mounds. When Victor returned from his patrol, he reported that he had ridden to Ctesiphon and found no obstacles or Persian relief force. Based upon Victor's report, the Roman generals were confident that the Persians posed no significant threat to the besieging army.

On the first day of the assault, the armies exchanged missiles with the Romans attempting to clear the fortress walls of defenders to allow their sappers to breach the walls and the Persians attempting to keep the Romans at bay. By midday, the heat forced hostilities to cease. The following morning, the battle continued with Julian supervising the battle within missile range of the walls to encourage his men in their endeavours. He and his generals were aware that they could not afford to expend a lot of time reducing this fortress without upsetting the campaign's timetable. As the armies were about to disengage due to the noonday heat, a Roman ram caused a tower and adjoining walls to collapse. The Romans immediately assaulted the breach and the Persians rushed reinforcements into the breach. The melee in this breach lasted the rest of the day until the Romans disengaged. Shortly after dark, Julian received a report that a mine had reached the foundations of a section of the city wall. With this news, the Romans decided to conduct a night assault to cover the noise of the miners tunnelling under the wall. The city was attacked from two sides to split Persian defenders and make them deploy their reserves. At sunrise, covered by the noise of the fighting, the tunnel was opened and Exsuperius, a soldier from a *numero* (cohort) of the legion *Victores*, charged out of the tunnel followed by his Tribune Magnus, the unit notary Jovianus, and a small band of stalwart legionaries. Silently, they moved into the city killing the watch under the cover of the morning hymns of praise to King Shapur. The assault from within unhinged the Persian defence, and soon the Romans assaulting the breaches broke into the city. The defenders, civilian and military, were put to the sword.[22] Nabdates and eighty followers were captured and their lives spared, but they remained in custody. Each member of the small band from the legion *Victores* was awarded the mural crown (*coronae murals*) for valour.[23] The loot from the city was divided among the army according to estimates of merit and hard service, except that Julian took only a mute boy valued at three gold *aurei*.[24]

Quickly recovering from the siege, the Romans marched on toward the Persian capital. One of Shapur's sons, with a force from Ctesiphon, confronted the advance guard led by Count Victor at a canal crossing but, upon seeing the size of the Roman army, retired without making contact. On approximately 15 May 363, the Romans established a hasty camp within the district of Ctesiphon, south of the Naarmalcha Canal and not far from the Tigris River.

Taking the district of Ctesiphon was a complicated military problem for the Romans, and Ammianus' and Zosimus' accounts fail to provide an analysis of the obstacles that had to be reduced for the Romans to clear the approaches to the capital on the east bank of the Tigris. Ammianus' account describes a series of unconnected small skirmishes where Julian repeatedly demonstrated his heroism in seemly reckless adventures. Yet, when viewed together, they reveal a calculated campaign to secure the site for the assault crossing of the Tigris. The fortress cities of Seleucia, Coche, Ctesiphon, and the walled town of Sabathad were within supporting distance of each other. Since the farthest of these built-up areas was less than 5kms from the

Naarmalcha Canal, all four built-up areas could be viewed as staging areas for raids against Roman forces working along the canal.

The Persian defence was centred around the fortified cities of Coche on the west bank of the Tigris and Ctesiphon on the river's east bank. The two cities had once been one city until the Tigris jumped its bank and split the city in two. In 363, both cities were well defended with walls of burnt brick and deep ditches. These man-made defences augmented the swamps and river to limit the approaches to the cities. The river separating the cities was swift and narrow such that ballista-launching projectiles would enfilade any ship attempting a passage or assault on either city's river walls.[25]

Coche could only be approached from the south along a narrow strip of land running north from the Naarmalcha Canal. The old river channel, which was then a swamp, reduced this approach to a frontage of a few kilometres. The walled town Sabathad, and possibly an additional unnamed fort, defended this narrow strip of land. To capture this region the Romans had to first control the Tigris River south of Ctesiphon and Coche by moving the fifty Roman warships through the Naarmalcha Canal into the river. The canal had been blocked and considerable work was required to open a channel for the fleet to enter the Tigris. The working party opening the canal had to be protected from Persian raiders and, initially, the Romans underestimated Persian determination.

The army rested two days before work was started on digging out the channel. During this rest period, Roman patrols were sent north of the canal to scout the area. Patrols discovered one of the Persian king's game parks that provided entertainment for the troops and food for the commissariat as the game animals in the park were slaughtered. Julian rode the 4.7kms (30 stadia) with a unit of lightly armed skirmishers to Seleucia to explore the ruins. Along a stream that flowed into the Tigris, Julian's patrol found the family of Mamersides, who had surrendered Pirisabora, impaled on stakes.

After the two days of rest, a number of strong reconnaissance patrols were sent north of the dried canal to scout the area and determine the strength of the Persians in the vicinity of Seleucia, Coche, Ctesiphon, Sabathad, and an unnamed fort. An unexpected sally from Sabathad engaged three cohorts of skirmishers as a diversion for Persian raiders to cross the Tigris and butcher the army's pack animals while overwhelming foragers in the vicinity. At the time of the raid Julian, with a small bodyguard, was conducting a reconnaissance of the small fort north of the skirmish at Sabathad. His party, coming too close to the fort's wall, attracted the attention of the Persian garrison. Consequently they were showered with arrows and ballista bolts. Enraged by this event, Julian ordered the fort to be taken. A force moved out of the Roman camp and crossed the dry canal with mantelets and other siege equipment. The night was clear and the moon was bright. The Persians noticed the Roman preparations and sallied out the fort's main gate and fell upon a security cohort, killing a large number, including a tribune who attempted to stabilize the situation. While this fight was unfolding, a second Persian raid crossed the Tigris throwing the Roman camp into disorder.[26]

These skirmishes demonstrated that the Romans needed to control the Tigris River to prevent the Persians from raiding their camp and baggage trains. The underestimation of their enemy enticed the Romans to relax their vigilance and camp procedures. The cohort that disgraced itself during the fighting had its mounted members reduced to infantry service. The camp

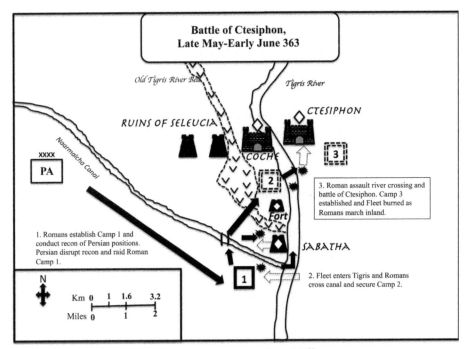

Map 18. The Battle of Ctesiphon, Late May-Early June 363[27]

was rebuilt properly, its weak points were reinforced, and a deep ditch dug around the camp's palisade. Work in the canal was completed and, when the retaining dams were broken, the fleet sailed into the Tigris. During this same period Sabathad was occupied and the offending fort destroyed. On or about 20 May 363, with the approaches to Coche cleared, the Romans threw bridges across the canal and moved their main army toward the fortress. They established a strong camp in an area of orchards, vineyards, and cypress groves just south of Coche.[28]

Ammianus and Zosimus agree that during the fight down the Euphrates the Persian and Saracen cavalry roughly handled the Roman cavalry of the security and reconnaissance screens. During these skirmishes, four Roman cavalry regiments were disgraced and the Roman baggage train was plundered twice. These skirmishes demonstrated that the Roman cavalry was not as effective as Surena's Persians and Emir Podosaces' Saracens. Julian's only successful long-range reconnaissance was Count Victor's patrol that reconnoitred the roads to Ctesiphon. Julian had lost the cavalry reconnaissance battle but, despite that fact, had successfully reached his objective, Ctesiphon, because Surena's raiders were operating out of supporting range of the Royal Army.[29]

Julian had the opportunity to take Ctesiphon in late May 363 by assault but failed to properly plan and support Victor's successful night river crossing of the Tigris. Ammianus, no friend of Victor, placed the blame for the failure squarely on Victor's shoulders. Zosimus provides key details of the critical battle, ignored by Ammianus as it did not enhance the prestige of Julian. Stripped of its artistic rhetoric, the details of the night assault river crossing and battle are impressive.

Julian unloaded fifteen of the largest barges carrying provisions and war engines and divided them into three squadrons. He formed a 'forlorn hope' of 800 armoured men, 80 of which were loaded aboard each barge. The lead squadron of five ships and 270 men was placed under the command of Count Victor. The Persian east bank was high and topped with a fence enclosing the king's garden, defended by Persian infantry and cavalry. To cause the Persians to lower their guard, Festus and Sozomen inform us that Julian called a rest day and held athletic contests and horse races to entertain his army.[30] After nightfall, Julian ordered Victor (over his generals' objections) to seize the eastern bank occupied by the Persians. Victor's five boats were quickly lost from sight in the dark until they were attacked near the eastern bank with fire pots and other incendiaries. Julian, seeing Victor's distress, ordered the remaining ten vessels to reinforce Victor's men. Fighting desperately, the Romans gained the east bank. Despite the strong current, undisciplined Rhineland *auxilia*, afraid they would miss the battle, swam the river using their shields as paddleboards.[31]

A general engagement started at midnight and continued though the next day. The Persians' attempt to drive Victor's beachhead back into the Tigris failed. As day broke the combatants disengaged and reformed. The Persians formed three lines of battle. The first line consisted of heavily armoured Savaran cavalry on leather-barded horses in close order. Infantry supported this line with large shields, also in close order. Elephants formed the Persians' third line. General Pigraxes (supported by Generals Tigranes, Surena, Anareus, and Narses) commanded the Persian army.[32] During the lull in the desperate fighting, Victor was able to organize his units into their traditional battle formation of three battle lines. The unreliable legions and regiments occupied positions in the second line (centre line). The light infantry manoeuvred between the lines as the situation required. After a preliminary skirmish, battle cries, war songs, and trumpets signalled the attack and the Romans quickly closed with the Persian formation. The quick attack negated the Persian archery and the battle developed into a general melee. The Roman generals on the opposite bank supported Victor's hard-pressed legions and cohorts by ferrying reserves off loaded in the beachhead and rushed into the battle. Julian crossed early cheering on the laggards as he ran around the battlefield with a guard of light *auxilia*. After fighting most of the day in extreme heat, the Persians wavered and finally retreated into their city. The Romans pursued the Persians to the gates of Ctesiphon. Taking advantage of the Persian retreat, the Romans attempted to capture a gate and fight their way into the city. Victor, while commanding the pursuing troops, was wounded in the shoulder by an arrow or bolt fired from the walls of the city. Most of the Romans stopped to plunder the Persian dead. Fearing that the few soldiers still with him would follow the routed Persians into the city and be overwhelmed by the mass of enemy, Victor called a halt to the attack. Had Julian reinforced Victor with his light *auxilia*, as he should have, the

Romans would have taken the gate and subsequently the city. Interestingly, Ammianus gives credit for the victory to Julian, not Victor. During the battle, 2,500 Persians were slain to the Roman losses of seventy.[33]

There are significant problems with Ammianus' version of the battle.[34] As events unfolded, this was the key engagement of the war as it was the only opportunity for the Romans to capture their objective: Ctesiphon. The Roman army was between 50,000 and 60,000 men. The garrison of Ctesiphon, with Surenas' cavalry, could not have numbered more than 20,000 men.[35] If the Roman army had been on the east bank of the Tigris in force, the garrison would not have given battle outside the city wall. Ammianus fails to mention the Roman cavalry, but Zosimus reports that Goths participated in the pursuit of the Persians.[36] Only fifteen vessels were unloaded for the river assault, carrying 800 armoured infantry. Germanic and Gallic *auxilia* swam the flooded Tigris using their shields as paddleboards, while the rest of the army passed over the Tigris with the wave of Ammianus' quill to fight the Persians in the morning. Zosimus alludes to the fact that Victor fought with a small division of the army and that Julian did not arrive with the main body over the Tigris until the day after the battle; his guard did not even cross until the second day after the battle.[37]

Ammianus either reported honestly as an eyewitness to the events or glossed over key facts at Victor's expense to enhance Julian's prestige. In either case, he failed to report honestly the time it took to pass soldiers and horses over an unbridged river at night and the difficulty of performing this manoeuvre without special horse transports. In 1066, William the Conquer performed a similarly difficult manoeuvre. As depicted in the Bayeux Tapestry, horses were off-loaded from ships or boats by jumping them over the side of the vessel into shallow water. The Romans would have utilized basically the same process, but they did so while actively engaged in combat, ducking fire pots and arrows. Controlling horses in such an environment explains why there was no cavalry present when the battle resumed at sunrise.

There is no indication that the Romans off-loaded any supplies or equipment other than the fifteen vessels used as assault boats/barges, which only had a maximum lift capacity of 800 men per trip across the Tigris. Unlike the first 800, there is no indication in the sources that additional legions were prepared to embark; neither did the Romans attempt to erect a pontoon bridge across the river that night. The only available means to deploy the follow-on legions across the river was to ferry them or have them swim. As the sun rose the next morning, Victor did not have the full army on his beachhead as Ammianus alleges and Zosimus refutes. During the night, Victor's 'forlorn hope' and the aquatic Germanic and Gallic *auxilia* established the beachhead. The remainder of the army was being ferried across. At best, Victor mustered between 5,000 and 10,000 infantry at sunrise without cavalry support. These numbers are supported by Ammianus as he reported that Julian was guarded by light *auxilia* rather than his mounted armoured bodyguard. The difficulty of loading and unloading horses made it impossible for the heavy armoured cavalry to begin crossing before first light. At sun up, lighter cavalry could have swum the Tigris, and the Goth *federates* referred to by Zosimus may have crossed in this manner.[38] Vegetius records that cavalry swimming rivers built small rafts of reeds to carry their arms and armour. These rafts were towed behind man and beast as they swam the river.[39] Earlier in the campaign, a similar canal crossing by the Roman armoured cavalry turned into a disaster when it was ambushed. This lack of preparation helps explain the Roman generals' objections to Julian's night river assault.

Zosimus reports that Julian supported Victor's hard-pressed legions and cohorts from the west bank of the river with reserves rushed from the ferry point. Ammianus claims that Julian was on the east bank with Victor running to different parts of the battlefield escorted by lightly armed *auxilia*.[40] With Julian's track record of reckless bravery, it is probable that he crossed with the *auxilia* but, apparently, did not take command of the beachhead or battle. By modern standards, ancient battle formations occupied a small area considering the masses of men involved. Ten thousand men in one battle line of six ranks deep in close order occupied a frontage of one Roman mile.[41] A Roman army of 10,000 in three lines would occupy a frontage of 300m or less than a third of a mile. When the Persian army broke at noon, the majority of the Roman Army was still on the west bank. If the majority of Victor's troops had not started to loot the 2,500 Persian dead, Victor could have captured the open gate into Ctesiphon. If Julian had been on the east bank commanding the battle instead of fighting it like a Homeric hero, he would have been less than 500m from Victor and could have reinforced the pursuit with his lightly armed *auxilia,* and captured the city gate. That did not happen. The evidence indicates that Ammianus' eyewitness account was tainted by his bias for Julian and against Victor. An opposed night assault river crossing requires detailed planning and a master's hand to control the operation. The Battle of Ctesiphon illustrates that Julian was a gifted tactician but still a novice at the operational art and someone who ignored the advice of his experienced generals. His failure to adequately prepare the river crossing and have a large force of cavalry to pursue the routed Persians into Ctesiphon was an operational error that cost him the campaign and led to the ultimate Roman strategic defeat. Youthful enthusiasm and audacity could not overcome stark reality. The principles of Sun Tzu surely apply: namely, that a general that is reckless leads his army to destruction.[42]

It took three days for the *Praesental* Army to cross the Tigris and encamp in the vicinity of the village of Abuzatha. Julian and his generals deliberated for five days while considering their options.[43] After the battle outside Ctesiphon, there appears to be a large lacuna at the end of Ammianus' Book XXIV, 7.2. Historian N J E Austin argues that there is a missing section that probably mentions King Arsaces' unreliability as the reason Procopius and Sebastianus failed to affect the link-up at Ctesiphon.[44] Libanius' *Funeral Oration* supports Austin's argument indicating that the 20,000 Armenian soldiers failed to join the Army of Mesopotamia. Austin's position is also supported by the seventh century Armenian historian Moses Kharenatsi. While Moses misidentified the King of Armenia in 363, he did record that the King of Armenia sent a cavalry contingent to join Julian's campaign. Moses specifically described Julian's fatal error in judgment. In accordance with Julian's pagan beliefs, he insisted that the Armenians put his picture or statue in their main church. Saint Yusik, an Armenian holy man, objected and was flogged to death. Upon hearing of the martyrdom of Saint Yusik, General Zawray deserted with the Armenian cavalry and rode home.[45] Support for this account is found in Ammianus where he states that 'There was another evil of no small weight, that the reinforcements which we were expecting to arrive under the command of Arsaces and some of our own generals, did not make their appearance, being detained by the causes already mentioned.'[46] Ammianus' mention of King Arsaces' 'failure to appear' corroborates Moses and places the blame for the failure not on Procopius and Sebastianus but on Julian. Despite the problems with Moses' account, his version rings true. Historically, statues of pagan emperors were placed in local temples of subjected and allied peoples. If Julian attempted to reintroduce this practice, it would explain the Christian Armenians' refusal to join the expedition. The letter Julian sent to King Arsacius before leaving Antioch, reinforces the argument that Julian's pagan views may have derailed the alliance. In the letter Julian praises the virtues of paganism and labels Arsacius '...a rascal and coward...'. It goes on to allege that Arsacius was colluding with the Persians, and Julian would look into that allegation at the conclusion of the campaign.[47] Not exactly the sentiments that would persuade Arsacius to send his loyal Christian Armenian troops to support a pagan emperor.

Libanius does not find Procopius and Sebastianus blameless. According to Libanius, the failure of the Army of Mesopotamia to link-up was due to the 'false play' of the Armenian prince and the quarrelling of the generals that bred cowardice within the Romans. One general was 'gaining victories' while the other recommended 'inaction'.[48] Sebastianus' character and his later actions support the argument that he was fighting and winning victories while the senior, inexperienced General Procopius recommended 'inaction' to please the men.[49]

A problem facing the Army of Mesopotamia, overlooked by historians, was the fact that Rome never recaptured Bezabde. With Count Aelianus dead and his legions destroyed, the Persians had uncontested control of the Trans-Tigris region for almost two years. It is questionable whether the region remained loyal to Rome. With Shapur's main army mustering in the region east of the Tigris, even if the Trans-Tigris princes remained loyal to Rome, it is unlikely they would have dispatched soldiers to join the Romans in Mesopotamia because their lands would have been left undefended. Without the Armenians, the Army of Mesopotamia would have numbered only 20,000 to 30,000 men without stripping the local garrisons of their legions. The Persian garrison of Bezabde and forces from nearby provinces would have been able to hold the fords of the Tigris against the invading Romans even if the river was not in flood.

The Christian historian Socrates informs us that, after the *Praesental* Army reached Ctesiphon, King Shapur sent repeated embassies to Julian offering portions of his kingdom and ending the war if the Romans withdrew from Persian territory. Socrates alleges that Julian rejected these peace overtures based upon non-Christian divinations and correspondence with the philosopher Maximus who deluded the young emperor into believing that he would exceed the accomplishments of Alexander.[50] Ammianus and Zosimus do not mention these peace negotiations but, because of the gaps in Ammianus' account at this point of the narration, these omissions cannot be used to rule out such peace overtures. Libanius does confirm that the negotiations took place.[51] The simple fact that Shapur was in communication with the Romans would indicate that he was within fifty miles of Ctesiphon. Fifty miles is the distance a courier could carry a message from the king and expect a reply within twenty-four hours.

Not all Roman units rested during these five days. After the battle of Ctesiphon, Duke Arintheus was sent with light infantry to lay waste to the rich agricultural land surrounding Ctesiphon and to hunt down the Persians who had been routed during the Battle of Ctesiphon and, failing to enter the city, were hiding in the vicinity. It was during these skirmishes that the myth of the Persian guides leading Julian astray seems to have had its genesis.[52] The local Persian leaders rallied their scattered units within a few days of their defeat outside Ctesiphon and started burning the surrounding area and skirmishing with Arintheus' light infantry and the Roman security screen. The Persian boldness in engaging in long-range archery engagements and their willingness to close into short melees deceived the Romans into thinking that the Royal Army had arrived and was in the vicinity.[53]

Having failed to capture Ctesiphon by 'coup de main', and considering the failure of the Army of Mesopotamia to arrive, the Roman generals met in late May to review their options. The boldness of the local Persian troops and the negotiations with the Persian representative indicated to the Roman leadership that Shapur and his Royal Army were within striking distance. The consensus was that it would be rash and foolish to besiege Ctesiphon as the terrain and weather rendered the city impregnable, and it was believed that Shapur would soon appear with a formidable host.[54]

The character and skill of a general are most tested in the chaos of war rather than during planning conferences. Julian faced a situation similar to that of Julius Caesar at the town of Alsea. Julius Caesar was cut off from his supplies and deep in enemy territory while one enemy army was trapped inside the town and a second army was marching to relieve it. Caesar managed to defeat the relieving army and capture the town. Julian's problem was larger, but similar. The enemy army was expected to materialize at any time. The June temperature was soaring, possibly as high as 120 degrees Fahrenheit, making construction of siege works only possible in the early morning and evening hours. The Persians had flooded the lands the Romans had traversed, cutting off their retreat back up the Euphrates, then in full flood. Instead of blockading Ctesiphon and using it as bait to force Shapur to relieve the city and fight a field battle on Roman terms, Julian and his generals took 'counsel of their fears'. They decided not to besiege or even blockade Ctesiphon while, at the same time, rejecting Shapur's peace overtures. Up to this point, Julian held the initiative forcing Shapur to react to Roman actions. With this decision, Julian handed the initiative to Shapur.

After rejecting the peace overture, on or about 5 June 363, the Roman high command held a second council of war to decide whether to march inland and seek a decisive battle with Shapur, retreat north along the Tigris back to Roman Mesopotamia, or march into the Persian heartland. Despite the later Christian writers' claims that Julian was delusional and attempting to become a new Alexander, in reality, the Romans had to decisively defeat the Royal Army to regain the freedom to manoeuvre away from Ctesiphon, move deeper into Persia, or march north to Roman territory.[55] The position of the Royal Army north of Ctesiphon and on the east bank of the Tigris prevented the *Praesental* Army from retreating up the Tigris or attacking into Persia along the Diyala River. Shapur had reduced the Roman operational options to one: seek a decisive battle on the terrain of the king's choosing.

The Roman fleet was burnt between 11 and 15 June 363, a deliberate decision made by Julian and his generals in preparation for the Romans marching away from Ctesiphon. Ammianus, Libanius, and Zosimus all record that Julian burned his boats, but only Libanius explains that the boats had to be burned regardless of whether Julian retreated or marched inland:[56]

This state of things [the Army of Mesopotamia failing to arrive], however, did not discourage the emperor; he did not approve of their being absent, yet he proceeded as he had planned to do if they had joined him, and extended his views as far as Hyrcania and the rivers of India…The flotilla, according to his original design, had been given for prey to the flames… because the Tigris, swift and strong, running counter to the prows of the boats, forced them to require a vast number of hands [to tow them up the stream]; and it was necessary for those engaged in towing to be more than half the army… the burning of the fleet removed every encouragement to laziness, for whoever wished to do nothing, by feigning sickness, obtained conveyance in a boat… but when there were no vessels, every man was under arms.[57]

As drastic as Julian's decision to burn his supply ships was, it was an accepted tactic recommended by Sun Tzu. Soldiers deep in enemy territory, in desperate straits, lose their sense of fear. 'If there is no place of refuge, they will stand firm. If they are in hostile country, they will show a stubborn front. If there is no help…they will fight hard', wrote Sun Tzu.[58] Theodoret (circa 393–466) the Greek ecclesiastical politician and historian, in his *Ecclesiastical History*, recorded that Julian 'burnt his boats so making his men fight not in willing, but in forced obedience'.[59] It was a dramatic gesture worthy of a new Alexander the Great. But, as only Libanius and Ammianus note, pulling the boats up the Tigris in flood, if possible, would have taken over 20,000 men. Libanius also notes that the fleet entered the Tigris south of Ctesiphon and Coche.[60] To move the fleet upriver, Julian had to take one or both cities, which Julian and his generals decided were impregnable.

Libanius also reports that one reason the Romans did not besiege Ctesiphon was that they were short of rations before the decision to march away from the river.[61] The Roman Army was very low on supplies when the boats were burnt; in fact, they were probably nearly empty. The *Praesental* Army had taken approximately ninety days to arrive and set up camp before the walls of Ctesiphon. The combat troops and cavalry horses alone had consumed 9,495 tons of grain. To veer from the Tigris River and march up the Diyala Valley, the Romans would have had to carry 3,150 tons of grain or pillage 105 tons of grain and 35 tons of fodder per day. With the exception of loading twelve to eighteen boats on wagons for bridging, Julian's supply trains were not reinforced or reorganized. Apparently, Julian's plan was to live off the land and consume the harvest then being collected from the fields. It was common practice for the Roman Army to issue twenty days' rations upon starting a major operation.[62] Issuing this ration in biscuit form (*bucellatum*) reduced its weight and considerably reduced the daily firewood requirement for the army.[63] Despite the fact that Ammianus claims the whole army suffered from lack of supplies, Libanius informs us that Julian issued the army twenty days' rations before the march started. At normal marching rates, this ration issue would have been sufficient to last the soldiers until they reached Roman territory. The cavalry horses and logistics animals would have suffered and died from a daily march rate of twenty miles a day, but the army had sufficient rations to march back to Roman territory. The biscuit ration would have been distributed to the army on or about 15 June 363. On 16 June 363, the Romans struck camp and started to march north toward the Diyala River and the region of Corduena. After crossing the Diyala, Julian turned east toward Barsaphtas and arrived there on 17 June 363, just in time to meet Shapur's Royal Army's vanguard.

Chapter 14

The March Up Country

The battles and skirmishes of late June and early July, 363 demonstrate Shapur's mastery of war. Shapur lead his army with the skill of a chess master, forcing the Romans to react to his moves. He used the land as a natural ally and his knowledge of the terrain and distances to great advantage.[1] He applied lessons learned fighting steppe nomads in the 350s, employing both the direct and indirect methods of attack. He placed particular effort on defeating the Roman reconnaissance effort and security screen. Shapur's tactics were selected to delay the Romans so their deteriorating supply situation would weaken their fighting ability. Even before the Romans departed Ctesiphon on 16 June 363, the Persians began burning the crops and grass along Julian's anticipated route of advance.[2] On 17 June 363, the Romans encountered Shapur's vanguard in a general engagement that turned out to be a draw or, at best, a 'pyrrhic victory' for the Romans.

On the night of 16 June 363, the Romans established a fortified camp in a grassy valley along an unidentified stream. At first light on 17 June 363, the glittering light from the Persian coats of mail confirmed that Shapur's Royal Army had arrived. The stream separated the two armies and skirmishes between opposing outposts and watering parties soon developed. During one of these skirmishes Duke Machameus was mortally wounded after killing four Persians. His brother, Maurus (later duke of Phoenicia) killed the Persian that wounded Machameus. Maurus' skill at arms forced the Persians to withdraw and, while wounded in the shoulder with an arrow, he gained the Roman lines with his dying brother.[3] At midday, the unendurable heat caused the skirmishes to stop as both sides withdrew to their respective camps. The Romans continued their march on 18 June 363. The Persians shadowed the march while Saracens harried the Roman column. The Romans halted for two days at an estate called Hucumbra. The Persians had not destroyed the harvest in this region and the Romans foraged for supplies and then burned what they could not use.

The first major engagement between the Romans and the Royal Army took place around mid-morning on 20 June 363. The Roman Army was fully deployed in march formation when, part-way through the day's march, the Persians attacked the rear guard division. During the swirling combat the *Equitis Tertiaci* disgraced itself in combat while failing to support the infantry. The *Tertiaci* retreated as the rear guard legions were pressing forward taking the spirit out of the Roman counterattack and most likely exposing the infantry's flank. The Roman reserve heavy cavalry arrived in time to save the rear guard infantry. A general engagement then developed with the Persian and Roman cavalry fighting in a confused melee over a large area. The Persian Satrap Adaces was killed, most likely in single combat. The soldier who killed him brought Adaces' armour to Julian who rewarded this Roman champion for his skill and bravery.[4]

For its cowardice, the *Equitis Tertiaci* was reduced to infantry baggage guards. The tribune of the *Equitis Tertiaci*, who had distinguished himself in the battle, was given command of another regiment. The commander of the valorous tribune's new regiment had cowardly fled the battle. Four other tribunes of cavalry regiments were also dismissed for disgraceful conduct. These five disgraced regiments appear to have been the cavalry initially detailed to support the rear guard legions. Their cowardice against their Persian counterparts may have caused the crisis that almost destroyed the rear guard and that was only stabilized when the heavy cavalry reinforcements arrived. This engagement is important because it undermined the confidence of the Roman light and general-purpose cavalry. These regiments were not only responsible for the security screens but also for scouting the route of march and preventing the Persians from burning the fields needed to secure fodder for the Roman animals. The demoralization of the security and scouting cavalry prevented them from effectively scouting the route of advance and detecting ambushes that contained elephants. The Romans advanced approximately six miles (10.9 kms, seventy *stadia*) through fields and grassland still smouldering from Persian scorched earth tactics. When the Romans entered the district of Maranga they established a camp.[5] On the morning of 22 June 363, the Romans discovered that their advance was blocked by elements of the Royal Army.

At the Battle of Maranga, the Persian General Merena commanded the Persian host, assisted by two of Shapur's sons and a large number of other magnates, paladins, and grandees. The Persian army deployed in three battle lines with squadrons of heavily armoured Savaran cavalry armed with kontos in the first line supported by squadrons of armoured horse archers in the second with war elephants in the third. Ammianus notes that the Persians, remembering their experience at the siege of Nisibis, ensured that the elephant mahouts had large knives strapped to their right hands in case their beasts turned in panic thereby disrupting and crushing their own men.[6]

Upon observing the Persian deployment, Julian deployed his army from its camp into a crescent formation, but Ammianus provides no additional details of the *Praesental* Army's deployment. It can be assumed that it fell into the standard Roman battle formation of two or three infantry lines with the cavalry on both flanks. The crescent formation indicates that the Roman battle lines were longer than the Persian lines and that the Romans outnumbered the Persians. Julian and his generals were well aware of the Persian tactic of using arrow storms to wear down their opponents. To counter this tactic, Julian ordered his men to advance rapidly in close order before the Persian archery could take its toll. Without finesse, the Romans and Persians made contact along the entire line. The Persians employed their traditional tactics of the armoured cavalry charging and then falling back covered by the horse archers, which Ammianus and other Romans mistook as the Persian lack of endurance for hand-to-hand combat. The battle lasted until midday when the heat forced the combatants to disengage.[7] The Battle of Maranga was the first and last traditional battle between the *Praesental* Army and the Royal Army. Ammianus claims that the Persians suffered higher casualties than the Romans and that the only Roman of note to die was the Tribune Vetranio who commanded the legion *Zianni*.[8]

Despite this claim of victory, the Romans and Persians agreed to a three-day truce to tend to the wounded. Because the Persians burned the surrounding fields, the Roman animals lacked fodder and the soldiers lacked fresh food. To raise morale, Julian had the delicacies from the tribunes' and generals' personal baggage animals distributed among the common soldiers while he set the example by subsisting on the common soldiers' porridge. On the last night of the truce, a brilliant shooting star was observed, which Ammianus reports the Roman/Etruscan soothsayers took as a bad omen. Between the lack of fresh rations, the three-day truce, and the bad omens, Ammianus was foreshadowing Julian's death the next day.

The fighting between 17 and 25 June 363, with the exception of the Battle of Maranga, were skirmishes that pitted Persian cavalry and elephants, supported by Saracens, against the van and rear guard of the Roman Army, which often marched in square formation. The square formation stretched over four miles from advance to rear-guard. The infantry marched in open order and closed formation when attacked. Julian daily rushed, with his armoured cavalry and bodyguard, from crisis to crisis, exhausting men and horses in the extreme heat. When the rear guard of the square was attacked, it took time to notify the front and sides to halt. Each time the rear guard was attacked a gap formed providing an opening for the enemy to cut off the rear guard and attack the baggage train in the centre of the square. Julian and his heavy armoured cavalry had to rush back and forth along the line of march stabilizing the situation. It would have taken an hour for an infantry formation to rush from the advance guard to the rear guard and about twenty minutes for a cavalry formation. But a fully armoured cavalry unit could only conduct the emergency redeployment a few times before the horses were exhausted.

Due to the Persian scorched earth policy, only a few days after marching away from the Tigris and crossing the Diyala River, the Romans began to suffer from lack of supplies for man and beast. Shapur refused a general engagement, burned the crops and vegetation, and kept up incessant attacks upon the Romans, slowing their rate of advance. During these skirmishes the Roman cavalry was clearly outclassed.[9] This may have been partly due to the exhaustion of the Roman cavalry mounts and the lack of remounts. Unable to dominate the cavalry skirmishes, the Romans had difficultly collecting the forage required for their animals. Underfed, the Roman cavalry mounts would have steadily grown weaker with each passing day. Not only were the cavalry mounts suffering, the draught oxen in particular suffered from lack of forage.[10] Most of the boats were lost as ox teams fell behind. At the time, this loss may have seemed inconsequential, but it doomed the Romans. Oddly,

Ammianus, an experienced staff officer, never discerns the significance of this loss. Shapur's indirect hit-and-run tactics, most likely based upon his experience fighting nomads in the 350s, maximized his army's strength and negated the Roman Army's cavalry.[11]

Traitorous local guides and advisors were traditionally blamed for Roman defeats against Parthia and Persia. Julian joins Crassus as an experienced general who, allegedly, was led to defeat by these dastardly characters.[12] However, Crassus' and Julian's defeats cannot be blamed on misinformation of this type.[13] Crassus was allegedly misled in his 53 BCE campaign (by spies and guides) as he attempted to bring the Parthian Army to battle. Crassus was guided from the Roman-controlled Euphrates River to the Roman garrisoned cities of Carrhae, Ichnae, and Niceporium located along the Balikh River. The scouts were tracking what they believed to be the Parthian main army.[14] Plutarch argued that Abgar of Osrhoene had led Crassus through difficult terrain as an act of treachery. Sheldon correctly responds that the allegation is unsupported by the facts.[15] Plutarch failed to realize that since the campaign occurred in late spring, the rivers and intermittent streams would have been swollen from the mountain snowmelt.[16] The mean high temperature for the Carrhae area (modern Harran) in May and June is between 83 degrees Fahrenheit and 93 degrees Fahrenheit.[17] Abgar guided the Romans along the caravan track in pursuit of either a Parthian scouting force or their main army. The terrain was not difficult for acclimatized legionaries, and Crassus was not ambushed on the west side of the Balikh River in Roman Mesopotamia. A meeting engagement between the Romans and the Parthians occurred east of the river in Parthian Mesopotamia. There was no ambush and the Roman Army was not led astray. Crassus was exactly where he wanted to be: fighting the Parthians near a water supply.

The Persian guides could not have misled Julian either. Without taking Ctesiphon, the fleet had to be burned or it would have fallen into Persian hands when the Romans marched inland. The road to the Persian heartland (i.e. the Silk Road) followed the Diyala River. This road was no mere goat track but the route trade caravans and armies had tramped for hundreds, if not thousands, of years. The Roman Army leaving Ctesiphon could not have missed the road, with or without guides. Some famous ancient misguided historians blame Roman defeats on traitorous guides. Rather than performing a factual analysis of events, these historians report rumours or have ulterior motives to illustrate competent generals suddenly becoming gullible. Conversely, Ammianus employs references to traitorous guides and ill omens as a literary device to explain why the expedition was doomed to fail rather than blame the emperor's lack of military skill.[18] The slow rate of advance of the *Praesental* Army between 16 and 26 June 363, helps explain why later historians believed in the myth that a Persian defector allegedly led Julian astray into a waterless wasteland. If this myth were true, without hundreds of thousands of gallons of water daily, the Romans would have perished within forty-eight hours in the 120 degrees Fahrenheit heat, yet they remained a formidable fighting force during this entire period. That is why it is argued here that the spy myth, if it has any factual basis, belongs to the period between 1 and 5 June, 363, when Duke Arintheus' light infantry was pursuing the Persians in the vicinity of Ctesiphon and not the 16 and

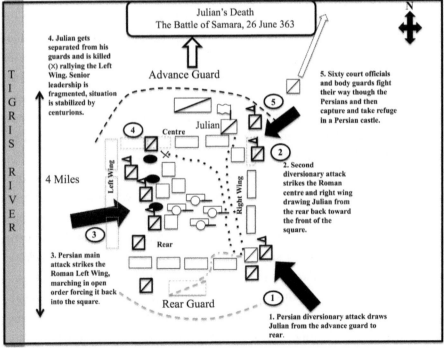

Map 19. Julian's Death, The Battle of Samara, 26 June 363[19]

26 June 363 period, when Julian was attempting to decisively engage the Persian Royal Army.

The Persians were not idle during the three-day truce. Anticipating the Roman route of advance, the Royal Army set a U-shaped ambush for the *Praesental* Army. The King's Royal Cavalry Corps was held in reserve.[20] Plains and steppes appear flat; in reality, they are undulating and crisscrossed with drainage channels and inner-visibility lines deep enough in the twenty-first century to hide companies of 70-ton tanks and, in the fourth century, squads of war elephants and squadrons of armoured cavalry. Ammianus describes the ambush site as surrounded by hills on both sides along the Roman route of advance. The Persians had planned a three-pronged ambush against the square, and the cowed Roman security forces around the square failed to detect thousands of Persians supported by elephants before the trap was sprung.

After the truce, on 26 June 363, the Romans resumed their march north in a square formation that stretched four miles and an unknown distance from the Tigris east bank. The infantry units marched in open order; the morning was so sweltering that the emperor had taken off his armour. Julian rode forward with his bodyguard to reconnoitre when he received word that the rear guard was under attack.[21] While en route, he discovered Persian elephant and cavalry units had attacked the centre and left wing. The left wing was overwhelmed and routed. With cavalry and elephants pouring into the centre of the square, Julian rushed to the breach and into the front lines to rally his light infantry and lead a counterattack against the elephants. The light infantry charged into the elephant formation hacking at the legs of the lumbering beasts forcing the elephants to retire. Julian, raising his arms and shouting, tried to rally the legionaries to pursue the withdrawing Persians. In the confusion and dust, Julian became separated from his *candidati* (bodyguards). A Persian cavalryman or possibly a Lakhmid Saracen, attacked Julian and, with a spear thrust, mortally wounded him knocking him from his horse. Julian was rushed from the battlefield as the battle raged on. Despite the heat and dust, the wounding of Julian enraged the Roman troops who rallied and re-engaged the Persians. On the Roman side, it became an uncoordinated soldiers' melee with centurions and tribunes leading their men from the front. Magisters and counts became little more than centurions as they physically fought with their bodyguards to re-establish the square's parameter. In the dust and confusion, one such group from the right wing under the *Magister Officiorum* Anatolius, Prefect Salutius, *Consiloaro* Phosphorius, and sixty other court officials found themselves outside the square and isolated from the Roman main body. These men stormed the small fortress of Sumara to seek a defensible position. Anatolius and Phosphorius were lost in the storming or in the vicinity of the fort. The Persians pressed their attack on the Roman main body with their elephants and the combatants only disengaged at dusk.[22] Ammianus does not name this battle but later historians refer to it as the Battle of Samara. Both sides sustained heavy casualties. Persian loses included the Generals Merena and Nohodares, fifty paladins, satraps and grandees, along with a large number of common soldiers. The Roman casualties were also heavy and included the Emperor, who expired from his wounds in the middle of the night.[23]

With Julian's death during the early morning of 27 June 363, Julian's army was left leaderless, out of supplies, and surrounded. For the rest of 27 and 28 June 363, the Romans took care of their wounded while the army's leaders deliberated. During this lull, the Persians were swarming about the Romans and a new emperor was desperately needed. Representatives of the western and eastern divisions of the army could not agree on a successor and, as a result, Jovian, a nonentity, was selected emperor.[24]

This meeting must have taken place in the early morning hours. At sun up on 29 June 363, Persian cavalry and elephants attacked the Romans as they marched out of their camp near the fort of Sumere. The Battle of the Elephants was a significant event as recorded by Ammianus and could have led to the defeat and total destruction of the Roman Army. The fact that Ammianus provided details of the elephant attack indicates that he may have been present with the Joviani and Herculiani Legions during the fight.

The standard bearer of the legion Joviani, was an enemy of the new Emperor Jovian. With Jovian's elevation to emperor, this soldier deserted to the Persians and reported the situation in the Roman camp to Shapur. Upon hearing this information, Shapur added his Royal Cavalry Corps to the next attack upon the Roman rear guard. On the morning of 29 June 363, after sacrifices, the Roman Army marched out of the camp to continue its march up the Tigris. Rather than waiting for the Romans to

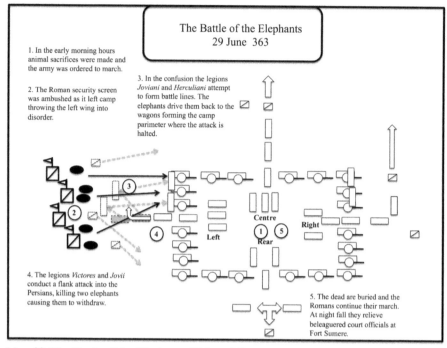

Map 20. The Battle of the Elephants, 29 June 363.

deploy, the Persian general attacked as the square was being formed. The Roman left wing included the traitor's legion, *Joviani*, and its sister legion Herculiani, which were marching out of the camp when the attack struck home. The attacking elephants threw the Roman's left wing cavalry and infantry into disorder, but the steadfastness of the legions *Joviani* and *Herculiani* prevented disaster. These two legions were pushed back to a rise (possibly the camp wall) where Roman logistics wagons were located. Availing themselves of the high ground and wagons, the legionaries threw darts from above wounding the elephants and fought the Savaran cavalry to a standstill. The legions *Jovii* and *Victores* reinforced the legionaries holding the elephants at bay and, together, routed the elephants into the Persian cavalry. In the desperate fighting, a number of elephants were killed along with the legionary Tribunes Julianus, Maximianus, and Macrobius.[25] Later in the day, the advancing Roman army rescued the soldiers and court officials taking refuge in the fortress of Sumara.[26] That night, the Romans stopped in a wooded area and built a traditional camp. After dark, the

Persian cavalry broke through the praetorian gate and almost fought their way to the emperor's tent.[27]

On 1 July 363, the heavy Roman cavalry, with their horses exhausted and riders walking, fell behind the army and were surrounded by Saracens. The Saracens were driven off by Roman light cavalry.[28] On the night of 1 July 363, the Romans camped near the town of Dara. Constant Persian attacks pinned the Romans at Dara for four days.[29] Persian successes at the Battle of the Elephants, the night raid on the camp, and the surrounding of the Roman heavy cavalry demonstrate that, not only had the Romans lost the initiative to the Persians, they had lost the security and reconnaissance fight as well.

As a result of these setbacks, the Romans decided to escape across to the Tigris' west bank. On or about the night of 5 July 363,500 Germanic and Gallic *auxilia* swam the flooded Tigris, killed the Persian guards, and established a beachhead on the west bank. Due to the earlier loss of the boats, Roman engineers attempted and failed to build a bridge of inflated animal skins. While Ammianus notes that the army was starving, the soldiers should have had about five days' rations remaining. Sun Tzu states that a soldier fights because he has no choice but to fight or die. A soldier quits fighting because he can quit and live instead of fighting and dying.[30] Clearly, Shapur understood this principle because he offered terms to end the war that would both save the Roman Army and achieve his war objectives. To save the army, Jovian had no choice but to agree to Shapur's peace terms. These terms were surprisingly lenient under the circumstances.

Blockley summarizes the new treaty in four main points: first, the Persians acquired the Roman Trans-Tigris regions of Arzanene, Moxoene, Zabdicene, and Corduene, together with fifteen forts on both sides of the Tigris; second, the Persians acquired Nisibis, Singara, and Castra Maurorum; third, the Romans were permitted to withdraw the Roman garrisons from the region and civilian populations of Nisibis and Singara. While Ammianus claims that Shapur insisted, as he had done in the letter to Constantius, that he wanted all the lands ceded in the treaty of 298, the list of principalities acquired in 363 does not match those lost in 298. Ingilene and Sophene would remain under Roman control. This division recognized the strategic and cultural orientation of the region and created a stable and defensible settlement for both sides.[31] Shapur proved that not only was he a superior military strategist and operational artist but also a superior diplomat. As Tom Holland observed, after Julian's defeat and death in 363, Roman leadership was forced to accept that Persia could not be defeated by short-term application of the combined resources of the united empire. Eventually Rome would agree to pay a yearly subsidy. It was simpler to purchase coexistence. These subsidies over the next 150 years funded the Persian fortifications on their northern frontier.[32]

Chapter 15

Conclusion

The loss of the Trans-Tigris region humiliated Rome, but the loss of Nisibis breached and seriously weakened its eastern defences. As a result, the *limites* moved west from the Tigris to the Khabur River. The new *limites* were anchored in the south by the fortress city of Circesium (garrisoned by IV Parthia and closely supported at *Apedna* by III Parthia) located near the confluence of the Khabur and Euphrates Rivers, and in the north by the fortress of Constantina (garrisoned by I Parthia). This breach in the empire's defence would not be repaired until construction of the fortress of Dura during the sixth century. This readjustment of the *limites* begs the question of why Jovian honoured a treaty he entered into under duress. The accepted explanation is that Jovian felt duty-bound to do so under the rules of chivalry and honour because Jovian… 'was an honourable man'. If correct, it would be the first and only time in history that an emperor complied with a treaty that was not in his self-interest. Evidence suggests that, contrary to the accepted explanation, Jovian acted from self-interest.

After the treaty was concluded, Jovian led the survivors of Julian's expedition back to Roman Mesopotamia. He dispatched Tribune Mauricius to Nisibis requesting provisions from Duke Cassianus. Other messengers were sent to family, friends, and select officials to gather support of his unexpected rise to the throne. After a six-day forced march, the Romans crossed the desert and reached pasturelands. Duke Cassianus met Jovian's army at Fort Ur with provisions. At Fort Ur the Tribune Memoridus and the Secretary Procopius were dispatched to Illyricum and Gaul to announce Julian's death and the elevation of Jovian to emperor. They were instructed to visit Jovian's father-in-law, Lucillianus, who had retired from military service, at Sirmium. The messengers carried a commission appointing Lucillianus as *Magister Equitum et Peditum*.[1] He was instructed to hasten to Milan and assume the duties of Jovian's representative in the West. In a secret dispatch, Jovian encouraged his father-in-law to bring with him picked men of tried energy and fidelity to assist him in establishing Jovian's administration in the West. Jovian sent a messenger to Malarichus, who was in Italy, with the commission appointing him *magister militum* in Gaul, with the objective of removing a *magister* of merit, who was considered a potential challenger. Messengers were dispatched to spread the news that the Persian campaign had been honourably concluded and that Jovian had been elevated. Messengers were tasked to secretly assess the dukes and governors for potential loyalty and support. The news of the treaty and loss of Nisibis travelled faster than the couriers, and the citizens of Nisibis prayed Jovian would reconsider relinquishing Roman control of their city. Their prayers fell on deaf ears. Supplies provided to the *Praesental* Army at Fort Ur did not last long. As the army marched toward Nisibis it consumed its remaining animals and abandoned its baggage and weapons.

When the *Praesental* Army reached the town of Thilsaphata it linked up with Sebastian, Procopius, their command staff, and the legionary tribunes of the Army of Mesopotamia. Jovian received them kindly and they accompanied the *Praesental* Army on its march to Nisibis. While not mentioned by Ammianus, a series of meetings between the senior leadership of both armies must have occurred. During these meetings, Jovian would have secured the loyalty of the military leadership of the field armies. Securing the support of the military would have been critical to the establishment of Jovian's legitimacy as emperor. In its weakened state, the *Praesental* Army was no match for the Army of Mesopotamia had Sebastian and Procopius contested the election of the new emperor. Jovian lacked connections with the House of Constantine, while the leadership of both armies owed their positions and fortunes to Constantine heirs. The only listed descendant of Constantine present during these meetings was Count Procopius, joint commander of the Army of Mesopotamia. It was rumoured that Julian had selected Procopius as his successor and had even given him an Imperial robe. The failure of Procopius and the Army of Mesopotamia to link up with the *Praesental* Army in Persia had prevented Procopius from pressing his claim to the throne and his default resulted in the selection of Jovian to replace Julian. Procopius probably met with Jovian early during this multi-day conference and surrendered the Imperial robe. Procopius remained with the army until after Julian's funeral and then unceremoniously left the army. Jovian allowed him to return to his family estates in the vicinity of Caesarea in Cappadocia. By allowing Procopius to peaceably depart Jovian succeeded in neutralizing the first challenge to his throne without reverting to bloodshed.

Jovian's next challenge was to gain support from the *magisters*, counts, and dukes and convince them to surrender the bastions of Rome's eastern defence: Nisibis and Castra Maurorum and the forts on both sides of the Tigris River. Jovian had entered into the treaty to save the *Praesental* Army, but the military situation in Roman Mesopotamia had changed. Nisibis' defences were strong, adequately provisioned, and the region was garrisoned by over 40,000 fresh soldiers (*comitatenses* and *limitaneus*). Jovian's *Praesental* Army had suffered heavy casualties (possibly as high as fifty per cent), and the Persian Royal Army had also sustained heavy losses. The Persians were unable to proceed with an offensive campaign against Nisibis until the next campaign season. Jovian had the combat power to negate the treaty (entered into under duress) and successfully defend the Roman East, but he chose to honour the treaty. Jovian was not motivated by honour and chivalry to enforce the Treaty of 363.[2] Simple self-interest and greed motivated him.[3]

Jovian's primary objective was to secure the throne, not protect the empire's people or its borders. He had to close down the Persian War to focus on securing his throne. His first act as emperor was to send out messengers to family, friends, and prospective supporters to help him secure the civil bureaucracy. With the massed military might of the whole empire, Jovian had to convince the *magisters*, counts, and dukes to support him. Convincing the battle-hardened professional soldiers of the *Praesental* Army may have been as simple as ratifying their current positions and promising large donatives to the rank and file. Most had no real property interest in the region. For the leadership of the Army of Mesopotamia, who owned estates in the lands to be surrendered, it may have required the promise of replacing those confiscated estates. But, no matter the details, by the time the *Praesental* Army reached Nisibis, the leadership of the *Praesental* Army and Army of Mesopotamia were nominally behind the new emperor. Upon arriving at Nisibis, Jovian refused to enter the city because of the terms of the treaty. He camped the army on the plains surrounding the city.

The next day Bineses, the Persian grandee, hastening to execute his king's commission, demanded Jovian's immediate performance of the treaty obligation. With Jovian's permission, Bineses entered the city and raised the Persian standard over the citadel. This act notified the citizens of the city that their worst fears were true and they would be forced to emigrate from the city. While in camp, Jovian received delegations from the city's leading citizens attempting to persuade him to negate the treaty. They reminded the new emperor that Nisibis had held out three times against Shapur's best efforts. The leading citizens would have pointed out that the city's defences and garrison were strong, the storehouses well stocked, and that the Persians had failed to take the city on three different occasions. When all of the legitimate arguments were exhausted and failed to persuade Jovian, Count Sabinus (aka Silvanus), a magistrate of the city, then requested permission to defend the city as an independent city. In anger, Jovian rebuffed the count's entreaties and ordered the magistrates and the rest of the population to leave the city within three days. Officials were appointed to oversee the evacuation. Every road toward Roman territory was soon crowded with refugees. When the population had evacuated, the Tribune Constantius delivered the city to the Persian nobles present.[4] Jovian, escorted by the Imperial Guard, rode to Antioch. He did not stop in any city or village because the inhabitants of these settlements had become unruly due to grief, fear, and the loss of their homes. In some villages, the official ordering the evacuation was stoned.

The remains of the *Praesental* Army escorted Julian's body into the Province of Cilicia where it was entombed at Tarus. Julian's epitaph was inscribed: '[H]ere rests in peace, [retired] from Tigris wave, Julian the wise, the virtuous, and the brave.'[5] The Persian occupation force was hot on the heels of the withdrawing *Praesental* Army. They first took control of the outlying fortresses and villages before the population could evacuate and, as a result, some of the Roman civilians were mistreated. The majority of the Nisibines repopulated Amida, while the remainder dispersed to other settlements in the region.

Upon reaching Antioch, Jovian continued to focus his efforts to consolidate his hold on the throne. In August or September 363, he reinstated Christianity, began replacing Julian's pagan administrators with Christians, and enforced new anti-pagan policies.[6] One of his early actions was to reinstate Count Valentinian (future emperor) who had been dismissed by Julian from his command of the legions *Herculiani* and *Joviani* for failure to participate in pagan rights.[7] Valentinian joined Jovian's father-in-law's party to secure the West for the new emperor. Lucillianus, Valentinian, and Secretary Procopius ran into opposition when they attempted to perform their duties at the key Imperial supply depot and court city Sirmium.[8] Lucillianus informed units of the Army of Pannonia of the death of Julian and the elevation of Jovian. Upon hearing the sad news, the men of the *Auxilium Bavarian* rushed Lucillianus and killed him.[9] Valentinian just managed to escape with his life …or did he? In hindsight, the limited facts available point to a conspiracy within the military and civil bureaucracy to prevent Lucillianus from enforcing Jovian's change of administration. It was rumoured that a low ranking tax collector in Sirmium spread the rumour that Julian was alive and Jovian was a usurper.[10] The murder of Lucillianus was not the first indication that Jovian was not popular with the western rank and file. It should be remembered that the standard bearer of the legion *Joviani*, a western legion, was an enemy of the new emperor and deserted to the Persians prior to the Battle of the Elephants.

Valentinian's father had been a count in the West, had been a leading citizen, and owned estates northwest of Sirmium. During Valentinian's military career he had commanded a cavalry regiment in Gaul and most likely had maintained his father's connections with the civil and military leadership in the West. After Jovian's death, he would rule the western half of the empire. It is significant that, while being a Christian, after becoming emperor, his policy toward pagans was extremely liberal proscribing only certain sacrifices and banning magic.[11]

Undoubtedly, Julian's *magister militum* of Gaul had no interest in being replaced or in supporting an emperor who was going to oust him from his command. Julian's pagan civil administrators would not have had cause to celebrate the elevation of a new conservative Christian emperor who would replace them. Valentinian's escape from death at the hands of the *Auxilium Bavarian* does not seem so lucky when these facts are revealed. Lucillianus' death demonstrates that there was an undercurrent of opposition within the bureaucracy and army to Jovian's attempts to consolidate his hold on the throne. Valentinian's survival and later elevation to emperor raises the possibility that he was a member of the plot to displace Jovian. With Lucillianus' death, there is no record of a second mission to the West to establish Jovian's administration.

When Jovian proceeded from Antioch toward Constantinople, in February 364 he suddenly fell ill at Dadostana in Bithynia and died after a reign of only eight months. His attempt to consolidate his rule failed. It has not been established whether he was assassinated or died of natural causes. Jovian was a conservative Christian and during his limited reign he started reversing Julian's pagan policies. A few months later the new Emperor Valentinian, a liberal Christian, was struck ill, while a general malady was not reported within the massed recovering *Praesental* Army. Valentinian suspected his sickness was an assassination attempt caused by some charm or poison administered by some of Julian's friends, but his recovery seems to have placated these fears.

When viewed from the eyes of an emperor, not a statesman, the Treaty of 363 was the correct strategy. Jovian's primary threat was not the Persians but the Roman military and civil establishment. If Jovian wanted to survive he had to make peace with Persia and focus all of his resources on gaining control of the Roman civil and military establishment. While his decision was correct, he did not have the support to hold the throne and his regime was terminated before it really started.

An analysis of the reign of King Shapur indicates that he was one of the great captains of Late Antiquity and a great statesman of his era. As a young monarch, he focused the military might of Persia on defeating the Saracen tribes raiding the Tigris-Euphrates Valley and absorbing the Arab coastal kingdoms. As a result, Persia gained control of the two major trade routes between Rome and the East. With the Arab challenge resolved, Shapur focused on Rome and the humiliating Treaty of 298. The Nisibis War began in 337 when Shapur was about twenty-seven years of age. Over twenty-five years of war, Shapur developed from a general who utilized conventional, simple direct attacks (ignoring terrain and weather) into a skilled master of the indirect approach. He employed diplomacy as effectively as the sword to separate the Trans-Tigris regions and Albania from the Roman sphere of influence. His campaigns of 359 to 361 are textbook examples of the advantages to be gained by utilizing all the tools of the kingdom (military, diplomatic, and economic) to achieve his goals. During the 363 Campaign, Shapur knew his enemy's capabilities and weakness and understood his countrymen and their capabilities. He considered time, distance, weather, and terrain, and he factored these elements into his campaign to defeat Julian. He capitalized on Roman mistakes that alienated the Armenians and some of the Saracen tribes, as well. Yet, Shapur's greatest achievement was that of peacemaker. The Treaty of 363 recognized the strategic and cultural orientation of the region and created a stable and defensible settlement for both sides that lasted almost two centuries.[12]

The Emperor Constantius initially assumed the strategic defence because he only controlled one-third of Rome's resources. The pagan and Christian elite no longer served in the Roman military. It is, therefore, not surprising that Constantius' military policy, with regard to the defence of the empire, was held in contempt and misunderstood by the elite. The elite, educated on Caesar's *War Commentaries* and Polybius, and Levy's account of the Punic Wars, expected the empire to be expanded or defended by direct legionary attrition warfare. They failed to understand the shift of eastern frontier defensive policy by Constantius because of limited resources. The Roman Imperial defence strategy established during the Nisibis War developed into an indirect Byzantine policy of strategic defence and subsidies to 'pay off' opponents.

Rome's strategic defence during the Nisibis War had a significant influence on the development of the Eastern Roman Army when compared to the Western Roman Army. Policing the *limes* in the East required cavalry because of the extended distances and mounted opponents. As a result, there was a higher ratio of cavalry to infantry units in the ducats of the East. Without the ability to recruit Germanic *auxilia* units, the *limitanei* armies relied on locally recruited legions and units, including organic archers and light infantry. While considered second-class by the Roman pay system, these eastern infantry units were specialized in the use of artillery and defending fortresses and cities. They were also fully capable of fighting Persians in open battle. The poor performance of both eastern and western cavalry against the Persians during the Nisibis War led to a gradual improvement of eastern Roman cavalry by the subsequent recruitment of soldiers from Goths, Huns, Saracens and other horse tribes. This innovation resulted in the development of a new Roman cavalry tradition within the military colonies of veterans within the Eastern Empire. During the next series of Roman-Persian wars in the sixth century, cavalry became the decisive arm of the Roman Army despite the fact that the ratio of cavalry to infantry did not increase from the fourth century.[13] The *limitanei* legions and cavalry of the sixth century were fully capable of marching out and defeating raiders and were important to Justinian I's offensive to reclaim Africa.

Constantius' critics failed to comprehend the resources required to decisively defeat Persia and underestimated the abilities of Shapur. Julian's 363 offensive was similar to Constantine's in 337, including the ultimate goal of replacing Shapur with a client prince. Julian massed between 85,000 and 95,000 men for the invasion, supported by three *limitanei* armies (totalling between 18,000 and 27,000 men), to hold his fortified cities. Militarily, he had sufficient combat power to accomplish his objectives. However, his logistical, intelligence, and diplomatic efforts failed to meet his requirements. Diplomatically, Julian failed to gain and maintain the support of Armenia and a number of the Saracen tribes. The failure in Armenia (due to Julian's religious policies and/or Shapur's diplomatic efforts) denied the Army of Mesopotamia 20,000 Armenian soldiers and resulted in the failure of the Army of Mesopotamia to fight their way to Ctesiphon. The inability to bind all of the Saracen tribes to the Roman cause resulted in the reinforcement of Surena's Persian frontier covering force with desert raiders. These diplomatic failures unhinged Julian's campaign plan, and he was not skilled enough to adapt to the new situation.

Julian's intelligence operations failed to provide him with critical information. 'Foreknowledge' can only be obtained from people with accurate intelligence of the situation.[14] The dukes of the East could not provide Julian with the location of the main Persian army or determine whether it wintered in the Tigris-Euphrates Valley or disbanded and returned home to the Zagros Mountains. Julian also lacked basic information regarding the fortifications and size of Ctesiphon.[15] At the tactical level, the Persian and Saracen cavalry out-classed Julian's cavalry. The problems commenced as the Roman Army marched into Persia and steadily worsened as they advanced. Roman scouts failed to provide intelligence needed to defeat the Persian covering force. As the Romans advanced, the situation became so critical that Roman scouts could not even report the presence of elephants in ambush until they attacked. Roman cavalry could not protect fields from Persian fires. These intelligence failures left Julian's army blind, capable of only reacting to Shapur's attacks.

Julian's logistical system was insufficient to supply his army in the heart of enemy territory. He had the resources of the entire empire at his disposal, but could not deploy supplies forward in sufficient quantity. Instead of spending his first year establishing a forward supply base 100 miles south at Circesium on the Euphrates and retaking Bezabde, he attempted to feed his army on the Persian harvest. As the Persian cavalry burned the fields and grasslands, his army starved. Julian had the resources to succeed had he taken the time to develop the logistical infrastructure for the theatre of operation. Rather, he rashly attempted to achieve all his objectives in one campaign season and failed to develop his diplomatic, intelligence, and logistical foundations.

The long-term impact of Julian's defeat and the Nisibis War was 150 years of relative peace. Due to King Shapur's diplomatic skills in dictating the peace terms, the Treaty of 363 wisely recognized the strategic and cultural orientation of the region and created a stable and defensible settlement for both sides.[16] Rome was forced to acknowledge that Persia was a peer. Rome and Persia fenced diplomatically and militarily over Armenia until it was partitioned by the two powers in the 380s.[17] Julian's campaign during the Nisibis War was Rome's last opportunity to decisively defeat Persia as Rome afterward lacked the necessary resources.

Appendix I

Glossary

Ala (pl. alae). Roman cavalry regiments dating from the early and mid-empire. Alae surviving into the fourth century were assigned to the *limitanei.*

Aurei. A Roman gold coin of the fourth century valued at twenty-five silver denarii.

Auxilia Cohors. Roman Auxiliary cohorts were battalions raised from non-citizens during the early to mid-empire. Auxiliary cohorts surviving into the fourth century were assigned to the *limitanei.*

Auxilia or Auxilium. Infantry regiments initially organized and raised during the fourth century from tribal warriors lead by their war chiefs. They evolved into regular Roman army units with a Roman command structure.

Antique Legion. In the early and mid-empire an infantry division of five to six thousand men divided into ten cohorts of six centuries. During the late third and early fourth century reorganization cohorts were detached to form small *comitatenses* legions while the remaining two to four cohorts would become downgraded to a *limitaneus* legion.

Bacaudae. Rural bandits.

Ballista (pl. ballistae). Roman bolt throwing torsion artillery.

Ballistarii. Artilleryman. The soldiers of the legion of *Ballistarii* may have been siege artillerists but they also operated as light infantry, armed with an *archballista* or *manuballista* (crossbow).

Barritus. German war song or chant used by Germanic units in the Roman Army.

Bucellatum. Army biscuits.

Caltrop. A four point spike designed so that when thrown on the ground one spike always points up. A horse or elephant that steps on one becomes disabled.

Candidatus (pl. candidati). Hand-chosen personal bodyguard of the emperor.

Caput-contubernii. Squad leader of a contubernium that probably had the pay grade of *semissalis* allowing him to draw more rations.

Cataphractus (pl. *cataphractarii*). Heavily armoured cavalryman riding a barded horse armed with a cavalry pike (*kontos*).

Century (*centuria*). A 'century' was the infantry company of the Roman Army and numbered approximately eighty men divided into ten squads (*contubernium*) of eight.

Centurion. Commander of a century of infantry.

Clibanarius (pl. Clibanarii). Heavily armoured cavalryman riding a barded horse armed with a *kontos* and bow. The term derives from *clibanarii* meaning 'bake oven'. The difference between a *cataphractarii* and *clibanarii* remains unclear.

Comes rei militaris. Literarily meaning military companion. *Comes* is translated as count. In the Roman Army of the fourth century a military count equated to a modern brigadier to lieutenant general. They were often given command of independent brigades or key cities. They were left in charge of whole regions when the emperor or a *magister* was not present.

Comitatensis (pl. Comitatenses). A Roman field army consisting of both cavalry and infantry of all types.

Comitatus. (1) From *comes* literally 'escort', applied to the entourage of the emperor. (2) Field army in the fourth century.

Contubernium (pl. contubernia). Tent party, usually of six to ten men, that share a tent on campaign or room in a fortress. An infantry century contained ten *contubernia*.

Coronae Murals (Mural Crown). Award for Roman soldiers that were first to force their way into a besieged city.

Comites. Elite cavalry units.

Ducatus. The region commanded by a duke.

Dux (pl. *duces*) In English duke. The term means commander. Generally refers to a commanding general of a *limitanei* army and *ducatus*.

Decurio. Commander of a cavalry *turma* or troop.

Decurions. Members of a city council.

Denarii. A Roman silver coin. According to Diocletian's Edict on Maximum prices it cost 100 denarii for a new pair of military boots without hobnails;

two denarii for a pint of beer; thirty denarii for a pint of high quality wine; and 100 denarii for an army *modius* of wheat.

Draco. Dragon standard.

Draconarius. Standard bearer of the *draco*.

Eques (pl. *Equites*). Cavalry regiment of the fourth century.

*Eques Sagittarius (*pl. *equites sagittarii).* Roman horse archers.

Exploratores. Scouts.

Fabricae. Imperial weapons factory.

Federates or *Foederati.* Allied barbarian soldiers under the leadership of their own chiefs. During the fourth century they could be German, Goth or Arab.

Gentiles. Non-Romans.

Helepolis. 'Taker of Cities.' Massive siege tower on wheels. Ammianus provides a brief description but fails to mention most of the details. Classical examples approximately 41.1m (130ft) high and 20.6m (65ft) wide and had a number of internal levels. A heavy battering ram occupied the lowest level while archers and torsion artillery occupied the higher levels that allowed the attackers to shoot down on the defenders and clear the fortress walls.

Kontos or *contos.* Cavalry pike approximately 3.6m or 12ft long and required two hands to fight with in combat.

Laeti. Small Germanic tribes settled in small groups on Roman territory in exchange for military service. They provided some *auxilia* and guard units.

Limes. (pl. Limites). Frontier.

Limes Arabicus. Roman eastern border incorporating the Syrian Desert and running south to modern Arabia. It included the *Strata Diocletian*.

Limitaneus (pl. Limitanei). Roman border troops.

Magister equitum. Master of cavalry. In modern terms a junior field marshal.

Magister militum. Master of soldiers.

Magister officiorum. Master of Offices. The senior civil/administrative official of the emperor's court.

Magister peditum. Master of infantry. In modern terms a senior field marshal.

Mithras. One of the eastern religions followed by members of the Roman Army during the second to fourth centuries. The cult of Mithras was thought to have evolved from the Persian god of light and wisdom.

Modius. A dry measure of 8.73 litres. One *modius* is the wheat rations for an eight man unit (*contubernium*) for one day. It roughly weighed 24lbs.

Optio. Second in command of a Roman century.

Protectores domestici. A guard regiment part staff and cadet corps, which functioned to train future legion and higher commanders for the Late Roman Army. Amminaus was a member of this regiment at least up to 363.

Plumbata (pl. plumbatae). A lead weighted dart carried by some legionaries. They were approximately 18ins long (0.5m) and three to five were clipped to the inside of a legionary's shield. Thrown before combat their ranges was approximately 90ft or 30m.

Primus Pilus. Senior centurion of a legion.

Naarmalcha Canal. Connected the Euphrates and Tigris Rivers in the vicinity of Ctesiphon.

Numero/Numerus. General term for military units and as used by Ammianius could refer to a century, maniple, cohort or regiment. Normally used for sub-unit of a legion or regiment.

Palantini. Highest paid and most elite category of the field army. The term came into general use after 364.

Praesental Army. The army 'in the presence' of the emperor.

Promoti. Former legionary cavalry formed into independent regiments.

Pseudocomitatenses. Legions and regiments transferred from the *limitanei* to serve with the *comitatenses*.

Savaran. Persian noble cavalryman. This corps included knightly horsemen that were adept at fighting in close order as *clibanarii* or as skirmishing horse archers.

Spatha. Standard 3ft long cavalry and infantry sword.

Surena. An official second only to the Persian and Parthian King of Kings. During the Nisibis War, the unidentified grandee and general headed the second most powerful family of the seven noble houses in the Persian kingdom.

Tirones. Recruit.

Tribunus (pl. tribune). Tribune. Legion or regimental commander.

Turma. A troop of cavalry containing approximately thirty-two men and commanded by a *decurio*. In a *promote* unit the *turma* could have been commanded by a centurion.

Vexillarius. The bearer of a *vexillum* standard.

Vexillation. A detachment of soldiers.

Vexillationes. Fourth century Roman cavalry unit containing approximately 500.

Vellillum. The standard of a *Vexillation* or *Vexillationes.* The standard consisted of a square red or purple tasselled flag which was hung from a cross bar of a lance.

Appendix II

Eastern Armies of the *Notitia Dignitatum*

A detailed study of the Eastern *Limitanei* Armies can be found in Dodgeon and Lieu, Appendix 5, 340–348, 397–400. Dodgeon's and Lieu's study focused on where the various *limitanei* units were stationed. Using this study with the *Barrington Atlas*, the Roman defensive templates within this book were created.

The Gothic incursions and defeat of the Roman Army at Adrianople had little impact on the infantry and cavalry units of the East. Unlike the Danube and Rhine *Limes*, after the Treaty of 363, no eastern *limitanei* units were destroyed. On the Rhine and Danube *Limesmilites* (infantry) and *cuneus* (cavalry) units were created to replace the destroyed units by the various barbarian incursions. The Eastern *Limitanei* Armies contained no *milites* or *cuneus* units raising the inference that that new units were needed to maintain the eastern defence after Adrianople. Due to the manpower shortages caused by these events the eastern *limitanei* legions and regiments may have been tapped for soldiers and or recruits.

1. Limitanei Armies of the East

Limitaneus Army of Mesopotamia

Limitanei Units	Station
1. *Legio primae Parthicae Nisibenae*	Constantina
2. *Legio Secundae Parthicae*	Cefa (Cepha)
3. *Equites scutarii Illyriciani*	Amida
4. *Equites promoti Illyriciani*	Rhesaina-Theodosioplis
5. *Equites ducatores Illyriciani*	Amida
6. *Equites felices Honoriani Illyriciani*	Constantina
7. *Equites promoti indigenae*	Constantina and Apadna
8. *Equites sagittarii indigenae Arabanenses*	Mefana-Cartha
9. *Equites scutarii indigenae Pafenses*	Assara

Limitanei Units	Station
10. *Equites sagittarii indigenae Thibithenses*	Thilbisme
11. *Equites sagittarii indigenae*	Thannuri
12. *Ala secunda nova Aegyptiorum*	Cartha
13. *Ala octava Flavia Francorum*	Ripaltha
14. *Ala quintadecima Flavia Carduenorum*	Caini
15. *Cohors quinquagenaria Arabum*	Bethallaha
16. *Cohors quartadecima Valeria Zabdenorum*	Maiocariri

Limitaneus Army of Osrhoenae

Limitanei Units	Station
1. *Legio quartae Parthicae*	Circesium
2. *Legio III Parthica?*[1]	Apatna
3. *Equites Dalmatae Illyriciani*	Ganaba
4. *Equites promoti Illyriciani*	Callinicum
5. *Equites Mauri Illyriciani*	Dabana
6. *Equites promoti indigenae*	Banasa
7. *Equites sagittarii indigenae*	Oraba
8. *Equites sagittarii indigenae Medianenses*	Mediana
9. *Equites sagittarii primi Osrhoeni*	Rasis
10. *Ala septima Valeria praelectorum*	Thillacama
11. *Ala prima Victoriae*	Touia
12. *Ala secunda Paflagonum*	Thillafica
13. *Ala prima Parthorum*	Resaia
14. *Ala prima nova Diocletiana*	Thannuris and Horaba
15. *Cohors prima Gaetulorum*	Thillaamana
16. *Cohors prima Eufratensis*	Maratha
17. *Ala prima salutaria*	Duodecimus

Limitaneus Army of Syriae and Eufratensis Syriae

Limitanei Units	Station
1. *Legio quartae Scythicae*	Oresa
2. *Legio sextaedecimae Flaviae firmae*	Sura
3. *Equites scutarii Illyriciani*	Serianae
4. *Equites sagittarii indigenae*	Matthana and Anatha
5. *Equites promotii Illyriciani*	Occariba
6. *Equites promoti indigenae*	Adada and Rosafa
7. *Equites sagittarii*	Acadama and Acadama

Limitanei Units	Station
8. *Equites Dalmatae Illyriciani*	Barbalisso
9. *Equites Mauri Illyriciani*	Neocaesareae
10. *Ala prima nova Herculia*	Ammuda
11. *Ala prima Iuthungorum*	Salutaria
12. *Cohors prima Gotthorum*	Helala
13. *Cohors prima Ulpia Dacorum*	Claudiana
14. *Cohors tertia Valeria*	Marmantharum
15. *Cohors prima victorum*	Ammattha

Limitaneus Army of Phoenica (Foenicis)

Limitanei Units	Station
1. *Legio I Illyricorum*	Palmyra
2. *Legio III Gallica*	Danaba
3. *Equites Mauri Illyriciani*	Otthara
4. *Equites scutarii Illyriciani*	Eurhari
5. *Equites promoti indigenae*	Saltatha, Avatha, and Nazala
6. *Equites Dalmatae Illyriciani*	Lataui
7. *Equites sagittarii indigenae*	Adatha, Abina, Casama and Calamona
8. *Equites Saraceni indigenae*	Betproclis
9. *Equites Saraceni*	Thelsee
10. *Ala prima Damascena*	Mons Iovis
11. *Ala noun Diocletiana*	Veriaraca
12. *Ala prima Francorum*	Cunna
13. *Ala prima Alamannorum*	Neia
14. *Ala prima Saxonum*	Verofabula
15. *Ala prima Foenicum*	Rene
16. *Ala secunda Salutis*	Arefa
17. *Cohors tetria Herculia*	Veranoca
18. *Cohors quinta pacta Alamannorum*	Onevatha
19. *Cohors prima Iulia lectorum*	Vallis Alba
20. *Cohors secunda Aegyptiorum*	Vallis Diocletiana
21. *Cohors prima Orientalis*	Thama

2. Regional Field Armies of the East

The Eastern Field Armies contained no *milites* infantry units and only one *cuneus* cavalry regiment raising the inference that no new units were needed to maintain the eastern defence after Adrianople.

Thracian Field Army

While the Thracian Field Army and Valen's *Praesental* Army were defeated at Adrianople and sustained heavy casualties, they were not destroyed. It appears Theodosius I rebuilt this army after the Gothic wars since four of its seven cavalry units bear his or his sons' names.[2] The majority of the legions bear names of units that predate Theodosius I's reign and appear in sources to predate the battle of Adrianople.

Palatinae Cavalry	Comitatenses Cavalry	Legions Comitatenses
1. *Comites Arcadiaci*	1. *Equites catafractarii*	1. *Solenses seniores*
2. *Comites Honoriaci*	*Albigenses*	2. *Menapii*
3. *Equites Theodosiaci*	2. *Equites sagittarii seniors*	3. *Prima Maximiana*
iuniores	3. *Equites sagittarii iuniores*	*Thebaeorum*
	4. *Equites primi Theodosiani*	4. *Tertia Diocletiana*
		Thebaeorum
		5. *Tertiodecimani*
		6. *Quartodecimani*
		7. *Prima Flavia gemina*
		8. *Secunda Flavia gemina*
		9. *Constantini seniores*
		10. *Divitenses Gallicani*
		11. *Lanciarii Stobenses*
		12. *Constantini*
		13. *Dafnenses*
		14. *Balistarii Dafnenses*
		15. *Balistarii iuniores*
		16. *Pannoniciani iuniores*
		17. *Taanni*
		18. *Solenses Gallicani*
		19. *Iulia Alexandria*
		20. *Augustenses*
		21. *Valentinianenses*

Pannonian/Illyrcium Field Army

Comitatenses Cavalry	Palatina Units	Legions Comitatenses	Pseudocomitatenses
1. Equites sagittarii seniors	**Legions** 1. Britones seniores	1. Matiarii constants 2. Martii	1. Timacenses auxiliarii 2. Felices Theodosiani
2. Equites Germaniciani seniors	**Auxilia** 2. Ascarii seniores	3. Dianenses 4. Germaniciani seniores	iuniores 3. Bugaracenses
	3. Ascarii iuniores	5. Secundani	4. Scupenses
	4. Petulantes iuniores	6. Lanciarii	5. Ulpianenses
	5. Sagittarii lecti	7. Augustenses	6. Merenses
	6. Invicti iuniores	8. Minervii	7. Secundi Theodosiani
	7. Atecotti	9. Lanciarii iuniores	8. Balistarii Theodosiani iuniores
			9. Scampenses

Eastern Field Army

Comitatenses Cavalry	Legions Comitatenses	Pseudocomitatenses
1. Comites catafractarii	1. Felices Arcadiani seniores[3]	1. Prima Armeniaca
2. Bucellarii iuniores	2. Felices Honoriani seniores[4]	2. Secunda Armeniaca
3. Equites armigeri seniores Orientales	3. Quinta Macedonica	3. Fortenses auxiliarii
4. Equites tertio Dalmatae	4. Martenses seniores	4. Funditores
5. Equites primi scutarii Orientales	5. Septima gemina	5. Prima Italica
6. Equites secundi stablesiani	6. Decima gemina	6. Quarta Italica
7. Equites tertii stablesiani	7. Balistarii seniores	7. Sexta Parthica
8. Equites promoti clibanarii	8. Prima Flavia Constantia	8. Prima Isaura sagittaria
9. Equites quarti clibanarii Parthi	9. Secunda Flavia	9. Balistarii Theodosiaci
10. Equites primi sagittarii	10. Constantia Thebaeorum	10. Transtigritani
11. Cuneus equitum secundorum clibanariorum Palmirenorum	11. Secunda Felix Valentis Thebaeorum	
	12. Prima Flavia Theodosiana	

Bibliography

I. Primary Sources

Ammianus Marcellinus History, Volumes I, II, and III. Translated by John C Rolfe. London, Cambridge: Harvard University Press, Leob Classic Library, 2006.

Ammianus Marcellinus, The Later Roman Empire (A.D. 354–378). Translated and edited by Walter Hamilton. London: Penguin Books, 2004 [1986].

Al-Tabari, *The History of al-Tabrai, Volume V, The Sassanids, The Byzantines, The Lakmids, and Yemen.* Translated and edited by C E Bosworth, (Albany: University of New York Press, 1999).

Ancient Strategists, Sun Tzu's The Art of War and Vegetius' Epitoma Rei Militaris. Edited by Gareth Simon. United Kingdom: The Society of Ancients, 1994.

Dennis, George T, trans., *Three Byzantine Military Treatises* (Washington D.C.; Dumbarton Oaks Research Library and Collection, 1985).

Dodgeon, Michael H and Lieu, Samuel N C, ed. *The Roman Eastern Frontier and the Persian Wars AD 226–363, A Documentary History.* London and New York: Routledge, 2002.

—— and Greatrex, Geoffrey, ed. *The Roman Eastern Frontier and the Persian Wars, Part II, AD 363–630,* London and New York: Routledge, 2008.

The Chronicle of Joshua the Stylite. Translated and edited by William Wright. Amsterdam: Philo Press, 1968.

The compilation *'notitia dignitatum,'* http://members.ozemail.com.au/~igmaier/webnotve.htm

Herodian of Antioch, History of the Roman Empire 1961, 108–134 Book 4, Chapter XV, 1–4. Translated by Edward C Echols; http://www.tertullian.org/fathers/index.htm#Herodian_Roman_Histories.

Libanius' Funeral Oration Upon the Emperor Julian. Transcriber Roger Pearse. Ipswich, UK: Public Domain Copy, Early Church Fathers – Additional Texts. http://www.tertullian.org/fathers/index.htm.

Maurice's Strategikon, Handbook of Byzantine Military Strategy. Translated by George T Dennis. Philadelphia: University of Pennsylvania Press, 1984.

Procopius, History of the Wars, Books I–IV. Translated by H B Dewing. Charleston: BiblioBooks, 2007.

Plutarch. *The Parallel Lives, The Life of Crassus.* Vol. III: Loeb Classic, 1916, 380–421. Transcribed by William Thayer. Online Public Edition. http://penelope.uchicago.edu/Thayer/E/Roman/Texts/Plutarch/Lives/Crassus*.html.

Robertson, Rev. A., ed. *Nicene and Post-Nicene Fathers, Series II, Vol. IV, Athanasius: Selected Works.* Includes Zosimus, *New History.* London: Green and Chaplin (1814) Online Version. http://www.bible.ca/history/fathers/NPNF2-04/Npnf2-04-08.htm.

The Works of the Emperor Julian, Volumes I, II, III. Translated by Wilmer Cave Wright. London and Cambridge: Harvard University Press, 1954.

Socrates. *The Ecclesiastical History of Socrates Scholasticus,* Nicene and Post Nicene Fathers Series II, Volume 2, Philip Schaff, Editor. Grand Rapids, MI: Christian Ethereal Library, ca. 1893.

Sozomen. *The Ecclesiastical History of Sozomen: Comprising a History of the Church from A.D. 324–440,* Edward Walford, trans. London: Henry G Bohn, 1855.

Sunzi: The Art of War and Sun Bin: The Art of War. Translated by Lin Wuaun. Beijing: Foreign Languages Press, 2007.

Zosimus. *The History of Count Zosimus, Sometime Advocate and Chancellor of the Roman Empire.* Unknown translator. London: W Green and T Chaplin, 1814.

II. Secondary Sources

Austin, Michel, Harries, Jill and Smith, Christopher, ed. *Modus Operandi, Essays In Honour of Geoffrey Rickman.* London: University of London, 1998.

Blockley, R C, *East Roman Foreign Policy, Formation and Conduct from Diocletian to Anastasius.* Leeds: Francis Cains, 1992.

Braund, David. *Georgian Antiquity, a History of Colchis and Transcaucasian Iberia, 550 BC–AD 562.* Oxford: Clarendon Press, 1994.

British Naval Intelligence Division. *Persia.* Geographic Handbook Series, September 1945 [Declassified].

Burton, Sir Richard F, trans. *The Book of the Thousand Nights and a Night,* Story of Prince Behram and the Princess Al-Datma, online version, http://www.wollamshram.ca/1001/Vol_1/vol1.htm.

Cameron, Averil, ed. *The Byzantine and Early Islamic Near East.* Princeton: The Darwin Press, Inc., 1995.

Cantrell, Robert L. *Understanding Sun Tzu on the Art of War.* Arlington: Center for Advantage, 2003.

Carey, Brian Todd. *Road to Manzikert: Byzantine and Islamic Warfare, 527–1071.* Barnsley: Pen & Sword, 2012.

Charlesworth, M P. *Trade-Routes and Commerce of the Roman Empire.* London: Cambridge University Press, 1924.

Charlton, James, ed. *The Military Quotation Book.* New York: Thomas Dunne Books, 2002.

Coello, Terence. *Unit Sizes in the Late Roman Army.* Oxford: BAR International Series 645, 1996.

Cowan, Ross. *Roman Battle Tactics 109 BC–AD 313.* Oxford: Osprey Publishing, 2007.

Cromwell, Richard. *The Rise and Decline of the Late Roman Field Army.* Shippensburg: White Mane Publishing Company, Inc., 1998.

Crump, Gary A. *Ammianus Marcellinus as a Military Historian.* Wiesbaden: *Historia 27* Franz Steiner Verlag GMBN, 1975.

D'Amato, Raffaele. *Roman Centurions 753–31 BC, the Kingdom and the Age of Consuls.* Oxford and New York: Osprey Publishing, 2011.

———. *Roman Centurions 31 BC–AD 500, the Classical and Late Empire.* Oxford and New York: Osprey Publishing, 2012.

Daryaee, Touraj. *Sassanian Iran (224–651 CE).* Costa Mesa: Mazda Publishers, 2008.

Delbruck, Hans (1848–1929). *History of the Art of War, Volume II, The Barbarian Invasion,* Walter J. Renfroe, Jr., Walter J. trans., Lincoln and London: University of Nebraska Press, 1990.

Dignas, Beate and Winter, Engelbert. *Rome and Persia in Late Antiquity, Neighbours and Rivals.* Cambridge: Cambridge University Press, 2008.

Dixon, Karen R & Southern, Pat. *The Roman Cavalry.* London: Routledge, 1992.

Dodgeon, Michael H and Lieu, Samuel N C, ed. *The Roman Eastern Frontier and the Persian Wars AD 226–363, A Documentary History.* London and New York: Routledge, 2002.

Drijvers, Jan Willem and Hunt, David, ed. *The Late Roman World and its Historian, Interpreting Ammianus Marcellinus.* London and New York: Routledge, 1999.

Elliott, Paul. *The Last Legionary, Life as a Roman Soldier in Britain AD 400.* Gloucestershire: Spellmount Publishers, 2012.

Elton, Hugh. *Warfare in Roman Europe, AD 350–425.* Oxford: Clarendon Press, 1997.

———. *Frontiers of the Roman Empire.* Bloomington and Indianapolis: Indian University Press, 1996.

Engels, Donald W. *Alexander the Great and the Logistic of the Macedonian Army.* Berkeley: University of California Press, 1980.

Farnum, Jerome H. *The Positioning of the Roman Legions.* Oxford, UK: BAR International Series 1458, 2005.

Farrokh, Kaveh. *Shadows in the Desert: Ancient Persia at War.* Oxford: Osprey Publishing, 2004.

———. *Sassanian Elite Cavalry AD 224–642.* Oxford: Osprey Publishing, 2005.

Freeman, Philip and Kennedy, David, ed. *The Defence of the Roman and Byzantine East, Proceedings of a Colloquium Held at the University of Sheffield in April 1986.* Oxford: BAR International Series 297(i), 1986.

French, D H and Lightfoot, C S, ed. *The Eastern Frontier of the Roman Empire, Proceedings of a Colloquium Held at Ankara in September 1988.* Oxford: BAR International Series 553(i), 1989.

Gibbon, Edward. *The Decline and Fall of the Roman Empire, Volume I.* Bury, J.B., ed. New York: The Heritage Press, 1946 reprint.

Giuseppe, C Di. *Constantine's Arch.* trans., MacAlways, C & Pope, A. Rome: Tipografia Ceccarelli, Grotte di Castro, 2000.

Goldsworth, Adrian. *The Complete Roman Army.* London: Thames and Hudson Ltd., 2003.

——. *Roman Warfare.* New York: Smithsonian Press, 2005.

——. *How Rome Fell, Death of a Superpower.* New Haven and London: Yale University Press, 2009.

Gott, Kendall, D. *In Search of an Elusive Enemy: The Victorio Campaign* (Fort Leavenworth, Kansas: Combat Institute Press, 2004).

Greatrex, Geoffrey. *Rome and Persia at War, 502–534.* Leeds: Francis Cairns, 1998.

Gregory, Shelagh. *Roman Military Architecture on the Eastern Frontier, Vol. I, II and III.* Amsterdam: Adolf H. Hakkert, 1997.

Haldon, John. *The Byzantine Wars.* Gloucestershire: The History Press, 2011.

Howard-Johnson, James. *East Rome, Sassanian Persia and the End of Antiquity.* Burlinton and Surrey: Ashgate Publishing, 2010.

Isaac, Benjamin. *The Limits of Empire: The Roman Army in the East.* Oxford: Clarendon Press, 1990.

James, Elizabeth. *Constantine The Great: Warlord of Rome.* Barnsley: Pen & Sword Books, Ltd., 2012.

James, Simon. *Excavations At Dura-Europos, 1928–1837, Final Report VII, The Arms and Armour and other Military Equipment.* London: British Museum Press, 2010.

Johnson, Stephen. *Late Roman Fortifications.* Totowa, NJ: Barnes and Noble Books, 1983.

Jones, A H M. *The Later Roman Empire 284–602, Volumes I and II.* Baltimore: Johns Hopkins University Press, 1964.

Lee, A D. *Information & Frontiers, Roman Foreign Relations in Late Antiquity.* Cambridge: Cambridge University Press, 2006.

——. *War In Late Antiquity: A Social History.* Oxford: Blackwell Publishing, 2007.

Lewin, Ariel S and Pellegrini, Pietrina, ed., *The Late Roman Army in the Near East from Diocletian to the Arab Conquest: Proceedings of a Colloquium Held at Potenza Acerenza and Matera, Italy (May 2005),* Oxford: British Archaeological Reports International Series 1717, 2007.

Luttwak, Edwin N. *The Grand Strategy of the Roman Empire.* Baltimore and London: Johns Hopkins University Press, 1979.

—— *The Grand Strategy of the Byzantine Empire.* Cambridge, Massachusetts, and London, England: Harvard University Press, 2009.

MacDowall, Simon. *Late Roman Infantry AD 236–565.* Oxford UK: Osprey Publishing, 1994.

McLaughlin, Roul. *The Roman Empire and the Indian Ocean, The Ancient World and The Kingdoms of Africa, Arabia & India.* South Yorkshire: Pen & Sword, 2014.

MacMullen, Ramsay. *Corruption and the Decline of Rome.* New Haven and London: Yale University Press, 1988.

Matthews, John. *The Roman Empire of Ammianus.* Baltimore: The Johns Hopkins University Press, 1989.

Matyszak, Philip. *Imperial General, the Remarkable Career of Petellius Cerialis.* Barnsley: Pen & Sword Books, Ltd., 2011.

McLaughlin, Roul. *The Roman Empire and the Indian Ocean, The Ancient World and The Kingdoms of Africa, Arabia & India.* South Yorkshire: Pen & Sword, 2014.

Millar, Fergus. *The Roman Near East 31 B.C.E.-A.D. 337.* Cambridge, Massachusetts and London: Harvard University Press, 1993.

Miller, J Innes. *The Spice Trade of the Roman Empire, 29 B.C. to A.D. 641.* Oxford: Clarendon Press, 1969.

Mitchell, Stephen, ed. *Armies and Frontiers in Roman and Byzantine Anatolia, Proceedings of a Colloquium Held at University College, Swansea, in April 1981.* Oxford: BAR International Series 156, 1983.

Morlillo, Stephen and Pavkovic. Michael F. *What is Military History?* Malden and Cambridge: Polity Press, 2006.

Nicasie, M J. *Twilight of Empire: The Roman Army from the Reign of Diocletian until the Battle of Adrianople.* Amsterdam: J.C. Gieben, Publisher, 1998.

Nossov, Konstantin. *War Elephants.* China: Osprey Publishing Ltd., 2008.

Parker, S Thomas. *The Frontier in Central Jordan, Final Report on the Limes Arabicus Project,* Volume I. Washington D.C.: Dumbarton Oaks, 2006.

Peddie, John. *The Roman War Machine.* Gloucestershire: Sutton Publishing, 1997.

Potter, David S. *The Roman Empire at Bay AD 180–395.* London and New York: Routledge, 2004.

Rawlinson, George. *The Seven Great Monarchies of the Ancient Eastern World, Volume VII.* http://www.gutenberg.org/files/16167/16167-h/16167-h.htm#linkBimage-0002.

Ross, Jonathan P. *The Roman Army at War, (264 B.C.–A.D. 235).* Leiden, Boston, and Koln; Brill, 1999.

Rowell, Henry T. *Ammianus Marcellinus, Soldier-Historian of the Late Roman Empire.* Cincinnati: The University of Cincinnati, 1964.

Simpson, Gareth C. *The Defeat of Rome in the East: Crassus, the Parthians, and the Disastrous Battle of Carrhae, 53 B.C.* Drexel Hill: Casement, 2008.

Shahid, Iran. *Byzantium and the Arabs in the Fourth Century.* Washington D.C.: Dumbarton Oaks Research Library and Collection, 2006.

Sheldon, Rose Mary. *Intelligence Activities in Ancient Rome, Trust in the Gods, But Verify.* London and New York: Routledge, 2005.

——. *Rome's Wars in Parthia: Blood in the Sand.* Portland: Vallentine Mitchell, 2010.

Southern, Pat and Dixon, Karen R. *The Late Roman Army.* New Haven and London: Yale University Press, 1996.

——. *The Roman Army, A History 753 BC-AD 479*. Gloucestershire: Amberley Publishing, 2014.

Stewart, Richard W. *American Military History Volume 1, the United States Army and the Forging of a Nation, 1775–1917*. Washington D.C.: Center of Military History, United States Army, 2005.

Smith, Sir William. *A New Classical Dictionary of Greek and Roman Biography, Mythology and Geography*. New York: Harper & Brothers, 1851.

Stephenson, I P. *Roman Infantry Equipment*. Gloucestershire: Tempus Publications Inc., 2001,

Summers, Jr. Harry G. *On Strategy: The Vietnam War in Context*. Carlisle Barracks: US Army War College, 1982.

Tafazzoli, Ahmed. *Sassanian Society*. New York: Bibliotheca Press, 2000.

Talbert, J A., et al eds. *Barrington Atlas of the Greek and Roman World*. Princeton and Oxford: Princeton University, 2000.

Tomber, Roberta. *Indo-Roman Trade, From Pots to Pepper*. London: Duckworth, 2008.

Treadgold, Warren. *Byzantium and Its Army, 284–1081*. Stanford: Stanford University Press, 1995.

Turabian, Kate L. *A Manual for Writers of Research Papers, Theses and Dissertations 7th Edition*. Chicago: University of Chicago Press, 2007.

Ueda-Sarson, Luke. 'Late Roman Shield Designs Taken from the Notitia Dignitatum.' *Luke Ueda-Sarson's Wargame Pages*, 2006. http://www.ne.jp/asahi/luke/ueda-sarson/NotitiaPatterns.html.

Whittaker, C R. *Frontiers of the Roman Empire, a Social and Economic Study*. Baltimore and London: The Johns Hopkins University Press, 1994.

III. Articles

Austin, N J E. 'Julian at Ctesiphon: A Fresh Look at Ammianus' Account.' *Athenaeum*, Volume 50, (1972): 301–309.

Anderson, J G C. 'The Road System of Eastern Asia Minor with the Evidence of Byzantine Campaigns.' *The Journal of Hellenic Studies*, Vol. 17 (1897), 22–44. http://www.jstor.org/stable/623816.

Barnes, T D. 'Constantine and the Christians of Persia.' *The Journal of Roman Studies*, Vol. 75 (1985), 126–136, 131. http://www.jstor.org/stable/300656.

——. 'Imperial Chronology, A. D. 337–350.' *Phoenix*, Vol. 34, No. 2 (Summer, 1980), 160–166. http://www.jstor.org/stable/1087874.

Banchich, Thomas M. 'Gallus Caesar 15 March 351–354 A.D.' *De Imperatoribus Romanis*, 1997. http://www.roman-emperors.org/gallus.htm.

Bivar, D.H. 'Cavalry Equipment and Tactics on the Euphrates Frontier.' *Dumbarton Oaks Papers*, Vol. 26 (1972) 271–291. http://www.jstor.org/stable/1291323.

Blacker, L V S. 'Travels In Turkistan.' *The Geographical Journal*, Vol. 58, No. 3 (Sep. 1921), 178–197. http://www.jstor.org/stable/1780485.

Blockley, R C. 'Festus' Source on Julian's Persian Expedition.' *Classical Philology,* Vol. 68, no. 1 (Jan., 1973), 54–55. http://www.jstor.org/stable/268792.

——. 'Ammianus Marcellinus on the Battle of Strasburg: Art and Analysis in the 'History.' *Phoenix,* Vol. 31, No. 3 (Autumn, 1977), 218–231. http://www.jstor.org/stable/1087102.

Burgess, R W. 'The Summer of Blood: The Great Massacre of 337 and the Promothion of the Sons of Constantine.' *Dumbarton Oaks Papers,* Vol. 62 (2008), 5–51. http://www.jstor.org/stable/20788042.

——. 'Ammianus Marcellinus on the Persian Invasion of A.D. 359.' *Phoenix,* Vol. 42, No. 3 (Autumn, 1988), 244–260. http://www.jstor.org/stable/1088346.

Chalmers, Walter R. 'Ammianus Marcellinus, and Zosimus on Julian's Persian Expedition.' *The Classical Quarterly,* New Series, Vol. 10, no. 2 (Nov., 1960), 152–160. http://www.jstor.org/stable/628046.

Coulston, J C. 'Roman, Parthian and Sassanid Tactical Development.' 59–75. in Freeman and Kennedy.

——. 'How to Arm a Roman Soldier.' In Austin, Harries and Smith.

Edie, John W. 'The Development of Roman Mailed Cavalry.' *The Journal of Roman Studies,* Vol. 57, no. 1/ 2 (1967), 161–173. http://www.jstor.org/stable/299352.

Fornara, Charles W. 'Julian's Persian Expedition in Ammianus and Zosimus.' *The Journal of Hellenic Studies,* Vol. 111 (1991), 1–15, http://www.jstor.org/stable/631884.

Daryaee, Touraj. 'A Review of the Encyclopaedia Iranica.' *Iranian Studies, Vol. 31,* no. 3/4. (Summer-Autumn 1988), 431–461.

——. 'The Persian Gulf Trade in Late Antiquity.' *Journal of World History,* Vol. 14, No. 1 (Mar. 2003), 1–16. http://www.jstor.org/stable/20079006.

Dunstervill, L C. 'Baghdad to the Caspian in 1918.' *The Geographical Journal,* Vol. 57, No. 3 (Mar. 1921), 153–164. URL: http://www.jstor.org/stable/1780858.

Felix, Wolfgang. 'Chionites.' *Encyclopaedia Iranica, Vol. V, Fasc.5, 485–487, 2012.* http://www.iranicaonline.org/articles/chionites-lat.

Fry, Richard Nelson. 'The Sassanian System of Walls for Defence.' *Studies in Memory of Gaston Wiet,* (1977), 7–15.

Hamblin, William. 'Sassanian Military Science and its Transmission to the Arabs.' *BRISMES Proceedings of the 1986 International Conference on Middle Eastern Studies.* Oxford: Brismes, (1986), 99–106.

Heath, Peter. 'Ammianus on Jovian, History and Literature.' 105–114. in Drijvers and Hunt.

Herrmann, Georgina, Kurbansakhatove, K. and Simpson, St. John. 'The International Merv Project. Preliminary Report on the Fourth Season' (1995). *Iran,* Vol. 34 (1996), 1–22. http://www.jstor.org/stable/4299941.

Howard-Johnson, James. 'The Two Great Powers in Late Antiquity.' 157–226. in Cameron.

Howard-Johnson, James. 'The Sassanian Strategic Dilemma.' *Commutatio et contentio, Studies in the Late Roman, Sassanian, and Early Islamic Near East; in Memory of Zeev Rubin.* Dusseldorf: Wellem, 2010.

Isaac, Benjamin. 'Bandits in Judea and Arabia.' *Harvard Studies in Classical Philology*, Vol. 88 (1984), 171–203, 200. http://www.jstor.org/stable/311452.

Kaegi, W E. 'Constantine's and Julian's Strategic Surprise against the Persians.' *Athenaeum*, Vol. 59, (1981).

Kagan, Kimberly. 'Redefining Roman Grand Strategy.' *The Journal of Military History*, Vol. 70, No. 2 (Apr. 2006), 333–362. http://www.jstor.org/stable/4137956.

Kleiss, Wolfram. 'Fortifications.' *Encyclopaedia Iranica*, 2012, http://www.iranicaonline.org/.

Kropotkin, P. 'The Old Beds of the Amu-Daria [Oxus].' *The Geographical Journal*, Vol. 12, No. 3 (Sep. 1898), 306–310. http://www.jstor.or/stable/1774317.

Lee, A D. 'Campaign Preparation in Late Roman-Persian Warfare.' 257–265. in French and Lightfoot.

——. 'Embassies as Evidence for the Movement of Military Intelligence between the Roman and Sassanian Empire.' 455–461. in Freeman and Kennedy.

Lightfoot, C S. 'The Site of Roman Bezabde.' 189–202. in Mitchell.

——. 'The Third Siege of Nisibis.' *Historia: Zeitschrift fur Alte Geschichte*, Bd. 37, H. 1 (1st Qtr, 1988), 105–125. http://www.jstor.org/stable/4436041.

Loewe, Michael. 'Spices and Silk: Aspects of World Trade in the First Seven Centuries of the Christian Era.' *Journal of the Royal Asiatic Society of Great Britain and Ireland*, No. 2 (1971), 166–179. http://www.jstor.org/stable/2503290.

Margabandhu, C. 'Trade Contacts between Western India and the Graeco-Roman World in the Early Centuries of the Christian Era.' *Journal of Economic and Social History of the Orient*, Vol. 8, No. 3 (Dec. 1965), 316–322. http://www.jstor.org/stable/3596384.

Millar, Fergus. 'Emperors, Frontiers and Foreign Relations, 31 B.C. to A.D. 378.' *Britannia*, Vol. 13 (1982), 1–23. http://www.jstor.org/stable/526487.

Monteith, Colonel. 'Journal of a Tour through Azerbaijan and the Shores of the Caspian.' *Journal of the Royal Geographical Society of London*, Vol. 3 (1833), 1–58. http://www.jstor.org/stable/1797594.

Napier, G.S.F. 'The Road from Bagdad to Baku.' *The Geographical Journal*, Vol. 53, No. 1 (Jan., 1919), 1–16. http://www.jstor.org/stable/1780395.

Nathanson, Barbara Geller. 'Jews, Christians, and the Gallus Revolt in the Fourth-Century Palestine.' *The Biblical Archaeologist*, Vol. 49, No. 1 (Mar., 1986), 26–36. http://www.jstor.org/stable/3209979.

Negin, A E. 'Sarmatian Cataphracts as Prototypes for Roman Equites Cataphractarii.' *Journal of Roman Military Equipment Studies*, Vol. 6, (1995), 65–75.

Nokandeh Jebrael, Sauer Eberhard W, et. al. 'The Enigma of the Red Snake, Revealing one of the World's Greatest Frontier Walls.' *Current World Archaeology*, No. 27, (February/March 2004), 12–22.

———. 'Linear Barriers of Northern Iran: The Great Wall of Gorgan and the Wall of Tammisher.' *Iran*, Vol. 44 (2006), 121–173. http://www.jstor.org/stable/4300707.

Poidebard, A. 'Les routes anciennes en Haute-Djezireh.' *Syria*, *T. 8, Fasc. 1* (1927), 55–65, figure 1 60 and figure 2 62. http://www.jstor.org/stable/4195320.

Rawlinson, H C. 'The Road to Merv.' *Proceedings of the Royal Geographical Society and Monthly Record of Geography*, New Monthly Series, Vol. 1, No. 3 (Mar., 1879), 161–191. http://jstor.org/stable/1800653.

Reade, Julian. 'An Eagle from the East.' *Britannia*, Vol. 30 (1999), http://www.jstor.org/stable/526684.

Rekavandi, Hamid Omrani and Sauer Ederhard W. Sauer et. al. 'An Imperial Frontier of the Sassanian Empire: Further Fieldwork at the Great Wall of Gorgan.' *Iran*, Vol. 45 (2007), 95–136. http://www.jstor.org/stable/25651414.

Seager, Robin. 'Perceptions of Eastern Frontier Policy in Ammianus, Libanius, and Julian (337–363).' *The Classic Quarterly*, New Series, Vol. 47, No. 1 (1997), 253–268. http://www.jstor.org/stable/639612.

Shahbazi, A S. *Sassanian Army*. Iranian Chamber of Chamber. http://www.iranchamber.com/history/sasanids/Sassanian_army.php.

Sidebotham, Steven E. 'Late Roman Berenike.' *Journal of American Research Center in Egypt*, Vol. 39 (2002), 217–240, http://www.jstor.org/stable/40001157.

Thompson, E A. 'Ammianus' Account of Gallus Caesar.' *The American Journal of Philology*, Vol. 64, No. 3 (1943), 302–315. http://www.jstor.org/stable/291014.

Thorley, John. 'The Roman Empire and the Kushans.' *Greece & Rome*, Second Series, Vo. 26, No. 2 (Oct. 1979), 181–190, http://www.jstor.org/stable/642511.

Tomlin, Roger. 'Seniores-Iuniores in the Late-Roman Field Army.' *The American Journal of Philology*, Vol. 93, No. 2 (Apr. 1972), 253–278. http://www.jstor.org/stable/293251.

Trombley, Frank. 'Ammianus and Fourth Century Warfare,' 17–28 in Drijvers and Hunt.

Warmington, B H. 'Objectives and Strategy in the Persian War of Constantius II.' 509–520, 512, In *Limes: akin des XI Internqtionalen Limeskongresses*. Budapest: Akade miai Kiado, (1977).

Wheeler, Everett, L. 'Methodological Limits and the Mirage of Roman Strategy: Part II.' *The Journal of Military History*, Vol. 57, No. 2 (Apr. 1993), 215–240. http://www.jstor.org/stable/2944057.

Whitby, Michael. 'Recruitment in Roman Armies from Justinian to Heraclus (c.a. 565–615).' 61–124, in Averil Cameron.

IV. Unpublished Doctoral Dissertations

Caldwell, III, Craig H. *Contesting Late Roman Illyricum: Invasions and Transformations in the Danubian-Balkan Provinces*. Ph.D. Dissertation: Princeton University 2007 (Publication No. 3273508).

Hunt, James Michael. *Constantius II in the Ecclesiastical Histories.* Ph.D. Dissertation: Fordham University, New York, 2010. Retrieved 25 September 2011, from Dissertations & Theses: The Humanities and Social Sciences Collection (Publication No. 341914).

Lightfoot, C S. *The Eastern Frontier of the Roman Empire with Special reference to the reign of Constantius II.* Ph.D. Dissertation (or British Equivalent): St, John's College, Oxford 1982. http://ora.ox.ac.uk/objects/uuid%3A68c9ad0a-7a8a-4c3e-a48f-73f4530f7b18/datastreams/ATTACHMENT1. Accessed 24 July 2014.

Pavkovic, Michael. *The legionary horsemen: An essay on equites legionis and equites promote.* Ph.D. Dissertation: University of Hawaii, 1991.

Toplyn, Michael Richard. *Meat for Mars: Livestock, limitanei, and pastoral provisioning for the Roman Army on the Arabian frontier* (A.D. 284–551), Ph.D. Dissertation, Harvard University, 1994. (Publication No. UTM 9514861).

Van Nort, R. *The Battle of Adrianople and the Military Doctrine of Vegetius.* Ph.D. Dissertation, City University of New York, United States — New York. Retrieved August 25, 2011, from Dissertations & Theses: The Humanities and Social Sciences Collection (Publication No. AAT 3283191).

Williams, Sean Robert, '*Ammianus and Constantius: The Portrayal of a Tyrant in the Res Gestae.* Master's Thesis, University of Tennessee, 2009. http://www.trace.tennessee.ed/utk_gradthes/572.

Wynn, Phillip Gerald. *War and Military Service in Early Western Christian Thought, 200–850.* Ph.D. Dissertation, University of Notre Dame, 2011. (Publication No. 342609).

V. United States Army and Navy Manuals (Open Source)

Landing Force Manual 1920, United States Navy, Washington D.C.: Government Printing Office, 1921.

Student Text 101–5, Command and Staff Decision Process, Fort Leavenworth, Kansas: United States Army Command and General Staff College Publication, January 1994.

Notes

Chapter 1

1. Richard W Stewart. *American Military History Volume 1, The United States Army and the Forging of a Nation, 1775–1917* (Washington D.C.: Center of Military History, United States Army, 2005), 1.

2. See generally Edwin N Luttwak, *The Grand Strategy of the Roman Empire* (Baltimore and London: John Hopkins University Press, 1979); Geoffrey Greatrex, *Rome And Persia At War, 502–534* (Leeds: Francis Cairns, 1998); Warren Treadgold, *Byzantium and Its Army, 284–1081* (Stanford: Stanford University Press, 1995); and Edward N Luttwak, *The Grand Strategy of the Byzantine Empire* (Cambridge Mass, and London, England: Harvard University Press, 2009).

3. Gareth C Sampson, *The Defeat of Rome in the East: Crassus, The Parthians, and the Disastrous Battle of Carrhae, 53 B.C.* (Drexel Hill: Casement. 2008); Rose Mary Sheldon, *Rome's Wars in Parthia: Blood in the Sand* (Portland: Vallentine Mitchell, 2010).

4. John C Rolfe's Introduction to *Ammianus Marcellinus, The Later Roman Empire Vol. I*, ix–xiv.

5. Frank Trombley, 'Ammianus and Fourth Century Warfare,' 17–28, Jan Willem Drijvers and David Hunt, eds. *The Late Roman World and Its Historian, Interpreting Ammianus Marcellinus* (London and New York: Routledge, 1999).

6. Iran Shahid, *Byzantium and the Arabs in the Fourth Century* (Washington D.C.: Dumbarton Oaks Research Library and Collection, 2006), 142–175.

7. Iran Shahid, *Byzantium and the Arabs in the Fourth Century*, 268–269.

8. Ibid, 272–274.

9. Peter Heath, 'Ammianus on Jovian, History and Literature.' 105–114, in Drijvers and Hunt; and Sean Robert Williams, 'Ammianus and Constantius: The Portrayal of a Tyrant in the *Res Gestae*.' Master's Thesis, University of Tennessee, 2009. http:..trace.tennessee.ed/utk_gradthes/572.

10. Frank Trombley, 'Ammianus Marcellinus and Fourth-Century Warfare.' 17–27 in Drijvers and David Hunt; and AM, XXIV 5.10, XXV 1.9, 1.7, 1.16, 1.19, 3.4.

11. Michael H Dodgeon and Samuel N C Lieu, *The Roman Eastern Frontier and the Persian Wars AD 226–363, A Documentary History* (London and New York: Routledge, 2002), ix, xiv; Zosimus, *The History of Count Zosimus, Sometime Advocate and Chancellor of The Roman Empire,* unknown translator (London: W Green And T Chaplin, 1814).

12. Dodgeon and Lieu, xiii, 268–269; Sozomen, *The Ecclesiastical History of Sozomen: Comprising A History of the Church From A.D. 324–440,* Edward Walford, trans., (London: Henry G. Bohn, 1855).

13. Ibid., xi, 255–261.

14. Charles W Fornara, 'Julian's Persian Expedition in Ammianus and Zosimus,' *The Journal of Hellenic Studies*, Vol.111 (1991), 1–15, 14, http://www.jstor.org/stable/631884.

15. Dodgeon and Lieu, xi, 261–265.

16. Dodgeon and Lieu, xx, xxi and 4–8; Geoffrey Greatrex and Samuel N C Lieu, *The Roman Eastern Frontier and the Persian Wars, Part II, AD 363–630* (London and New York: Routledge, 2008).

17. Beate Dignas and Engelbert Winter, *Rome and Persia in Late Antiquity, Neighbors and Rivals* (Cambridge: Cambridge University Press, 2008).

18. Terrence Coello, *Unit Sizes in the Late Roman Army* (British Archaeological Reports S645, 1996), 44–50.

19. Adrian Goldsworthy, *How Rome Fell* (New Haven and London: Yale University Press, 2009), 285–290; Treadgold, 43–59.

20. *Sunzi: The Art of War, Sun Bin: The Art of War.* trans. Lin Wuaun (Beijing: Foreign Languages Press, 2007), 1–11. On his influence, see Harry G Summers, Jr., *On Strategy: The Vietnam War in Context* (Carlisle Barracks: US Army War College, 1982); and Robert L Cantrell, *Understanding Sun Tzu on the Art of War* (Arlington: Center for Advantage, 2003).

21. *Maurice's Strategikon, Handbook of Byzantine Military Strategy,* trans. George T Dennis (Philadelphia: University of Pennsylvania Press. 1984), xvii.

22. *The Tactics of Aelian,* trans. Christopher Matthew (South Yorkshire: Pen & Sword Books Ltd. 2012).

23. *Vegetius: Epitome of Military Science,* trans. N M Milner (Liverpool University Press: Liverpool).

24. George T Dennis, trans., *Three Byzantine Military Treatises* (Washington DC.; Dumbarton Oaks Research Library and Collection, 1985), viii, ix.

25. Edward Gibbon, *The Decline And Fall Of the Roman Empire, Volume I,* J B Bury, ed. (New York: The Heritage Press, (1946 reprint); George Rawlinson, *The Seven Great Monarchies Of the Ancient Easter World, Volume VII,* http://www.gutenberg.org/files/16167/16167-h/16167-h.htm#linkBimage-0002. Ebook reprint 2005.

26. L V S Blacker, 'Travels In Turkistan,' *The Geographical Journal*, Vol. 58, No. 3 (Sep. 1921), 178–197. URL: http://www. Jstor.org/stable/1780485; P Kropotkin, 'The Old Beds of the Amu-Daria [Oxus],' *The Geographical Journal*, Vol. 12, No. 3 (Sep. 1898), 306–310. URL: http://www.jstor.or/stable/1774317. Accessed 26 June 2012; and L C Dunstervill, 'Baghdad to the Caspian in 1918,' *The Geographical Journal*, Vol. 57, No. 3 (Mar. 1921), 153–164. URL: http://www.jstor.org/stable/1780858.

27. A H M. Jones, *The Late Roman Empire 284–602 Volumes I and II* (Baltimore: Johns Hopkins Press, 1964).

28. Benjamin Isaac, *The Limits of Empire, the Roman Army in the East* (Oxford: Clarendon Press, 1992); Fergus Millar, *The Roman Near East 31 B.C.E.-A.D. 337* Cambridge Mass. and London: Harvard University Press, 1993); and John Mathews, *The Roman Empire of Ammianus* (Ann Arbor: Michigan Classical Press, 2007).

29. Richard Cromwell, *The Rise and Decline of the Late Roman Field Army* (Shippensburg: White Mane Publishing Company, Inc., 1998); Karen R Dixon and Pat Southern, *The Roman Cavalry* (London: Routledge, 1992); Pat Southern and Karen R Dixon, *The Late Roman Army* (New Haven and London: Yale University Press, 1996); M J Nicasie, *Twilight of Empire, The Roman Army from The Reign of Diocletian until the Battle of Adrianople* (Amsterdam: J C. Gieben, Publisher, 1998); Treadgold; Hugh Elton, *Warfare In Roman Europe, AD 350–425* (Oxford: Clarendon Press, 1997); Hugh Elton, *Frontiers of the Roman Empire*, (Bloomington and Indianapolis: Indian University Press, 1996); Brian Todd Carey, *Road to Manzikert: Byzantine and Islamic Warfare, 527–1071* (Barnsley: Pen & Sword, 2012).

30. Greatrex (1998) *Rome And Persia At War, 502–534*; and John Haldon, *The Byzantine Wars* (Gloucestershire: The History Press, 2011).

31. C S Lightfoot, *The Eastern Frontier of the Roman Empire with Special Reference to the Reign of Constantius II*. Ph.D. Dissertation (or British Equivalent): St, John's College, Oxford 1982. http://ora.ox.ac.uk/objects/uuid%3A68c9ad0a-7a8a-4c3e-a48f-73f453 0f7b18/datastreams/ATTACHMENT1.

32. R C Blockley, 'Ammianus Marcellinus on The Persian Invasion of A.D. 359,' *Phoenix*, Vol. 42, No. 3 (Autumn, 1988), 244–260. http://www.jstor.org/stable/1088346. Accessed 9 December 2011 14.11; C.S. Lightfoot, 'The Third Siege of Nisibis,' *Historia: Zeitschrift fur Alte Geschichte*, Bd. 37, H. 1 (1st Qtr., 1988), 105–125. http://www.jstor.org/stable/4436041.

33. W E Kaegi, 'Constantine's and Julian's Strategies of Strategic Surprise Against the Persians,' *Athenaeum*, Vol. 59, (1981), 209–213; B H Warmington, 'Objectives and Strategy in the Persian War of Constantius II,' *Limes: akten des XI Internationalen Limeskongresses*, (Budapest: Akademiai Kiado, 1977), 509–520.

34. Donald W Engels, *Alexander The Great and the Logistics of the Macedonian Army* (Berkeley, Los Angeles and London: University of California Press, 1980).

35. Jonathan P Ross, *The Roman Army At War, (264 B.C. –A.D. 235)* (Leiden, Boston and Koln: Brill, 1999).

36. Simon James, *Excavations at Dura-Europos, 1928–1837, Final Report VII, The Arms and Armor and other Military Equipment* (London: British Museum Press, 2010); Peter M Edwell, *Between Rome and Persia* (Routledge: New York, 2008), 63–92.

37. Shelagh Gregory's work *Roman Military Architecture on the Eastern Frontier, Vol. I, II, and III* (Amsterdam: Adolf H Hakkert, 1997).

38. Al-Tabari, *The History of al-Tabrai, Volume V, The Sassanids, The Byzantines, The Lakmids, and Yemen*, C E Bosworth, trans., (Albany: State University of New York Press, 1999).

39. James Howard-Johnson, 'The Two Great Powers in Late Antiquity: a Comparison.' 157–226, 169–173, ed., Averil Cameron, *The Byzantine And Early Islamic Near East* (Princeton: The Darwin Press Inc., 1995).

40. Touraj Daryaee, 'A Review of the Encyclopedia Iranica.' *Iranian Studies, Vol. 31*, No. 3/4 (Summer-Autumn 1988): 431–461.

41. Touraj Daryaee, *Sasanian Iran (224–651 CE)* (Costa Mesa: Mazda Publishers, 2008); Ahmad Tafazzoli, *Sasanian Society* (New York: Bibliotheca Press, 2000); Kaveh

Farrokh, *Shadows In the Desert, Ancient Persia At War*(Oxford: Osprey Publishing, 2007); and James Howard-Johnson, *East Rome, Sasanian Persia and the End of Antiquity* (Burlinton and Surrey: Ashgate Publishing, 2010).

42. William Hamblin, 'Sasanian Military Science and its Transmission to the Arabs.' *BRISMES Proceedings of the 1986 International Conference on Middle Eastern Studies* (Oxford: Brismes, 1986), 99–106.

43. Richard W Stewart, Ed. *American Military History, Volume I, 1775–1917* (Washington D.C.: U.S. Army Center of Military History, 2005), 1.

44. Stephen Morillo and Michael F Pavkovic, *What is Military History?* (Malden and Cambridge: Polity Press, 2006), 1.

45. James Charlton, eds., *The Military Quotation Book* (New York: Thomas Dunne Books, 2002), 95.

46. James Charlton, eds., *The Military Quotation Book*, 125.

47. Morillo, 1–9.

48. Richard W Stewart, ed., *American Military History, Volume I, 1775–1917*, 12–13.

49. Harry G Summers, Jr., *On Strategy: The Vietnam War in Context* (Carlisle Barracks: US Army War College, 1982), 57.

50. See John Haldon, *The Byzantine Wars* (Gloucestershire: The History Press, 2011), 7.

51. Student Text 101–5, Command and Staff Decision Process, Fort Leavenworth Kansas: United States Army Command and General Staff College Publication, January 1994 excerpts from Field Manuel 34–130. Intelligence Preparation of the Battlefield II-2-1 to 54.

53. Colonel Monteith, . 'Journal of a Tour Through Azerbaijan and the Shores of the Caspian.' *Journal of the Royal Geographical Society of London*, Vol. 3 (1833), 1–58. http://www.jstor.org/stable/1797594; H.C. Rawlinson. 'The Road to Merv.' *Proceedings of the Royal Geographical Society and Monthly Record of Geography*, New Monthly Series, Vol. 1, No. 3 (Mar., 1879), 161–191. http://jstor.org/stable/1800653; G.S.F. Napier. 'The Road from Bagdad to Baku.' *The Geographical Journal*, Vol. 53, No. 1 (Jan., 1919), 1–16. http://www.jstor.org/stable/1780395. J.G.C. Anderson. 'The Road System of Eastern Asia Minor with the Evidence of Byzantine Campaigns.' *The Journal of Hellenic Studies*, Vol. 17 (1897), 22–44. http://www.jstor.org/stable/623816; and Georgina Herrmann, K Kurbansakhatove, and St. John Simpson. 'The International Merv Project. Preliminary Report on the Fourth Season (1995).' *Iran*, Vol. 34 (1996), 1–22. http://www.jstor.org/stable/4299941.

Chapter 2

1. Rose Mary Sheldon, *Rome's Wars In Parthia, Blood In The Sand*, 2–9, 231–249.

2. Farrokh (2004), *Shadows in the Desert*, 184–190, 194–197.

3. The modern village of Sadak is in the province Gümüshane, Turkey. MAVORS, Institute for Ancient Military History, http://www.mavors.org/en/projects_3.htm.

4. Dodgeon and Lieu, 133; Dignas and Winter, 122–130.

5. C S Lightfoot, 'The Site of Roman Bezabde.' 189–202, ed. Stephen Mitchell, *Armies and Frontiers in Roman and Byzantine Anatolia, Proceedings of a colloquium held at University College, Swansea, in April 1981* (Oxford: BAR International Series 156, 1983).

6. R C Blockley, *East Roman Foreign Policy, Formation and Conduct from Diocletian to Anastasius* (Leeds: Francis Cains, 1992), 6.

7. Blockley (1992), 6–7.

8. Al-Tari, *Annales*, ed., Barth, Noldeke, Trans, 290–291.

9. Wolfram Kleiss, 'Fortifications,' *Encyclopaedia Iranica*, 2012, http://www.iranicaonline.org/.

10. Shapur has a second bridge built across the Tigris at Ctesiphon to ease traffic congestion while still a boy. al-Tabri, 290.

11. Irfan Shahid, *Byzantium And The Arabs In The Fourth Century* (Washington D.C.: Dumbarton Oaks Research Library and Collection, 1984, 2006), 66–68.

12. Ibid., 68, fn 155.

13. Ibid., 71–72.

14. Map adapted from Dignas and Winter, 198–199.

15. Roberta Tomber, *Indo-Roman Trade, From Pots To Pepper* (London: Duckworth, 2008), 62–64.

16. T D Barnes, 'Constantine and the Christians of Persia,' *The Journal of Roman Studies*, Vol. 75 (1985), 126–136, 131. http://www.jstor.org/stable/300656.

17. Ibid., 132.

18. Ibid., 136.

19. Philip Matyszak, *Imperial General, The Remarkable Career Of Petellius Cerialis* (Barnsley: Pen & sword Books, Ltd., 2011), 42–43.

20. Blockley, (1992), 9.

21. Cromwell, 5–12.

22. Shahid, 72.

23. Potter, *The Roman Empire at Bay*, 460.

24. W E Kaegi Jr., 'Constantine's and Julian's Strategic Surprise Against the Persians,' *Athenaeum*, Vol. 59, (1981), 209–213.

25. A D Lee, *Information & Frontiers, Roman Foreign Relations in Late Antiquity* (Cambridge: Cambridge University Press, 2006), 113, 119.

26. At this point the Army of the Orient was not a *comitatus* field army. See Cromwell, 5–12.

27. Julian, 'Oration I, Panegyric In Honor Of The Emperor Constantius,' *The Works Of The Emperor Julian*, Vol. I Wilmer Cave Wright, trans., (London: Loeb Classical Library, 1913), 33; Dodgeon and Lieu, 152–162.

28. Festus, *Breviarium* and Theophanes, *Chronographia*, translated in Dodgeon and Lieu, 154.

29. AM, XVIII, 9.1, 73–75.

30. Barnes, T D. 'Constantine and the Christians of Persia,' *The Journal of Roman Studies*, Vol. 75 (1985), 126–136, 131. http://www.jstor.org/stable/300656.

31. Isaac, 416.

32. Craig H Caldwell, III, *Contesting Late Roman Illyricum: Invasions and Transformation in the Danubian-Balkan Provinces* (Doctoral Dissertation, Princeton University September 2007) 82.

33. R W. Burgess, 'The Summer of Blood: The Great Massacre of 337 and the Promotion of the Sons of Constantine,' *Dumbarton Oak Papers*, Vol. 62 (2008), 5–51, 10. Http://www.jstor.org/stable/20788042.

34. Caldwell, 85.

35. Ibid., 87.

36. Timothy D Barnes, *Athanasius and Constantius: Theology and Politics in the Constantinian Empire*, Ph.D. Dissertation (Cambridge, MA: Harvard University Press, 1993), 218–26.

37. Caldwell, 88; T.D. Barnes, 'Imperial Chronology, A. D. 337–350,' *Phoenix*, Vol. 34, No. 2 (Summer, 1980), 125–166, http://www.jstor.org/stable/1087874. Accessed 3 July 2012, 20.12; T.D. Barnes, 160–166.

38. Dodgeon and Lieu, 165.

39. Barnes (1985), 133. In the alternative, these events took place in 338.

Chapter 3

1. Vegetius, 48.

2. Farrokh (2007), 198–207.

3. Rawlinson, 41.

4. A D Lee. *Information & Frontiers, Roman Foreign Relations in Late Antiquity* (Cambridge: Cambridge University Press, 1993), 49.

5. Map adapted from Dignas and Winter, 198–199; and Talbert, 3, 4, 5, 6, 67, 69, 68, 71, 86–99.

6. Donald W Engels, *Alexander the Great and the Logistics of the Macedonian Army* (Berkeley: University of California Press, 1980), 67–68; Geoffrey Greatrex, *Rome and Persia At War, 502–532* (Leeds: Francis Carina Ltd., 1998), 19–21. The author is an olive farmer.

7. Lee, (1993) 91–92.

8. Jones (1964), 844–846.

9. James Howard-Johnson, 'The Two Great Powers in Late Antiquity.' 157–226, 189, ed. Jan William Drijvers, *The Late Roman World And Its Historian, Interpreting Ammianus Marcellinus* (London and New York: Routledge, 1999).

10. James Howard-Johnson (1995), 180–181; Colonel Monteith, . 'Journal of a Tour Through Azerbaijan and the Shores of the Caspian,' 1–58; H.C. Rawlinson. 'The Road to Merv,' 161–191; G.S.F. Napier. 'The Road from Baghdad to Baku,' 1–16; and Georgina Herrmann, K Kurbansakhatove, and St. John Simpson. 'The International Merv Project. Preliminary Report on the Fourth Season.'1–22.

11. James Howard-Johnson (1999), 'Heraclius' Persian Campaigns and the Revival of The Eastern Roman Empire,' *War In History*, Vol. 6, 1991, 1–44, 17.

12. Charlesworth, 58.

13. The Oxus River changed course in the late thirteenth century. Ernst Herzfeld, *Zoroaster and His World*, Vol. II (1947). Cited in Sylvia Volk's internet page *Page of Asian* 'The Course of the Oxus River,' http://www.iras.ucalgary.ca/~volk/sylvia/Asia.htm.

14. M P Charlesworth, *Trade-Routes and Commerce of the Roman Empire.* (London: Cambridge University Press, 1924), 104–109.

15. Ibid., 102–103; Monteith, 1–58; H C Rawlinson, 161–191;Napier, 1–16; and Herrmann, 1–22.
16. Ibid., 60, Roul McLaughlin, *The Roman Empire and the Indian Ocean, The Ancient World and The Kingdoms of Africa, Arabia & India* (South Yorkshire: Pen & Sword, 2014), 76–77, 150–151.
17. Ibid., 67–71.
18. Ibid., 101–111.
19. Wolfgang Felix, 'Chionites,' *Encyclopaedia Iranica, Vol. V, Fasc.5, 485–487, 2012 http://www.iranicaonline.org/articles/chionites-lat.*
20. Michael Loewe, 'Spices and Silk: Aspects of World Trade in the First Seven Centuries of the Christian Era.' *Journal of the Royal Asiatic Society of Great Britain and Ireland,* No. 2 (1971), 166–179. http://www.jstor.org/stable/2503290.
21. Roul McLaughlin, *The Roman Empire and the Indian Ocean, The Ancient World and The Kingdoms of Africa, Arabia & India,* 14–17.
22. John Thorley, 'The Roman Empire and the Kushans,' *Greece & Rome,* Second Series, Vo. 26, No. 2 (Oct., 1979), 181–190, http://www.jstor.org/stable/642511; C. Margabandhu, 'Trade Contacts between Western India and the Graeco-Roman World in the Early Centuries of the Christian Era,' *Journal of Economic and Social History of the Orient,* Vol. 8, No. 3 (Dec., 1965), 316–322, http://www.jstor.org/stable/3596384.
23. J Albert Morales, 'The Curious Career of Aurelius Gaius,' *Ancient Warfare VI-5,* (Dec. 2012), 40–41.
24. Steven E. Sidebotham, 'Late Roman Berenike,' *Journal of American Research Center in Egypt,* Vol. 39 (2002), 217–240, http://www.jstor.org/stable/40001157.
25. Touraj Daryaee, 'The Persian Gulf Trade in Late Antiquity,' *Journal of World History,* Vol. 14, No. 1 (Mar., 2003), 1–16, http://www.jstor.org/stable/20079006.
26. Peter Crawford, *The War of Three Gods, Romans, Persians and the Rise of Islam* (Pen & Sword: South Yorkshire, 2013), 54, map Heraclius' Campaigns of 624–628.
27. Howard-Johnson (1999), 16–27; A D Lee, *Information & Frontiers, Roman Foreign Relations In Late Antiquity* (Cambridge: Cambridge University Press, 1993), 94–95.
28. British Naval Intelligence Division, *Persia,* (Geographic Handbook Series, September 1945. [Declassified]), 544.
29. James Howard-Johnson. 'The Two Great Powers in Late Antiquity.' 157–226, 189, ed. Jan William Drijvers, *The Late Roman World And Its Historian, Interpreting Ammianus Marcellinus* (London and New York: Routledge, 1999); and AM, XXIV.2.9–22, 413–421.
30. Ibid., 190.
31. John Matthews. *The Roman Empire of Ammianus* (Baltimore: The John Hopkins University Press, 1989), 151–155.
32. Map adapted from Dignas and Winter, 198–199; and Talbert, 3, 4, 5, 6, 67, 69, 68, 71, 86–99.
33. Fourth century Ctesiphon was 30km^2 while Rome was 13.7km^2.
34. J Innes Miller, *The Spice Trade of the Roman Empire, 29 B.C. to A.D. 641* (Oxford: Clarendon Press, 1969), 120–123, 132, 176–177, 238, 239.
35. Matthews, 148–159.

36. Ibid., 150–158.
37. Ctesiphon was taken by Trajan in 116; Avidius Cassius in 164; Septimius Severus in 197; and Carus in 283. See generally, Sheldon (2010), *Rome's Wars In Parthia.*
38. R. Van Nort, *The Battle of Adrianople and the Military Doctrine of Vegetius.* Ph.D. Dissertation, City University of New York, United States--New York. Retrieved August 25, 2011, from Dissertations & Theses: The Humanities and Social Sciences Collection. (Publication No. AAT 3283191), 105–106.

Chapter 4

1. The term *ripeness* was used for the higher-grade frontier unit (legions, equites, cunei and equitum). Pat Southern & Karen R. Dixon, *The Late Roman Army* (New Haven and London: Yale University Press, 1996) 36; Cod. Th. 7.1.18; and Potter, *The Roman Empire At Bay, A.D. 180–395,* 451.
2. Southern and Dixon (1996), 36–37.
3. The designation *Palatini* did not appear until after 365. The *Pseudocomitatensei* regiments, which were *limitanei* units attached to a field army. The term first appears after Roman fortresses of Mesopotamia were ceded to Persia in 363 and the displaced *limitanei* were seconded to the field army. Cromwell, 31–33.
4. Cromwell, 31–33; and Potter, 457.
5. Cromwell estimates the army contained sixty-four comitatensian legions, six scholae (bodyguards), thirty-six cavalry and thirty-one *auxilia* regiments. The legions are estimated as 1,000 men and all other regiments as 500. At Naissus in the summer of 364 this army may only have mustered 30,000 men before the division of the empire between Valentinian I and his brother Valens. Cromwell, 11, 18–19. Potter estimates the total for the *comitatus* armies spring 363 as 120,000 men. Potter, 455–459.
6. Nicasie, 204.
7. Cromwell, 13–15.
8. At the time Arbito was Constantius' *magister equitum.* Potter, 481.
9. Zosimus as translated in Dodgeon and Lieu, 203; and AM, XVIII, 9.1–4, 463–467.
10. The compilation 'Notitia Dignitatum,' http://members.ozemail.com.au/~igmaier/webnotve.htm. Accessed 10 September 2012, 09.00.
11. Hugh Elton, 'Warfare and the Military,' 325–346, 332 in Noel Lenski, *The Cambridge Companion To The Age of Constantine* (Cambridge and New York: Cambridge University Press, 2012).
12. Gray A Crump, *Ammianus as a Military Historian* (Wiesbaden: Franz Steiner Verlag GMBH, 1975), 85.
13. AM, XIX, 3.1–3, 483, 485.
14. A 'vexillation' initially was a legionary detachment. In the fourth century some cavalry regiments in the field army were named *vexillationes* after their regimental standard. Cromwell, 71.
15. Parker, 148. Either two standard cohorts (Cohorts II-X) or one double cohort (Cohort I).
16. The compilation 'notitia dignitatum,' http://members.ozemail.com.au/~igmaier/webnotve.htm.; and Luk Ueda-Sarson. *Late Roman Shield Patterns taken from the Notitia Dignitatum,* www.lukeuedasarson.com/NotitiaPaterns.html.

17. The alternative theory argued by Donald O' Reilly is that the European legion in Thrace was the remains of Saint Mauricius' Theban Legion of Christians, sent to Gaul as a full antique legion in 286. Both theories could be correct. Four legions, (I Maximiana Thebeorum, II Flavia Constantia Thebeorum, III Diocletiana Thebeorum and I Flavia Constantia (originally named IV Galeriana Thebeorum) are recorded with the title 'Thebeorum'. St. Mauricius' legion could have been any of these legions. See Donald O'Reilly, *Lost Legion Rediscovered, The Mystery of the Theban Legion* (Barnsely: Pen & Sword Military Books Ltd., 2011), xiv-xv, 128–145.
18. AM., XVIII, 8.2, and XXIV, 1.2.
19. Vetetius list the antique cohorts II-IX as 550 infantry and 66 cavalry and cohort I as 1, 105 infantry and 132 armoured cavalry. Vetetius, Book II, 6–8.
20. Following Vegetius it would be 1,100. Vegetius, Book II, 6–8.
21. Jones, 640.
22. Treadgold, 87–89; Jones, 640.
23. The strength estimates are based upon, the first double cohort of 1,000 men and four standard cohorts of 500 remaining in the legion. In the alternative 3,000 to 4,000 men would have been the average daily strength (versus authorized strength) of an antique legion with all ten cohorts.
24. In March 363 the garrison of Circesium on the Euphrates was 6,000 men. Magnus of Carrhae (Malalas XIII, 5–337, 11), 226.
25. Michael P Speidel, 'Raising New Units for the Late Roman Army: Auxilia Palatine,' *Dumbarton Oaks Papers*, Vol. 50 (1996), 163–170, http://www.jstor.org/stable/1291742.
26. Nicasie, 188–193.
27. I.P. Stephenson, *Roman Infantry Equipment, The Later Empire* (Charleston and Gloucestershire: Tempus Publishing Ltd., 2001) 111–113.
28. AM XVI 11.9, 261, XXIV, 6.4–7, and XXV, 6.10–15.
29. Speidel, 167; and Treadgold, 90.
30. Vegetius, Book II, 3.
31. Letki, 75–81; Southern and Dixon (1996), 188; and Treadgold, 89–92.
32. Vegetius, Book II, 6. The first cohort had 132 cavalrymen while the remaining nine cohorts had sixty-six cavalrymen for a total of 704 men. The additional twenty-two men reported by Vegetius may have been additional horsemen not in the *turmae* or his math was in error. The *decurio* (decurion) may actually have been a centurion. See Pavkovic.
33. Piotr Letki, *The Cavalry of Diocletian* (Oswiecim: Napoleon V, 2012), 43–47; and Coello, 8–17.
34. Letki, 71–77.
35. Treadgold, 43–86; and Southern and Dixon (1996), 67–75.
36. Elton (1997), 128–134; and Southern and Dixon (1996), 67–75.
37. This requirement was lowered to 5'7" Roman Feet in 367. Clyde Pharr, Trns. *The Theodosian Code and Novels and Sirmondian Constitutions* (Princeton, NJ: Princeton University Press), 1952, 170; and Jones, 616. A Roman foot is 0.971feet or 296mm. A Roman mile was 0.919 standard miles or 1.48km. Sir William Smith, *A New Classical*

Dictionary of Greek and Roman Biography, Mythology and Geography (New York: Harper & Brothers, 1851), Tables, 1024–1030.

38. Vegetius, Book I, 2; and Southern and Dixon (1996), 67–75.
39. A D Lee, *War In Late Antiquity, A Social History* (Oxford: Blackwell Publishing, 2007), 176–187, 193–211.
40. Vegetius, Book I, 2–6.
41. Isaac, 145.
42. Abinnaeus, 16–17, 61–65.
43. Theodosian Code, 157, 183.
44. Jones, 620–623; and Southern and Dixon (1996), 67–75.
45. Southern and Dixon (1996), 67–68.
46. Vegetius, Book I, 1.
47. Ibid., Book I, 1.
48. Ibid., Book I, 9 and 19. A Roman mile equals 1,617yards or 1,478.5m. A Roman pound equals .07lb. or 327.45g. Sixty Roman pounds equals 43lb. 5 oz. or 19.6kg.
49. Ibid., Book I, 1–19.
50. Clyde Pharr, Trns. *The Theodosian Code and Novels and Sirmondian Constitutions* (Princeton, NJ: Princeton University Press), 1952, 170, 188.
51. Luttwak (2009), 285.
52. Vegetius, Book I, 8.
53. Dr Patricia Southern disagrees with this assertion and argues that the *contubernium* had no tactical function. See Patricia Southern, *The Roman Army, A History 753 BC-AD 479* (Gloucestershir: Amberley Publisshing, 2014) 218.
54. Zosimus, 89; AM XXV, 5.1–4.
55. Luttwack, (2009), 285.
56. Vegetius, Book I, 20, 21fn3, Book II, 3; AM, XVIII, 2.6
57. Some authorities argue that this organization was one regiment, while others list it as two: *protectors* and *domesticus*.
58. Jones, 637–639.
59. Ibid., 639.
60. Jones, 623–635.
61. Jones, 629–630; and Southern and Dixon (1996), 76–88.
62. Ibid.
63. J C N Coulston, 'How to Arm a Roman Soldier,' 167–190, ed. Michel Austin, Jill Harries and Christopher Smith. *Modus Operandi, Essays in Honour of Geoffrey Richman* (London: University of London 1998), 167–190, 178–179.
64. J Albert Morales, 'The Curious Career of Aurelius Gaius,' 40–41.
65. Jones, Vol. II fn. 31, 1257–1258; and Terence Coello. *Unit Sizes in the Late Roman Army* (Oxford UK:BAR International Series 645, 1996), 2–10.
66. M J Nicasie, *Twilight of Empire, the Roman Army from the Reign of Diocletian Until the Battle of Adrianople* (Amsterdam: J C Gieben, 1998), 190–191, fn23.
67. AM., XVIII, 9.1–4, 463–467. Translators disagree as to whether these legions were cavalry or infantry. AM describes them as legions which does not preclude them containing cavalry.

68. John Malalas, as quoted in Dodgeon and Lieu, 262. As used in the passage it is not clear whether the *lanciarii* is a unit name or a term for light infantry.

69. Based upon his study of Late Roman infantry equipment, I P Stephenson concludes the Late Roman infantry converted to spearmen in the late third century. See I P Stephenson, *Roman Infantry Equipment, The Late Roman Empire* (Gloucester: Tempus Publishing, 2001), 52–60, 75 and 111–113.

70. *Vegetius' Epitoma Rei Militaris*, 24–25; and *Strategikon*, 138.

71. Dixon and Southern (1992), 34–53, 142–147.

72. Julian, *Oration I*, 37C-38A (30.15–28, pp. 54–5, Bidez) as quoted in Dodgeon and Lieu, 173–174; A D H Bivar, 'Cavalry Equipment and Tactics on the Euphrates Frontier,' *Dumbarton Oaks Papers*, Vol. 26 (1972), 271–291, http://www.jstor.org/stable/1291323.

73. Dixon and Southern (1992), 137–147.

74. Ross Cowan, *Roman Battle Tactics 109 BC-AD 313* (Oxford: Osprey Publishing, 2007), 4–41

75. The actual distance between lines is not clear. The flight range of a bow-shot would be 300m while the effective range would be closer to 80–100m. *Strategikon*, Book II, 13. (31fn3).

76. The pairs were the *Joviani-Herculiani, Divitenses-Tungrecani, Celtae-Petulantes, Eruli-Batavi, Jovii-Victores* and *Lancearii-Mattiarii*. The final pair, *Gentiles-Scutarii*, were guard units. Roger Tomlin, 'Seniores-Iuniores in the Late Roman Army,' *The American Journal of Philology*, Vol. 93, No. 2 (Apr., 1972), 253–278. http:www.jstor.org/stable/293251.

77. See Peter Crawford, *The War of the Three Gods, Romans, Persians and the Rise of Islam* (Pen & Sword: Yorkshire, 2013), 124; and Procopius, *History of the Wars, Books I and II The Persian Wars*, trans., H.B. Dewing (BiblioBazaar: London, 2007), Book I, XIII, 58–59.

78. Titus Livius, *The History of Rome, Books 1 to 8* (Online: Project Gutenberg, 2006), VIII, 512–514. www.gutenberg.org; Cowan (2007) 8, 23–32.

79. Vegetius, III, 14.

80. Ibid.

81. Sander van Dorst, 'Arrian's Array against the Alans,' http://s_van_dorst.tirpod.com/Ancient_Warfare/Rome/Sorces/ektaxis.html#orderofbattle. Accessed 2 December 2013, 14.00; Adrian Goldsworthy, *The Fall of Carthage* (Cassell Military Paperback: London, 2006), 48–49.

82. *Strategikon*, 138.

83. Lenski, 325.

84. Sita Ram, *From Sepoy To Subedar, The Life and Adventures of Subedar Sita Ram, A Native Officer of the Army of the Bengal Army, written and related by Himself*, ed., James Lunt (Archon Books: Hamden, 1970), 170–175.

85. AM, XX, 4.2.

86. Coello, 25–26.

87. *Strategikon*, Book XII, B, 8. 140. It was also the strength of Alexander the Great's basic infantry company. See Christopher Matthew, trans. *The Tactics of Aelian, A New*

Translation of the Manual that Influenced Warfare for Fifteen Centuries (South Yorkshire: Pen & Sword, 2012), 27 Plate 3.

88. The safety ditch was to keep men and animals out of the caltrop field. *Strategikon*, 164.

89. Zosimus, 89.

90. George T Dennis, trans. *Three Byzantine Military Treatises* (Washington DC: Dumbarton, 1985) in 'Campaign Organization and Tactics,' 247–335, 323–335.

91. Vegetius, 36.

92. Roth, 83, 206–209.

93. Engels, 18–21.

94. Roth, 210–212; and Jones (1964), 830–833.

95. Engels, 14–16; and Roth, 14–58, 210–212.

96. John Peddie. *The Roman War Machine* (Gloucestershire: Sutton Publishing Ltd., 1997), 40–58; and Adrian Goldsworthy (2003), 170.

97. *The Chronicle of Joshua The Stylite* Translated and edited by Wright, William (Amsterdam: Philo Press, 1968), 44; and Greatrex (1988), 96.

98. Roth, 22; A *modii* equates to approximately between 9–10 quarts or 8.7 litres with a weight of 20lbs depending on the grain.

99. Jones (1964), 629, 1261 fn 44.

100. AM, XIX., 9.9–10.

101. Hugh Elton, 'Cavalry in Late Roman Warfare,' 377–381. Ariel S Lewin and Pietrina Pellegrini. Ed., *The Late Roman Army in the Near East from Diocletian to the Arab Conquest: Proceedings of a colloquium held at Potenza Acerenza and Matera, Italy (May 2005)* (Oxford: British Archaeological Reports International Series 1717, 2007).

102. A D Lee, *War in Late Antiquity, A Social History* (Oxford: Blackwell Publishing, 2007), 91–93.

103. Ibid., 89–94.

104. Nicasie, 203–207.

105. Vegetius, 35; and Nicasie, 207.

106. During the 502–506 war two armies with a combined strength of 52,000 operated in the same region as one army of 40,000 and a second army of 12,000. Greatrex (1988), 96.

107. John Peddie, *The Roman War Machine*, (Gloucestershire: Alan Sutton Publishing Ltd., 1997), 72–76; and Goldsworthy (2003), 174.

108. The soldiers were trained to march 4mph, but the oxen could not maintain that speed.

109. AM, XXIV, 1.2, 401.

110. Vegetius, I.19.

111. *Landing Force Manual 1920, United States Navy* (Washington D.C.: Government Printing Office, 1921), Article 483–493.

112. Ibid., XXIV, 1.1–4, 401–403; and Nicasie, 201.

113. Edward N Luttwak, (1979); Everett L. Wheeler, 'Methodological Limits and the Mirage of Roman Strategy: Part I.' *The Journal of Military History*, Vol. 57, No. 1 (Jan., 1993), 7–41. http://www.jstor.org/stable2944221; Everett L Wheeler, 'Methodological Limits and the Mirage of Roman Strategy: Part II.' *The Journal of Military History*, Vol. 57, No. 2 (Apr., 1993), 215–240. http://www.jstor.org/stable/2944057; Kimberly

Kagan, 'Redefining Roman Grand Strategy.' *The Journal of Military History*, Vol. 70, No. 2 (Apr., 2006), 333–362. http://www.jstor.org/stable/4137956; and Edward N Luttwak, *The Grand Strategy of the Byzantine Empire* (Cambridge, Mass. and London: Harvard University Press, 2009).

114. C R Whittaker, *Frontiers of the Roman Empire, A Social and Economic Study* (Baltimore and London: The John Hopkins University Press, 1994), 132–133.

115. Isaac, 373–387, 416, 419–420, 424.

116. Zosimus, 51–55.

117. Stephen Johnson, *Late Roman Fortifications* (Totowa, NJ: Barnes and Noble Books, 1983), 253.

118. Robin Seager, 'Perceptions of Eastern Frontier Policy in Ammianus, Libanius, and Julian (337–363).' *The Classic Quarterly*, New Series, Vol. 47, No. 1 (1997), 253–268. http://www.jstor.org/stable/639612; and see generally Harry G Summers, Jr. *On Strategy: The Vietnam War in Context.* Carlisle Penn: Strategic Institute Studies, 1982.

119. Jones (1964), 610.

120. Hugh Elton (1997), 207–208; and Isaac, 147–148.

121. H I Bell, V Martin, E G Turner, D van Berchem. ed and trans. *The Abinnaeus Archive: The Papers of A Roman Officer in the Reign of Constantius II* (Oxford, UK: Oxford University Press, 1962), 13–15.

122. AM, XVIII, 6.8, 439; and Elton (1997), 207–208.

123. Elton (1997), 200–201.

124. AM, XXVII, 2.11, 13.

125. Benjamin Isaac. 'Bandits in Judaea and Arabia.' *Harvard Studies in Classical Philology*, Vol. 88 (1984), 171–203, 200. http://www.jstor.org/stable/311452.

126. O'Reilly, 34–39. Dodgeon and Lieu, 9–139.

127. Ibid., 136–154.

128. Jerome H Farnum. *The Positioning of the Roman Legions* (Oxford, UK: BAR International Series 1458, 2005) 9; Southern and Dixon (1996), 127–147;

129. Elton (1997), 163.

130. Ibid., 157–160.

131. AM, XXIII, 4.1–14, 325–333; and Southern and Dixon (1996), 153–160.

132. Ibid., XIX, 2.7; Adrian Goldsworthy, *The Complete Roman Army*, (London: Thames & Hudson, 2003), 188–192.

133. Goldsworthy (2003), *The Complete Roman Army*, 188–192.

134. AM, XIX, 6.3–13, 497–503.

135. Dodgeon and Lieu, 340–349 and 397–400; Talbert, 67, 69, 68, 71 and 86–99.

136. Excluding the legions, Phoenicia was garrisoned with nineteen cavalry regiments and five cohorts; Syria and Euphratensis, eleven cavalry regiments and four cohorts; Osrhoene, fifteen cavalry regiments and two cohorts; and Mesopotamia, thirteen cavalry regiments and two cohorts. See Dodgeon and Lieu, Appendix 5, 340–348.

137. See Appendix 1 for a complete listing of the *limitanei* armies of the provinces of Phoenicia, Syria, Euphratensis, Osrhoene, and Mesopotamia and their garrison locations c. 395.

138. Michael Pavkovic, *The legionary horsemen: An essay on equites legionis and equites promote* (Ph.D. Dissertation: University of Hawaii, 1991).

139. For simplicity sake, only the locations of the *limitanei* legions and *equistes promote* are depicted on the maps of this book.

140. See Appendix 1.

141. Close to Vegetius' 4 infantry to 1 cavalry ratio.

142. Dodgeon and Lieu, Appendix 5, 340–348.

143. Queen Mavia personally led her Saracen warriors in raids along the Roman *limes* from Phoenicia to Egypt and defeated the Roman Field Army in open battle then dictated the terms of the peace. *The Ecclesiastical History of Sozomen: Comprising A History Of The Church From A.D. 324–440*, trans., Edward Walford, (London: Henry G. Bohn, 1855) 307, 308.

144. AM, XIX, 9.2, 515.

145. Dodgeon and Lieu, 399 fn 35, 38 and 41; See also C S Lightfoot, 'The Third Siege of Nisibis (A.D. 350),' *Historia: Zeitschrift fur alte Geschichte*, Bd. 37, H 1 (1st Qtr., 1988), 105–125, 108; http//www.jstor.org/stable/4436041.

146. Dodgeon and Lieu, 340–349 and 397–400; and Talbert, 67, 69, 68, 71 and 86–99.

147. Julian Reade, 'An Eagle from the East', *Britannia*, Vol. 30 (1999), 286–288, http://www.jstor.org/stable/526684.

148. AM XVIII, 10.1–4, 467–469.

149. Reade argues that Seh Gubba is location of Castra Maurorum. See Read, 286–288.

150. AM, XIV, 7. 5; Julian, Vol. III, Ltr 58, March 10, 363, 'To Libanius, Sophist and Quaestor.' 201–209.,

151. Jones, 637–639.

152. S Thomas Parker, *The Frontier in Central Jordan, Final Report on the Limes Arabicus Project*, Volume I (Washington D.C.: Dumbarton Oaks, 2006), 544–545; Luke Ueda-Sarson. 'Late Roman Shield Designs Taken from the Notitia Dignitatum.' *Luke Ueda-Sarson's Wargame Pages*, 2006. http://www.ne.jp/asahi/luke/ueda-sarson/NotitiaPatterns.html.

153. Jones, 679–686. Jones estimates that *comitatenses* legions had an authorized strength of 1,000 and *limitanei* legions at between 1,000 and 3,000. *Auxilia Palatine* infantry regiments were authorized 600 to 700 and most other cavalry and infantry units at about 500.

154. The variance is dependent whether the two *limitanei* legions *tertiae Cyrenaicae* and *quartae Martiae* had 1,000 or 2000 men. Parker, 544–545.

155. Jones, 52–59, 96–100, 1257, fn 31and 1280 fn.170–173.

156. C S Lightfoot, *The Eastern Frontier of the Roman Empire with Special Reference to the Reign of Constantius II* (Oxford: St. James College Theise, 1982), 73–77. Based upon its name, the *pseudocomitatenses* legion *Transtigritani* (beyond the Tigris) would have originally occupied one of the fortresses on the east side of the Tigris. Very little is known about the history of this legion before the fifth century and is therefore not used in this template. The legion's existence supports the argument that there was a substantial Roman military establishment on the east side of the Tigris until 363. The legion was transferred from the Army of the East to Egypt shortly after 395. It

is mentioned on a papyrus dated February 14, 406. See Papyri. Info at http://papyri. info/ddbdp/sb;14;11574.

157. Ibid., XVIII, 9, 1–9, 463–467. The names of these legions are derivatives of Latin verbs: *Superventores* a derivative of *supervenio* (catch) and *Praeventires* may be a derivative of *praevenio* (intercept).

158. Another example is *Milites Exploratores.*

159. Kendall D Gott, *In Search of an Elusive Enemy: The Victorio Campaign* (Fort Leavenworth, Kansas: Combat Institute Press, 2004), 12–15.

Chapter 5

1. Blockley (1992), 101, 102.
2. British Naval Intelligence Division, *Persia* (Geographic Handbook Series, September 1945. Declassified), 245.
3. *Persia,* 245.
4. James Howard-Johnson, *East Rome, Sasanian Persia and the End of Antiquity* (Cornwall: Ashgate Publishing Ltd., 2006), 188–189.
5. James Howard-Johnson, 'The Sasanians' Strategic Dilemma', *Commutatio et Contentio; Studies in the Late Roman, Sasanian, and Early Islamic Near East; in memory of Zeev Rubin,* (Dusseldorf: Wellem, 2010), 37–70.
6. Howard-Johnson (2006), 188–189; AM, XXIV 2.1–3, 409–411.
7. Richard Nelson Frye, 'The Sasanian System of Walls for Defense', *Studies in Memory of Gaston Wiet,* 1977, 7–15, 10.
8. AM, XXV, 6.8, 523.
9. Howard-Johnson (2006), 190.
10. Fraye, 12–14; Jebrael Nokandeh, Eberhard W. Sauer et. al., 'Linear Barriers of Northern Iran: The Great Wall of Gorgan and the Wall of Tammisher', *Iran,* Vol. 44 (2006), 121–173. http://www.jstor.org/stable/4300707; and Hamid Omrani Rekavandi, Ederhard W Sauer et. al., 'An Imperial Frontier Of The Sasanian Empire: Further Fieldwork At The Great Wall of Gorgan', *Iran,* Vol. 45 (2007), 95–136. http://www.jstor.org/stable/25651414.
11. Al-Tabari, 54–57.
12. Based upon the accounts of Alexander the Great campaigns, we know he was assisted by experienced generals inherited from his father and his own companions. He could not have accomplished what he did alone; neither could Shapur.
13. Farrokh (2005), 6–8.
14. In 336 Narses, possibly the brother of Shapur, commanded an army that captured Amida and invaded Roman Mesopotamia. In 350 when Shapur moved east to face the Huns, Tamsapor, was left in charge of the Roman War. He also commanded a cavalry advance guard during Shapur's 359 invasion. In 363 'the Surena' commanded the Persian delaying force opposing Julian's advance south along the Euphrates River. Also in 363 Generals Merena and Nohodares commanded the tactical battles against Julian's retreating army. These events are discussed in detail in following chapters.
15. AM, XXIV 6.8, 468.

16. Kaveh Farrokh, *Sasanian Elite Cavalry AD 224–642* (Oxford: Osprey Publishing, 2005), 3–5; AM, XXIV 6.8, 461.

17. Farrokh (2005), 9–22; A.D.H. Bivar. 'Cavalry Equipment and Tactics on the Euphrates Frontier,' *Dumbarton Oaks Papers*, Vol. 26 (1972), 271–291. http://www.jstor.org/stable/1291323.

18. Farrokh (2005), 27–28.

19. AM, XXIV, 2.1, 2.7, 3.1, 3.7, 4.1.399–449.

20. Ibid., XXIV, 4.2, 431; J.C. Coulston, 59–75; and Bivar, 271–291.

21. A. Sh. Shahbazi. *Sasanian Army*. Iranian Chamber of Chamber. 2–3. http://www.iranchamber.com/history/sasanids/Sasanian_army.php. Accessed 10 December 2012, 08.26.

22. AM., XIX, 6.6–7.4, XXIII, 6.83 and XXIV, 6.8; Farrokh (2005), 23–24; Brain Todd Carey, *Road To Manzikert, Byzantine And Islamic Warfare 527–1071* (Barnsley: Pen and Sword Books Ltd., 2012), 6–10.

23. Carey, 59–66; and Crawford, 135–145,

24. Farrokh (2004), 201. Despite their size they were repeatedly used in ambush against Julian's army in June 363. See Chapter 10.

25. Andrew de la Garza, 'The Mughal Battlefield: Personnel. Technology and Tactics in the Early Empire, 100–1604,' *The Journal of Military History*, Vol. 78, No. 3 (July 2014) 927–960, 936.

26. Zonaras, XII, 23, 595–596.

27. Dodgeon and Lieu, 181.

28. Sir Richard F Burton, trans., *The Book of the Thousand Nights and a Night*, Story of Prince Behram and the Princess Al-Datma, online version, http://www.wollamshram.ca/1001/Vol_1/vol1.htm.

29. Historic Persian Women, http://mani.tk/queens.htm. This article does not follow western scholarly protocols.

30. Farrokh, (2005) 43.

31. Ibid., 6–8.

32. AM, XXV, 5.8–9.

33. Farrokh, (2005), 5–7.

34. AM, XVIII., 6, 22–23, XIX., 2.3.

35. *Procopius History of the Wars, Books I and II*. trans. H.B. Dewing (London: BiblioBazaar, 2007), 58; Howard-Johnson, 166–167; Lee 259–260; and A. Sh. Shahbazi, 2–3; Carey, 8–14. *Strategikon*, 113–115.

36. Edward C. Echols, trans. *Herodian of Antioch's History of the Roman Empire*, Book IV.15.1–9.

37. Farrokh (2005), 30; and A.D.H. Bivar, 289–291.

38. *Strategikon*, Book XI, 1; and *Herodian*, Book IV.15.2–3.

39. *Strategikon*, Book VI.1–5; Letki, 163–178; Dixon and Southern (1992), 132–134, 140–147; and A.D.H. Bivar, 289–291.

40. Ammianus makes it clear that he was afraid of the Persian elephants. AM, XIX, 2.1–3.

41. Simon, 11.

42. Zonaras XII, 23, 10–595, as cited in Dodgeon and Lieu, (2002) 55, 56.

Chapter 6

1. Christian tradition alleges Bishop Jacob defeated the Persian assault with the local mosquitoes and gnats. Theodoret, *Historia Religiosa* and *Historia Ecclesiastica,* in Dodgeon and Lieu, 165–168.
2. Ibid., 384, FN 6.
3. Ibid.
4. Simons James, *Excavations At Dura-Europos 1928–1937, Final Report VII The Arms and Armor and other Military Equipment,* (Oxford: Oxbow Books, 2004), 30–39.
5. Julian, *Or.* I, 18c; Neol Lenski, ed., *The Cambridge Companion to the Age of Constantine* (Cambridge and New York: Cambridge University Press, 2012), 332.
6. Blockley (1992), 23.
7. Ibid., 14–15.
8. Ibid., 14.
9. Barnes, 135–136.
10. Blockley, 15–16.
11. Julian, *Or.* I and Libanius, *Or.* LIX 176–179, 188 and 385 fn18 as translated in Dodgeon and Lieu.
12. Ibid.
13. Ibid.
14. Ibid.
15. The sources indicated the camps were one hundred fifty *stades* apart. One hundred fifty *stades* equals approximately sixteen miles.
16. Zosimus I, 50, 2–4; Dodgeon and Lieu, 93.
17. *Strategikon,* 113–115.
18. Standard Roman battle tactics. See: *Herodian of Antioch, History of the Roman Empire (1961, 108–134* Book 4, Chapter XV, 1–4, Edward C. Echols, trans; http://www.tertullian.org/fathers/index.htm#Herodian_Roman_Histories. Accessed 19 October 2012, 08.12; and Ross Cowan, *Roman Battle Tactics 109 BC-AD 313* (Oxford: Osprey Publishing, 2007), 9–10.
19. Zosimus, in Dodgeon and Lieu, 93–95.
20. Maxentius (Marcus Aurelius Valerius Augustus, c. 278– 28 October 312) was Roman emperor from 306–312. He was a son of the former Emperor Maximian and the son-in-law of Emperor Galerius. Elizabeth James, *Constantine the Great, Warlord of Rome* (Barnsley: Pen & Sword Books, Ltd., 2012), 54–55.
21. Dodgeon and Lieu, 181–190.
22. T D Barnes, 'Imperial Chronology, A.D. 337–350', *Phoenix,* Vol. 34, No. 2 (Summer, 1980), 160–166, 163. http://www.jstor.org/stable/1087874. Accessed 19 October 2012, 10.10
23. AM, XXV, 9, 3, 549.
24. Dodgeon and Lieu, 191, 192.
25. AM, XVIII, 9, 3; Dodgeon and Lieu, 193, 386 fn 20 and fn 25; Barnes (1980), 164.
26. AM, XIX, 2.8 and XX, 6.5.
27. Cromwell, 14; Zosimus, 58, Sozomen, 146, 147.
28. The term 'Nisibenae' was probably a battle honour earned during the siege of 350.

29. Dodgeon and Lieu, 193–206; Lightfoot (1988), 119–122.
30. Nossov, 12, 13; For a general discussion see Phillip Rance, 'Elephants In Warfare In Late Antiquity', *Acta Ant. Hung. 43*, 2003, 355–384, 361–369.
31. C S Lightfoot (1988), 105–125.

Chapter 7

1. James Howard-Johnson, 'The Sasanian Strategic Dilemma', *Commutatio et contentio, studies in the Late Roman, Sasanian, and Early Islamic Near East; in memory of Zeev Rubin,* (Dusseldorf: Wellem, 2010), 37–70, 41.
2. Howard-Johnson (2010), 41–42.
3. Ammianus describes the Persian attempt to raid the market town of Batnae in 354. AM, XIV, 3.1–4, 25–27; and B.H. Warmington, 'Objectives and Strategy in the Persian War of Constantius II', *Limes: Aken des XI Internationalen Limeskongresses* (Budapest: Akademiai, Kiado, 1977), 514.
4. Church historians relate tales of Saracen brigands disrupting life in Mesopotamia. See Irfan Shahid, *Byzantium and The Arabs in the Fourth Century* (Washington DC.: Harvard University Press, 2006) 284–293; AM, XIV, 4.1–7, 27–29.
5. AM, XXVI, 1.1–2, 565–567.
6. Howard-Johnston (2010), 43.
7. Richard Nelson Fry, 'The Sasanian System of Walls for Defense', *Studies in Memory of Gaston Wiet*, (1977), 7–15.
8. In his translation of *The History of al-Tabari, Volume I,* Bosworth indicates that these accomplishments were wild claims. Bosworth argues it would have been unlikely that Shapur would build a city in a disputed region with the Saka and almost impossible to have built a city in the Indian province of Sind. al-Tabari, 65 fn179. Historically, building a city or castle in a disputed area is how a kingdom established control. Roman colonies and Norman and English castles are prime examples of establishing control of a region.
9. AM, XXIII 6.14, 357.
10. Tourj Daryaee. *Sasanian Iran (224–651 CE)* (Costa Mesa: Mazda Publishers, 2008) 47–48; AM, XXIII.6.14, 357.
11. Fry, 13.
12. Jebrael Nokandeh et al., 'The Enigma of the Red Snake, Revealing one of the World's Greatest Frontier Walls', *Current World Archaeology*, No. 27, (February/March 2004), 12–22; Jebrael Nokandeh et al., 'Linear Barriers of Northern Iran: The Great Wall of Gorgan and the Wall of Tammishe', *Iran*, Vol. 44 (2006, 121–173. http://www.jstor.org/stable/4300707. Accessed 10 October 2012, 11.15.

Chapter 8

1. A H M Jones, J R Martindale and J Morris, *The Prosopography of the Later Roman Empire* (Cambridge: Cambridge University Press, 1971), 224–225.
2. A H M. Jones, J R Martindale and J Morris, *The Prosopography Of The Later Rome*, 224–225.
3. AM, XIV, 1–4.

4. Samuel N C Lieu and Dominic Montserrat, ed., *From Constantine to Julian, Pagan and Byzantine Views, A Source Book* (Routledge: London and New York, 1996), 211–212.
5. Jones (1971), *The Prosopography*, 222.
6. Ibid., 720.
7. Ibid., 886–887.
8. AM, XIV, 1.9.
9. Thompson, 308 fn 13. 311, 315
10. Thompson, 305.
11. Ryszard Kapuscinski, *Travels With Herodotus* (New York: Vintage Books, 2007), 112, 113.
12. AM, XIV.4.1–3.
13. Ibid., XIV, 4.4.
14. Ibid, XIV. 1.4–6; Libanius Ep. 391
15. Barbra Geller Nathanson, 'Jews, Christians, and the Gallus Revolt in Fourth-Century Palestine', *The Biblical Archeologist*, Vol. 49, No. 1 (Mar., 1986), 26–36. http://www.jstor.org/stable/3209979.
16. Matthews, 405–409.
17. AM, XIV, 7.6.
18. Matthews, 405–409.
19. E A Thompson, 'Ammianus' Account of Gallus Caesar,' *The American Journal of Philology*, Vol. 64, No. 3 (1943), 302–315, 305–307. http://www.jstor.org/stable/291014.
20. AM's timeline is confusing but, since Thalassus died in 353, the crisis must have been after the harvest in 353.
21. AM, XIV, 1.10.
22. E A Thompson, 307.
23. E A Thompson, 308.
24. AM., XIV, 2.14. The Isaurian region would cause the empire problems throughout the fourth century. In 395, the legions II and III Isauria are listed as its garrison. In 353, its garrison probably consisted of the legions I Isauria *sagittarii* along with II and III Isauria.
25. AM, XIV, 2.2–4.
26. Ibid., XIV, 2.5–6.
27. Ammianus uses the term *equestrium adiumento cohortium*. Since there are no records of independent cavalry units deployed to this region, this phrase could refer to mounted infantry or legionary cavalry. Ibid., XIV, 2.12.
28. Ibid., XIV, 2.10–12.
29. Ibid., XIV.15–17.
30. Ibid., XIV.16–17.
31. AM XIV, 7.6.
32. AM XIV, 7.6. Julian's initial personal bodyguard was 360 men, so Gallus' may not have been much bigger. The regiments *Scutarii* and *Gentiles* were cavalry and would have numbered approximately 500, if at full strength.
33. AM, XIV, 7, 9–12.

34. Ibid.
35. Ibid., XIV, 7, 20–22.
36. Ibid., XIV, 9.1–3; and Mathews, 34–35.
37. Ibid., XIV, 9, 3–9.
38. Ibid., XIV, 7, 18; Thompson, 310–311.
39. Samuel N.C. Lieu and Dominic Montserrat, ed., *From Constantine to Julian, Pagan and Byzantine Views, A Source Book*, 211.
40. AM, XIV, 3, 1–4.
41. Matthews, 35.
42. AM, XIV.9.1; and Matthews, 34.
43. AM, XIV, 11–25.
44. Ibid., XV, 23–7.
45. Libanius, 'Oration 59(LIX)', 33–47, in Samuel N.C. Lieu and Dominic Montserrat, *From Constantine To Julian, Pagan and Byzantine Views, A Source History* (London and New York: Routledge, 1996), 164–205.
46. AM, XV 3, 1–11.

Chapter 9

1. The alternative theory is that Gallus or Ursicinus created the Eastern Field Army from detachments from the eastern *limitanei* armies. In either case, a field army was created and employed by Ursicinus to suppress the Jewish revolt of 351, suppress Isaurian bandits in 353–354, and counter Persian raids in 353–354.
2. For an examination of non-military issues, see Timothy D Barnes, *Athanasius and Constantius, Theology and Politics in the Constantinian Empire* (Cambridge, Mass.: Harvard University Press, 1993).
3. Timothy D Barnes, *Athanasius and Constantius, Theology and Politics in the Constantinian Empire*, 101–102.
4. Zosimus, Book II 58.
5. Zosimus, Book II 57–58.
6. Zosimus, 58, Sozomen, 146–147, Socrates, I, 146–147.
7. Craig H Caldwell, III, *Contesting Late Roman Illyricum: Invasions and Transformation in the Danubian-Balkan Provinces* (Doctoral Dissertation, Princeton University September 2007), 123–124.
8. Zosimus, Book II, 42.
9. Zosimus, Book II, 42. Socrates claims these events took place at Sirmium. Socrates, I, 146.
10. Caldwell, III, *Contesting Late Roman Illyricum: Invasions and Transformation in the Danubian-Balkan Provinces*, 82–85 citing Eutr., Brev. 10.9, Aur. Vict., Caes. 41.25.
11. James Michael Hunt, *Constantius II In The Ecclesiastical Historians.* Ph.D. Dissertation (Fordham University, New York, April, 2010) 172–173.
12. David S Potter, *The Roman Empire At Bay, A.D. 180–395* (London and New York: Routledge, 2004) 472.
13. Ibid., 132.
14. Zosimus, Book II, 59.

15. Vetetius, Book I, 1. Spartacus' gladiators were successful against green Roman levies during the late republic. Their pampered fourth century counterparts were no match for professional soldiers.
16. Caldwell III, 136–137.
17. Zonaras, 13.7, page 165., Trans DiMaio.
18. Luke Ueda-Sarson, *Late Roman Shield Patterns taken from the Notitia Dignitatum*, 'Magister Militum per Thracias' at http://www.ne.jp/asahi/luke/ueda-sarson/ NotitiaPatterns.html. Last update 16 November 2014. This is an academically professional webpage dedicated to the study of the Late Roman Army.
19. McLaughlin, 95–112.
20. Vegetius, Book III, 3.
21. Sozomen, 148–149.
22. Zosimus, Book II, 59–60, Sozomen, I, 149.
23. Julian, *Or. II,* 1.31.
24. Zosimus, Book II, 59–60, Socrates, I, 151.
25. Julian, *Or. II,* 2.77.
26. Zonaras, 165. The losses reported by Zonaras to Constantius' forces appear to be too high for a battle of this period. See also Potter, 472–476.
27. Treadgold, 44–55. The *Notitia Dignitatum* has computed the Army of Illyricum (Pannonia) at 17,500; the Army of Thrace at 24,500 and the two *Praesental* Armies of the East at 21,000 each. It is assumed that in 395 as well as 351 two-field armies of totalling 42,000 men could reasonably be supplied without over taxing the region's food resources. Adding an additional two armies totalling 80,000 men (40,000 Rebels and 40,000 Imperials) would severely over tax the Balkan agricultural resources.
28. Julian, *Or. II,* 2.77.
29. Zonaras, 165. The losses reported by Zonaras to Constantius' forces appear to be too high for a battle of this period. See also Potter, 472–476.
30. Goldsworthy (2009) 286–290 and 307–313; Heather (2009), 175–177.
31. James, 50.
32. Sozomen, 149, Socrates, 152.
33. *Atrans* (modern Trojane) was a Roman town in the modern municipality of Lukovica in central Slovenia. It lies in the northern part of the Sava Hills. The Roman road connected it with Aquileia and Emona to the north and west and Celeia to the southeast.
34. Zosimus, II, 61–62.
35. Ibid.
36. Caldwell III, 146–147.
37. Ibid., 147
38. Zosimus, 62–64
39. AM, XXX, 7.1–4.
40. Constantius confiscated Gratian's estate due to his support of Magnentius. This may have been the real reason Valentinian was cashiered from the command of cavalry regiments. AM, XVI, 11.6–7, XXX, 7.1–4.
41. Zos., HN 2.93.3.
42. Caldwell III, 154–155; Zosimus II, 63–64.

43. Hugh Elton, *Warfare In Roman Europe, A.D. 350–425* (Oxford: Clarendon Paperbacks, 1997), 231.

44. Zosimus, II, 63.

45. Ibid.

46. Hugh Elton, *Warfare In Roman Europe, A.D. 350–425*, 233.

47. Q C Hunter, *Usurper, A Novel of the Late Roman Empire* (New York: Eyes and Ears Edition, 2013).

48. Zosimus, II, 64, 205; Cadwell, 150–158.

49. Caldwell, 150–158. Based upon Caldwell's analyses, the story was credited to churchmen who were hostile to Constantius' Arian Christian policies and attempted to portray Constantius as a coward and weak-minded. There is nothing in the contemporary pagan sources to indicate that Constantius was a coward or weak minded. A Christian emperor or general praying in a chapel as his army deploys for battle would have been as common an occurrence as a pagan conducting sacrifices before a battle. In the fourth century, Roman generals and emperors were not expected to lead cavalry charges and fight duels as in the sixth century. Their job was to direct battles and not exhibit Homeric heroics.

50. Julian, *Or. II*, 149–155; and AM, XVI, 12.33–51.

51. Zosimus, 63–64 and Julian, *Or. II*, 149–155.

52. Zosimus, Book II, 64, Julian, *Oration II, The Heroic Deeds of the Emperor Constantius*, 149–155.

53. Magnentius' location would have been known by his standard.

54. Julian, *Or. II*, 159.

55. Zosimus, II 64, Julian, *Or. II*, 159.

56. Ibid., 159.

57. Julian, *Or. II*, 159–160.

58. Zosimus, II, 64, Julian, *Or. II*, 161.

59. AM, XVI, 12.60–68, XXXI, 13.14.

60. Zosimus, II, 64–65.

61. Raffaele D'Amato, *Roman Centurions 753–31 BC, The Kingdom and the Age of Consuls* (Oxford and New York: Osprey Publishing, 2011), 21–22; and Raffaele D'Amato, *Roman Centurions 31 BC-AD 500, The Classical and Late Empire* (Oxford and New York: Osprey Publishing, 2012), 15–17.

62. Late Roman arms and armour were simpler to construct than the equipment of the early empire. That said, replacing 50,000 helmets, mail shirts, shields, and swords by the next campaign season was an impossible task for the empire's weapons factories.

63. Zosimus, 64–65.

64. Julian, *Or. I*, 102–103. This town could have been near the city of Tergeste. The towns in this region are surrounded by the sea on one side and mountains on the landward side and with a number of routes through the mountains from Pannonia. They also had a good supply road leading to Aquileia. See Barrington, Map 19.

65. Julian, *Or. I*, 102–103.

66. Cameron, Averil & Peter Garnsey editors, *The Cambridge Ancient History*, Volume XIII. CUP, Cambridge, 1998. ISBN 0-521-30200-5, Drinkwater, John F, *The Alamanni and*

Rome 213–496 (Caracalla to Clovis), OUP Oxford 2007. ISBN 0-19-929568-9 Potter, David S *The Roman Empire at Bay AD 180–395*, Routledge, New York, 2004, ISBN 0-415-10058-5; Zosimus, II, 66.

67. Elton (1997), 233.
68. Zosimus, II, 64.
69. With the exception of *XXX Ulpia*, the other legions disappear from the record about this time.
70. AM, XVI, 2.7–3.3. Legion *I Minerva* was stationed at Bonna (Bonn), a short distance from Cologne. This desperate siege may have resulted in *I Minerva's* destruction. Legion *VIII August's* home base was Strasbourg (Argentorate), and an inscription from 371 indicates the legion was not destroyed and that its survivors reformed based upon Julian's rallying the scattered legions.
71. Zosimus, II, 66, Cromwell, 14.
72. Isaac, 416.

Chapter 10
1. Libanius, *Or.* XIII, 28.
2. AM, XXV, 4.22, 299.
3. AM, XVI, 5.10, 219; 295–299.
4. Socrates, III, 195, 215–217 and 220; Sozomen, VI, 1.
5. AM, XVI, 5.10, 219; 295–299.
6. Libanius, *Or.* XIII, claims this force was 400 infantry.
7. Julian, 'Letter to the Athenians,' *Julian Vol. II*, 269.
8. Peter Heather, *Empires and Barbarians, the Fall of Rome and the Birth of Europe* (Oxford and New York: Oxford University Press, 2009), 81–82.
9. AM does not identify from what regiment these men were detached. They may have been from the *Scola Laeti, Gentiles,* and or *Scutarii* regiments, which feature prominently in Julian's campaigns in Gaul.
10. Julian, 'Letter to the Athenians,' *Julian Vol. II*, 269.
11. 1. The Army of Gaul strikes the Alamanni settlements; and 2. turns north and strikes the Franks while the warriors are raiding the Rhone *Limes.*
12. The fact that, in 357, the Army of Gaul contained 13,000 men and, in 354, Silvanus was leading a force of 8,000 *auxilia* raises the inference that the Army of Gaul was comprised mostly of *auxilia* solders and not legionnaires.
13. There were two *cataphractii* regiments at the Battle of Strossberg. Therefore, this force contained between 500 and 1,000 armoured horsemen and approximately 300 to 500 *Ballistari* infantry.
14. These regiments were part of Constantius' immediate bodyguard, and it appears that he provided detachments to both Gallus and Julian when they were elevated to Caesar. See Tomlin, 267, fn.2.
15. AM., XVI, 7. 1–3.
16. Ibid., XVI, 7. 1–3.
17. AM, XVI, 9.2.
18. Crump, 85–86.

19. See Hamilton, 490, 495 and 501.
20. This hostile Laeti war band should not be confused with Julian's guard squadron of the same name. The *Laeti,* referred to here, could be the band of Alamanni settled in Gaul by the Roman government that went rogue. See Tomlin, 267, fn 3. See also AM XVI, 11, 4 and XX, 8, 13.
21. Jones (1964), 614, 620.
22. AM, XVI, 11.6–7.
23. Ibid., XIV.11, XVI.11, XVIII. 3.
24. Ibid., XVI, 11.6–10.
25. 1. Julian and the Army of Gaul march to *Tes Tabernae* to establish a supply base and raid Germanic tribes along the Rhine. Barbatio's army marches out to trap the Alamanni along the Rhine. *Laeti* war band slips between the Roman armies and raids Gaul. Two-thirds of this war band were destroyed by Julian's cavalry. 2. Barbatio's army is decisively defeated and retreats from the field. 3. Julian decisively defeats the Alamanni, but the majority of the tribe escapes to the east side of the Rhine. 4. Julian raids across the Rhine and establishes a fort on the east bank.
26. AM, XVI, 11.15.
27. The deserter was from the Scutarii regiment. AM XVI, 11.11–12.21. There is a compelling argument that the Alamanni only mustered between 6,000 and 10,000 men. See Hans Delbruck, *History of the Art of War, Volume II, The Barbarian Invasion,* Walter J. Renfroe, Jr., trans., (Lincoln and London: University of Nebraska Press, republished 1990), 262.
28. For an alternative interpretation of Ammianus see Matthews, 90–92.
29. AM, XVII, 17.6.
30. See For an alternative interpretation of these events see Matthews, 90–92.
31. AM, XVI, 12.10–20. Some historians are of the opinion that this event was fictional. See Crump, 86–89.
32. AM XVI, 12.18.
33. Phillip Sabin, 'The Face of Battle', *The Journal of Roman Studies,* Vol. 90 (2000), 1–17, 8. Http://www.jstor.org/stable/300198. Accessed 12 December 2009,00.58.?
34. See Elton (1996), 256 for an alternative view of these events.
35. Elton and Crump have the Romans conducting two counterattacks to plug gaps in the line instead of a line exchange. See Crump, 87–89 and Elton (1997), 255–256.
36. Julian, 'Letter to the Athenians,' 273.
37. This estimate is based upon the timetable for the levy recorded by Julian in 358 to have reached the Eastern Theatre. See Julian, 'Letter to the Athenians', *Julian Vol. II,* 273.
38. AM, XVIII, 9.3–4. There was only one known XXX Legion and that was XXX *Ulpia Victrix.*
39. Ibid., XVIII, 1.1–4.

Chapter 11

1. Warmington, 515.
2. AM, XVIII, 5.1–8, 427–433.
3. Shahid, 284–285.

4. AM, XVIII, 5.6, 431.

5. Ibid., XVIII, 6.5–8, 437–439.

6. Stewart, 8.

7. AM, XVIII, 6.1–3, 435; and Henry T Rowell, *Ammianus Marcellinus, Soldier-Historian of the Late Roman Empire,* (Ohio: University of Cincinnati, 1964) 23.

8. Ammianus states that the Persians used siege artillery captured at Singara that were used at the siege of Amida. He does not indicate whether they were captured in 359 or during an earlier operation.

9. Ibid., XVIII, 9, 1–9, 443–467. The legions of the usurpers Magnentius and Decentius had been posted to the east after the civil war for disloyalty and ill-discipline. Neither legion is recorded on the eastern section of the *Notitia Dignitatum.* See Dodgeon, 193, 340–347. The parent legion XXX *Ulpia* may have been destroyed in 355 when the Rhine *limes* collapsed since it disappears from history at this point. Since historians have identified only one XXX Legion, and that is XXX *Ulpia,* the unit at Amida was probably a *comitatensis* legion created out of the old XXX *Ulpia.* See generally Cromwell, 14.

10. Ibid., XVIII, 8, 1–4, 457; and XVIII, 9, 1–9, 463–467; Julian, 'Letter to the Athenians,' *The Works of the Emperor Julian,* Vol. II, 273.

11. Ibid., XVIII, 9, 1–9, 463–467. *Superventors.* The Legion of Catchers. The root word for *superventores* is *supervenio* and, in English, means catching someone in a given activity. Catchers. *Praeventires.* The Legion of Preventers. The root word for *Praeventires* is *praevenio* and, in English, means to arrive first or beforehand; anticipate or forestall. Preventers.

12. This force had a maximum strength of 6,500 but was most likely under-strength . See Terence Coello, *Unit Sizes in the Late Roman Army* (Oxford: BAR Series 645, 1996), 23.

13. The fortress city of Mardin sits atop a mountain overlooking the Nisibis-Amida road. See A. Poidebard, 'Les routes anciennes en Haute-Djezireh', *Syria, T. 8, Fasc. 1* (1927), 55–65, figures 1 and 2. http://www.jstor.org/stable/4195320. Accessed 19 July 2012, 08.12

14. AM, XVIII, 10–17.

15. Ibid., XVIII, 17–18.

16. Ibid., XVIII, 7.1–7.

17. Ibid., XVIII., 7, 2–8.

18. Ibid., XVIII, 7, 5–8; and R.C. Blockley, 'Ammianus Marcellinus on the Persian Invasion of A.D. 359', *Phoenix,* Vol. 42, No. 3 (Autumn, 1988), 244–260, 255, http://www.jstor.org/stable/1088346. Accessed 19 July 2011, 08.12

19. Ibid., XVIII, 7, 8–11, 455.

20. 1. Shapur's advance to Bebase, 2. Shapur's halt at Bebase to consider his options, 3. Ursicinus' forced march to Amida, 4. Persian attack of Amida and supporting forts.

21. Ibid., XVIII, 7.8–11.

22. Ibid., XVIII, 7.8–11.

23. Ibid., XVIII, 7, 8.1–4.

24. What was the debt of Antonius that the *Magister Equitum* Ursicinus could not intercede? Was he being blackmailed for his part in the plot against Constantius that Gallus uncovered in 354?
25. Ibid., XVIII, 8, 4–7.
26. The women of lower rank would not have received such honourable treatment. See A.D. Lee, *War In Late Antiquity, A Social History*, 141–146.
27. AM, XVIII, 10.3–4.
28. Ibid., XIX, 1.1–2.12.
29. Geoffrey Greatrex, *Rome and Persia at War, 502–532* (Leeds: Francis Cairns, 1998), 73–115.
30. AM, XIX, 3, 1–3.
31. Coello, 25.
32. AM, XVIII, 9.3–4.
33. Most historians give the garrison strength of between 7,000 and 10,000 men. See R C Blockley, 'Ammianus on the Persian Invasion of A.D. 359', *Phoenix*, Vol. 42, No. 3 (Autumn, 1988), 244–260, 258, http://www.jstor.org/stable/1088346; and Coello, 21. The estimate here assumes the following strengths: V Parthia 1,000; X Fortenses 300; *Equites* 350; *Magnentius, Decentius*, and XXX *Ulpia* 2, 400; *comites sagittarii* cavalry 32; and *Superventores* and *Praeventires* 1,400. Total Roman strength would have been 5,320. This estimate assumes that the reinforcing legions strength were between seventy per cent and eighty per cent. This is a generous estimate since the three Gallic legions were survivors of the Rebel army and two still retained the name of the usurpers.
34. AM, XIX, 1.-9.1.
35. The excavations at Dura-Europos indicated that mines damaged a tower and sunk a wall. See James, 31–39.
36. AM, XIX, 1–8.12, 471–515.
37. Ibid., XIX, 9.4–5.
38. Ibid., XIX, 9.5–8.
39. AM, XX, 2.1–3.
40. The black arrows demonstrate Shapur's successful Summer 360 attack into Mesopotamia. The white arrows represent Constantius' failed fall 360 counterattack.
41. Ibid., XVIII, 6.20.
42. Ibid., XVIII, 6.20–23.
43. Sozomen, *Historia Ecclesiastica*, 4.23, 4–7.
44. AM., XX, 4.2.
45. Ibid., XX, 9.1–3.
46. Ibid., XX, 13.1–16.
47. Ibid., XX, 6.8–9.
48. Ibid., XX, 6.8.
49. Ibid., XX, 6.7.
50. Ibid., XX, 7.14. Unlike the legions and regiments at Amida, these units lived to fight against Persia for years and are found listed on the *Notitia*.
51. Ibid., XX, 7.14–17.
52. Ibid., XXI, 13. 8.

53. Warmington, 517.
54. AM, XX, 4, 4.
55. Ibid., XX., 4.2–3.
56. Ibid., XX, 4.10.
57. Ibid., XX, 4.11.
58. Despite Julian's efforts, it is unlikely that his legions were back to full strength.
59. AM, 4.16–17.
60. Libanius, *Or.* XVIII, 206.
61. AM., XXI, 16.15, 183; XXV, 9.2, 549.

Chapter 12
1. Isaac, 376, 377.
2. Ibid., 380, 381.
3. AM., XXII, 12.1–4. 263–265.
4. Blockley (1992), 24.
5. Ibid.
6. Zosimus, 75, 77.
7. Potter, 517.
8. Crawford, 147–195.
9. Kaegi, 209–213.
10. Gibbons, 706–707 and 722.
11. The sources are not clear about whether this detached force was the Army of the East or an ad hoc formation of eastern and western units. Because the identity of the force is unclear, this thesis will follow Gibbon when referring to this force as the Army of Mesopotamia. According to Ammianus, this army was 30,000 men; Libanius claims it was 20,000 men; and Magnus claims it was 16,000 men.
12. Elite legions *Herculiani and Joviani* (AM XXII, 3.2 and XXV, 6.2, AM XXII, 3.2 XXV, 6.2); *Lanciarii* and *Mattiarii* (Magnus of Carrhae [Malalas XIII, 5–337, 11) 226 and AM XXI, 13.6); *comitatenses* legion Zianni(AM XXV, 1.19)and *limitanei* legions *I Armenia* (Magnus of Carrhae [Malalas XIII, 5–337, 11) 227); *Auxilia Cornuti and Bracchiatii* (AM XXV, 5.30); *Celtae* (AM XXII, 12.6); *Cornuti* (AM XV, 5.30); *Eruli/ Heruli/Aeruli* (AM XXV, 10.19); *Jovii* (AM XXV, 6.3); *Petulates* (AM XXI, 3.2 and XXII, 12, 6) *Reges* (AM XVI, 12.45); and *Victores* (AM XXIV, 4.23 and XXV, 6.3).
13. Southern and Dixon (1996), 71–72.
14. *Domestici Protectores* (AM XV, 3.10); *Scutarrii* (AM XV. 4.9); *Promoti* (AM XV 4.10); and *Tertiaci* (XXV, 1.7).
15. Moses Kharenatsi as translated and quoted in Dodgeon and Lieu, 326 and 396 fn 67.
16. Julian, letter to Libanius, Dodgeon and Lieu, Vol. I, 210–211
17. Roth, (2012), 77–92.
18. Ibid., (2012), 119–120.
19. *Landing Force Manual 1920, United States Navy* (Washington D.C.: Government Printing Office, 1921), Article 483–493.
20. Ammianus records that he was forty years, ten months when he died in 366. AM, XXVI, 9.1–8.

21. Ibid., XXIII, 3.1–5.
22. Rev A Robertson, ed. *Nicene and Post-Nicene Fathers, Series II, Vol. IV, Athanasius: Selected Works.* Online Edition. Par. 59. http://www.bible.ca/history/fathers/ NPNF2-04/Npnf2-04-08.htm.
23. Lee, 199–202.
24. Dodgeon and Lieu, viii.
25. Robertson, Par. 59.
26. Henry T Rowell. *Ammianus Marcellinus, Soldier-Historian of the Late Roman Empire* (Cincinnati: The University of Cincinnati, 1964), 22–23.
27. Ramsay MacMullen. *Corruption and the Decline of Rome* (New Haven and London: Yale University Press, 1988), 194.
28. *Ammianus Marcellinus, The Later Roman Empire (A.D. 354–378)*, ed. Walter Hamilton (London: Penguin Books, 2004), 484.
29. A D Lee. 'Embassies as Evidence for the Movement of Military Intelligence Between the Roman and Sassanian Empire'. 455–461, 456–457, in Philip Freeman and David Kennedy, ed. *The Defense of the Roman and Byzantine East, Proceedings of a Colloquium Held at the University of Sheffield in April 1986* (Oxford: BAR International Series 297 {ii} 1986); and Lee (1993), 112–114 and 118–127.
30. Lightfoot, 190, in Mitchell.
31. A D Lee. 'Campaign Preparation in Late Roman-Persian Warfare'. 257–265. ed. D H French and C S Lightfoot. *The Eastern Frontier of the Roman Empire, Proceedings of a Colloquium Held at Ankara in September 1988* (Oxford: BAR International Series 553(i), 1989).
32. Dodgeon and Lieu, 262.
33. Plutarch, 'The Life of Crassus', in Plutarch, *The Parallel Lives*, Bernadotte Perrin, trns., Bill Thayer Webpage ed. (Loeb Classic Library, 1919). Online Edition, 22.1–3, http://penelope.uchicago.edu/Thayer/E/Roman/Texts/Plutarch/Lives/home. html.
34. AM, XXIV, 2, 4–6.

Chapter 13

1. The rough timeline used for Julian's expedition in this chapter is based upon that computed by Dodgeon and Lieu Vol. I (pages 201–207) with typographical errors corrected.
2. AM, XXIII, 3.7–9.
3. Shahid, 107–112.
4. Shahid, 120, 121.
5. Malalas, XIII, pp. 328, 5–337, 11 [Magnus of Carrhae] Liu Persian Wars Vol. 1, 226
6. Until the twentieth century, disease killed or incapacitated more soldiers than enemy action.
7. The Legion *Lanciarii* would translate as Spearmen or Spear Throwers. The Legion *Mattiarii* would translate as Clubmen or Macemen.
8. AM XXIV, 7.4.
9. Ibid., XXIII, 5.15–24.

10. Ibid., XXIV, 1.16 and 2, 2–3.

11. Ibid., XXIV, 2.4–5 and Zos. III 15.4–6.

12. This image or file is a work of a U.S. Air Force Airman or employee, taken or made as part of that person's official duties. As a work of the U.S. federal government, the image or file is in the public domain. http://www.au.af.mil/au/awc/awcgate/gabrmetz/romseig1.gif

13. AM.XXIV, 2–7–8.

14. Ibid., XXIV 3.1–2; Zos. III 19, 1–2; and Lib., *Or.* XVII, 229.

15. The prices are approximate values based upon Diocletian's Edit on Maximum Prices. Diocletian's Edit was not completely successful, but it is a useful tool in determining the approximate value of goods and services. Stephen Williams, *Diocletian and the Roman Recovery* (New York: Methuen Inc., 1985), 224–227.

16. AM, XXIV, 3.1–11.

17. Ibid., XXIV., 4.1–4

18. Ibid., XXIV, 4.7.

19. Ibid., XXIV, 4.10–11.

20. Ibid., XXIV, 4.12–15.

21. Ibid., XXIV., 4.22–25.

22. Ammianus states that this brave band was awarded the siege-crown. This award was reserved for a general that relieved a beleaguered city. The actual award should have been the *Coronae Murals.* Ibid., XXIV, 4.24, fn1.

23. The value of a new set of army boots.

24. Gregory Nazianenus, *Orations* V, 10–13, ed. Bernardi, Trans. Dodgeon and Lieu, Vol. I, 217.

25. AM, XXIV, 5.10. This passage indicates that not all infantry cohorts and legions had lost their cavalry elements with Diocletian's and Constantine I's reorganization.

26. Map modified from the map found in Dodgeon and Lieu, 232 and Matthews, 142.

27. AM., XXIV, 6.1–3.

28. Ibid., XXIV, 2.4–5, 3.1, 4.8–15, 5.5–10; and Zosimus, III, 15.

29. Festus, *Breviarum* 28–9., as trans. Lee and Doge Vol. I, 215; Sozomen, VI, 1, 243; Libanius, *Oration XVIII*, 249–252.

30. AM XXIV, 6.4–7, 459–461.

31. Ammianus and Zosimus disagreed as to which Persian generals were present. Zosimus, 86; AM XXIV, 6.12.

32. Ibid., XXIV, 6, 14–17.

33. Historian R T Ridley takes the alternate view and finds fault with Zosimus' account. R T Ridley, 'Notes on Julian's Persian Expedition (363)', *Historia: Zeitschrift fur Alte Geshichte*, Vol. 22, No. 2 (2nd Qtr., 1973), 317–330, 322. http://www.jstor.org/stable/4435340.

34. In the sixth century, Persian Nisibis provided 10,000 infantry and cavalry to General Firuz' Persian army. If this small city was garrisoned with over 10,000 men, Ctesiphon's garrison could have been considerably larger. Carey, 11.

35. Zosimus, 86.

36. Ibid., 86.

37. Dixon and Southern (1992), 114.
38. Vegetius, 39.
39. Absent in this battle are Julian's heavily armed and armoured guard cavalry. AM, XXIV, 6.9–11, 461–463 and Zosimus, 86.
40. Vegetius, III. 14.
41. Sunzi, 61.
42. Zosimus, Book III, 86.
43. N J E. Austin. 'Julian at Ctesiphon: A Fresh Look at Ammianus' Account'. *Athenaeum*, Volume 50 (1972), 301–309, 301.
44. Moses Kharenatsi as translated and quoted in Dodgeon and Lieu, Vol. I, 326 and 396 fn 67.
45. AM, XXIV, 7.8, 471.
46. Julian, Vol. III, Ltr. 57, Spring 363, 'To Arsaces, Satrap of Armenia,' 197–201.
47. Libanius, 26.
48. Ibid., 26.
49. Philip Schaff, ed, *The Ecclesiastical History of Socrates Scholasticus* (Grand Rapids: Christian Ethereal Library, Book III, 229, online edition).
50. Libanius, *Oration XVIII*, 255–258.
51. AM, XXIV, 6, 3–4; Festus, D&L 216; and Gregory Nazianzenus, *Orations,* D&L, 215–216.
52. AM, XXIV, 7.7–8.
53. AM, XXIV, 7.1–3. 467.
54. Socrates, III, 21., 229.
55. Ibid., XXIV 7.1–7, 467–471; and Zosimus, III, 26.
56. Libanius, 26–27; Matthews, 158.
57. Sunzi, 24 and 39.
58. Theodoret, translated and quoted in Dodgeon and Lieu, Vol. I, 271.
59. Libanius, 25; and Dodgeon and Lieu, Vol. I, 233.
60. Libanius, 27.
61. Elton (1997), 238.
62. Lee (2007), 96.
63. Libanius, *Oration XVIII*. 263–265.

Chapter 14
1. Sunzi, 75.
2. AM XXIV, 7.3–8; Zosimus, 83–84.
3. Ibid., XXV, 1.1–3 and Zosimus, 87.
4. Ibid, XXV, 1.5–9. Ammianus is not clear as to the details of this engagement and seems to have reversed the events. Here the events have been reordered based upon the most probable course of the battle.
5. This slow rate of advance of the *Praesental* Army between 16 and 26 June 363 helps us understand later historians' belief in the myth that a Persian defector allegedly led Julian astray into a waterless wasteland. If this myth were true, without hundreds of thousands of gallons of water daily, the Romans would have perished within forty-

eight hours in the 120 degree Fahrenheit heat, yet they remained a formidable fighting force during this entire period.

6. AM, XXV, 1.14–18.
7. AM, XXV, 1.14–18.
8. John C Rolfe thinks the *Zianni* was a Thracian tribe, which means this legion may have been from the Army of Thrace. AM, XXV, XXVI.19, fn1.
9. AM, XXV, 1, 1–2, 7–9. The authorized strength of Roman cavalry regiments is generally accepted as being 500 men. The disgraced eight cavalry regiments' combined strength was 2,400 men. See generally Terence Coello. *Unit Sizes in the Late Roman Army* (Oxford: BAR International Series 645, 1996).
10. Ibid., XXV, 1, 18–19, 2–3.
11. Sunzi, 81.
12. Ibid., XXIV., 7.1–8, 467–471; Matthews, 158.
13. Ridley agrees with this argument and points out that exiled Homizdas and his Persians were in the Roman army and would have known the area. See Ridley 322.
14. Plutarch, *The Parallel Lives*, Bernadotte Perrin, trns., Bill Thayer Webpage ed. (Loeb Classic Library, 1919). Online Edition, 22.1–3, http://penelope.uchicago.edu/Thayer/E/Roman/Texts/Plutarch/Lives/home.html.
15. Sheldon (2010), 35.
16. Simpson, 110.
17. Turkish Tourist Bureau. http://www.iwasinturkey.com.
18. Matthews, 158, 176–179.
19. Illustration based upon AM, XXV, 3.1–15, 491–497.
20. It is not clear whether the Immortals Corps of 10,000 cavalry existed during the reign of Shapur II, but a Royal Corps of elite savaran cavalry did exist during this campaign. Farrokh (2005), 5–7.
21. AM, XXV, 3.1–4; and 420 fn2 referring to Zonaras, XIII, 13, B.
22. Ibid., XXV, 1–27; and Zosimus, III, 88.
23. Ibid., XXV, 3.5–13, 493–497.
24. R C Blockley, *East Roman Foreign Policy, Formation and Conduct from Diocletian to Anastasius* (Leeds: Francis Cairns, 1992), 26–27.
25. Zosimus, 89; AM, XXV, 6.1–4, 521–523.
26. AM, XXV, 3.14 and 6.11.
27. Ibid., XXV, 6.10–13, 527.
28. Ibid., XXV, 6.5–13, 525–527.
29. Ibid.
30. Sunzi, 86, Robert L. Cantrell, *Understanding Sun Tzu* (Arlington: Center For Advantage, 2003), 15.
31. Blockley (1992), 27.
32. Tom Holland, *In the Shadow of the Sword, the Battle for Global Empire and the Ancient World* (London: Little Brown Book Group), 2012, 95.

Chapter 15

1. Hughes, 17.
2. Tabari, I, 843/62–3, in Greatrex and Lieu, Part II, 8–9.
3. Festus, *Breviarium* 29 and Eunapius frg. 29.1.3–6, 10–15 in Greatrex and Lieu, Part II, 4.
4. AM, XXV.8.13–17, 9.1–6, 12.
5. Zosimus, III, 92.
6. Hughes, 18.
7. Ibid., 16–17.
8. Ibid., 18.
9. AM., XXV, 10.6–7.
10. Hughes, 18.
11. Gibbon, 388.
12. Blockley (1992), 27.
13. Haldon, 21–25.
14. Sunzi, 96.
15. Lee (1993), 81–90, 112–115, 147–158, 170–184; and Austin and Rankov, 227–234.
16. Blockley (1992), 27.
17. Beate Dignas and Engelbert Winter, *Rome and Persia in Late Antiquity, Neighbors and Rivals* (Cambridge: Cambridge University Press, 2008) 185–186.

Index